A PLUME BOOK

SO SUE ME, JACKASS!

AMY EPSTEIN FELDMAN, ESQ., is a nationally syndicated legal correspondent and a legal contributor to the news programming at WXTF in Philadelphia. She is also the general counsel of the Judge Group, Inc., a $200 million international placement firm. Formerly an associate at Drinker Biddle & Reath, LLP, Amy specializes in employment and consumer-related issues. She received both a law degree and a masters in education from the University of Pennsylvania, and a bachelor of arts in history from Cornell University.

ROBIN EPSTEIN has written for publications including *The New York Times, Marie Claire, Real Simple, Glamour,* and *Teen People* magazines. A contributor to NPR's *This American Life,* Robin started her career as a stand-up comic, moved into sitcom writing, and served as the head writer (and on-air sidekick) for a game show for teenage girls. She cowrote the novel *Shaking Her Assets,* and has published numerous children's books. In addition to scripting video games, Robin currently teaches writing at NYU. She graduated from Princeton University and earned her MFA in nonfiction from Columbia University.

So Sue Me,
JACKASS!

Avoiding Legal Pitfalls That Can Come Back to Bite You at Work, at Home, and at Play

**Amy Epstein Feldman
and Robin Epstein**

A PLUME BOOK

PLUME
Published by the Penguin Group
Penguin Group (USA) Inc., 375 Hudson Street, New York, New York 10014, U.S.A. •
Penguin Group (Canada), 90 Eglinton Avenue East, Suite 700, Toronto, Ontario, Canada
M4P 2Y3 (a division of Pearson Penguin Canada Inc.) • Penguin Books Ltd., 80 Strand,
London WC2R 0RL, England • Penguin Ireland, 25 St. Stephen's Green, Dublin 2, Ireland
(a division of Penguin Books Ltd.) • Penguin Group (Australia), 250 Camberwell Road,
Camberwell, Victoria 3124, Australia (a division of Pearson Australia Group Pty. Ltd.) •
Penguin Books India Pvt. Ltd., 11 Community Centre, Panchsheel Park, New Delhi – 110 017,
India • Penguin Group (NZ), 67 Apollo Drive, Rosedale, North Shore 0632, New Zealand
(a division of Pearson New Zealand Ltd.) • Penguin Books (South Africa) (Pty.) Ltd.,
24 Sturdee Avenue, Rosebank, Johannesburg 2196, South Africa

Penguin Books Ltd., Registered Offices: 80 Strand, London WC2R 0RL, England

First published by Plume, a member of Penguin Group (USA) Inc.

First Printing, October 2009
10 9 8 7 6 5 4 3 2 1

Copyright © Amy Epstein Feldman and Robin Epstein, 2009
All rights reserved

Article on pp. 13–15 first published in *Gear* magazine as "The Sex Files," June 2002.

 REGISTERED TRADEMARK—MARCA REGISTRADA

LIBRARY OF CONGRESS CATALOGING-IN-PUBLICATION DATA

Feldman, Amy Epstein.
   So sue me, jackass! : avoiding legal pitfalls that can come back to bite you at work, at
home, and at play / Amy Epstein Feldman and Robin Epstein.
      p. cm.
   Includes index.
   "A Plume book"
   ISBN 978-0-452-29574-2 (pbk. : alk. paper) 1. Law—United States—Popular works.
2. Law—United States—Anecdotes. I. Epstein, Robin, 1972– II. Title.
   KF387.F454 2009
   349.73—dc22   2009017841

Printed in the United States of America
Set in Adobe Caslon Pro

PUBLISHER'S NOTE
The scanning, uploading, and distribution of this book via the Internet or via any other means
without the permission of the publisher is illegal and punishable by law. Please purchase only
authorized electronic editions, and do not participate in or encourage electronic piracy of
copyrighted materials. Your support of the author's rights is appreciated.

While the authors have made every effort to provide accurate telephone numbers and Internet
addresses at the time of publication, neither the publisher nor the authors assume any responsibility for errors, or for changes that occur after publication. Further, publisher does not have
any control over and does not assume any responsibility for author or third-party Web sites
or their content.

BOOKS ARE AVAILABLE AT QUANTITY DISCOUNTS WHEN USED TO PROMOTE PRODUCTS OR
SERVICES. FOR INFORMATION PLEASE WRITE TO PREMIUM MARKETING DIVISION, PENGUIN
GROUP (USA) INC., 375 HUDSON STREET, NEW YORK, NEW YORK 10014.

*To our parents, Marcia and Paul Epstein,
who taught us everything we know.*

Contents

Introduction xix

Chapter 1. Your Job
Hi Ho, Hi Ho, It's Off to Sell Your Soul to the Devil You Go! **1**

Can a company really make you take a personality test before hiring you? 2

What's legal (and illegal) for an employer to consider when making hiring decisions? 3

Can an employer refuse to hire you because you look a certain way? 4

Are companies allowed to judge you on your Facebook profile? 5

Once you've deleted something from your profile, employers can't find it . . . can they? 6

R'uh-r'oh. So if you posted (but later deleted) a photo of yourself mooning your old boss, are you screwed? 7

Are companies allowed to do background checks on you? 8

Will a criminal record follow you around for your whole life? 9

Why isn't a noncompete agreement a violation of the "life, liberty, and pursuit of happiness" thing? 11

If you and your boss talk about sex in the office, can you sue for sexual harassment? 16

What's a "hostile" work environment? 17

How could you lose a sexual harassment case if you've proven there's been a constant stream of sexual jokes, gestures, and discussions? 18

Can you protect yourself from claims of sexual harassment by letting people know in advance that you're a little bit harass-y?   18

What about porn on the job . . . okay to look as long as you don't show?   19

If your company serves alcohol at its Christmas party, getting bombed can't be held against you, right?   20

Can a person go to jail for sexual harassment?   24

Do you *really* need to read your company's policy manual?   25

Can you get fired for gaining weight?   26

Can a company randomly decide to drug-test you even if there's no sign of a problem?   27

Once you have a job, you don't need to worry about what's on your online profile, do you?   29

Do you have any rights when it comes to a smelly coworker?   30

Any way to stop a coworker from constantly whining?   31

Do you have the right to see your personnel file?   32

Is it illegal for a company to stop a worker's protest?   33

Can a company prevent people from talking politics on the job?   34

Employers can't censor you from expressing your beliefs on a lapel pin, can they?   34

Isn't it illegal to make people work on national holidays?   35

How much of a right to privacy do you have at your job?   36

How can companies get away without paying employees overtime if they work more than forty hours a week?   38

Can you demand vacation days instead of overtime pay if you've earned it?   40

Are there any laws to protect people from dangerous jobs?   41

Can a company really count sick days as part of your vacation time?   42

Do you have any rights if you need time off for medical reasons?   43

Are there any laws regulating nannies?   46

Are nanny cams legal?   47

The "My Sister Is Smarter than She Looks" Section   48

How to Complain at Work   48

Asking for a Raise   48

Dress Code for Office Parties   49

Responding to a Bad Review   50

Progressive Discipline   51

Fear of Firing   51

Flat-Out Fired   52

What to Say/What *Not* to Say in an Exit Interview   52

Deleting Computer Files as You Leave   52

Giving a Reference to a Departed Employee   53

Getting a Reference if You've Been Fired   54

Severance   54

Two Weeks' Notice   55

Collecting Unemployment   55

Chapter 2.   Your Money

Mo' Money, Mo' Problems . . . Unless It's No Money, in Which Case It's All Problems   57

People can't cash postdated checks until the date written on them, right?   58

How bad is it to send out a check you know will bounce?   58

Is there any way to make the calls from the collection agency stop?!   59

What do you do if you owe money to more than one creditor?   60

What does garnishing a paycheck mean?   61

If your paycheck is being garnished, is it possible that you'll work the whole week and wind up with no money at the end?   61

Is there any way to guarantee a friend will repay a loan?   62

What happens when a judge makes a ruling against you, but you *still* don't have the funds to repay the debt?   63

What's the downside to declaring bankruptcy?   64

If you're in dire need, can you get help to heat your home?   64

How long will bad credit bloopers haunt your credit rating?   65

Do you get saddled with your beloved's bad credit when you hitch the wagon?   67

What happens if you lose your ATM card and someone withdraws all your cash?   67

Do you need to prove you didn't make the false purchases that show up on your credit card bill?   68

Can you cancel payment on a mail-order purchase you don't like?   69

Is an extended warranty *really* a best buy, or is it a really stupid waste of money?   70

How come you never get back as much money in rebates as they promise in ads?   71

Is an expired gift certificate redeemable?   72

You don't have to pay taxes on the money you make selling your old junk online . . . do you?   73

Are winnings at a casino taxable?   74

How much dough can you get back for charitable giving come tax time?   74

How can you tell if telemarketing calls from charities are on the up-and-up?   76

If you work from home, how much of your bedroom set can you write off on your taxes?   78

How can tax prep offices offer instant rebates?   79

Can you conscientiously object and refuse to pay taxes if you disagree with government policies?   79

How do your tax returns change when you get married?   81

Are those work-at-home opportunities where you can supposedly make good cash "right from your kitchen table!" for real?   82

Do you pay taxes on bartered goods?   82

How can you get salary owed to you from a company that folds?   83

Some private colleges cost more a year than the average American household income. What's a family to do?   84

How do you know if a site can be trusted with your credit card and social security numbers?   85

Any chance those spam offers for great vacation deals are real?   93

Is there any reason to hold on to old bank statements and tax returns, and if so, how long should you keep them?   94

When you're ready to retire, how do you do it?   95

Once you've retired, does your pension vanish if your former employer files for bankruptcy?   97

Chapter 3.   Your "Love" Life
Bad Lovin', or, Breaking Up Is Hard to Do, Particularly if Your Partner's an Asshole   98

Who keeps the ring when your fiancé, the douche bag, breaks your engagement?   99

Who's responsible for paying those nonrefundable down payments for the wedding?   99

Can you get sued for damages incurred during sex?   100

Is crashing a wedding illegal?   101

Prenup: I do or I don't?   102

Can you get out of your marriage by claiming temporary insanity?   104

Are you officially "common law" married once you've lived together for seven years?   106

Is there really such a thing as a "no-fault" divorce?   108

Can one lawyer represent both the husband and the wife in a divorce?   108

Is nothing private, or are the sleazy details of your divorce available for all to see?   109

Can you stop your ex from posting nasty pictures of you on the Web?   110

Are you on the hook for the bill your vindictive money-grubbing ex charges to your joint credit card after you split?   111

Is there any kind of tax credit for alimony payments?   112

Who decides which (divorced) parent has to pay for their kid's college tuition?   112

Chapter 4.   Your Kids
Yes, Sir, That's My Baby . . . and Other Things You Might Not Want to Admit to Your Child's Arresting Officer   114

Can you get any cash back for having kids?   115

If Joe Camel was banned because he encouraged kids to smoke, why aren't cutesy beer ads censored for promoting underage drinking? 115

Are advertisers allowed to shill endlessly to children during Saturday morning cartoons? 116

Can teachers get insurance against lawsuit-happy parents? 117

Can a child bring medication to school these days? 118

Are there any regulations about traveling on planes with children (besides my fantasy "No crying!" rule)? 119

What's the youngest age you can make your kid get a job? 120

Can parents get busted if minors drink alcohol in their home? 122

Are schools allowed to ban girls from prom because they look too slutty? 123

Can parents be fined and/or imprisoned for the crimes of their kids? 124

What if your idiot child goes wild on your credit card—are you liable for all the charges? 125

When you drop your kid off at college, does the school assume legal responsibility for his stupid decisions? 126

Beyond selling organs, how can you legally defray college expenses? 130

Can both divorced parents "write off" their kids on their tax returns? 131

What should you do if you can no longer afford your child support payments? 132

Can an ex stop paying child support if he suspects he's not the baby daddy? 133

What the hell's a parenting plan? 134

Do grandparents get visitation rights? 135

Chapter 5. Your Online Profile
A.k.a. What the Whole Wide World *Knows About You!* 137

Do you have any rights or recourse in yanking pictures of you off the Web? 138

What if you're photographed or videotaped without your knowledge or consent—any options? 138

What can you do if someone anonymously posts really mean shit about you?   139

Can you sue dating sites (or the daters) for fraud if members lie on their profiles?   141

How can you be sure a Web site is secure when you make a purchase?   143

What should you do if a hacker steals your identity?   144

Can you stop Web sites from monitoring your movements and purchasing history online?   147

Are stores legally allowed to sell your info to advertisers?   148

What should you do if you think you're being wiretapped?   149

Aren't those police cameras that take pictures of you at intersections a violation of privacy rules?   150

How can you be sure Johnny Geeksquad won't snoop through your personal files and make them public when you get your computer repaired?   151

Is spamming illegal?   152

Is it wrong to let people believe someone with your name *is you* when they do a Google search on your qualifications?   154

How can you protect yourself from getting conned in an online auction?   158

Why can hotel staff enter a room at any time if you've rented it for that period of time?   159

Why don't the casinos jam cell signals on the gaming floor?   160

Cn u txt-n-drive?   161

Chapter 6.   Your Home
Your Castle, Your Casa, the Cage You Call Home   **162**

Isn't it discrimination for a landlord to reject you for bad credit?   163

How can you evict a crazy-ass roommate?   163

Who do you sue for the damages to your apartment caused by your upstairs neighbor?   164

If someone's horsing around in your home and gets hurt, can you get sued for his klutziness?   165

Are you responsible for Calamity Jane's injuries if she hurts herself while playing with one of your toys?   167

When your landlord isn't returning your security deposit, how do you get your money back?   168

Why do mattresses have tags that say "Do not remove under penalty of law"?   170

Without making me sit through a lecture, can you explain the differences between a time-share condo and buying a "vacation interval"?   171

Are there any weird laws that govern the purchase of foreclosed property?   172

Are home sellers required to disclose if their property is on top of a burial ground?   173

Are online real estate broker services a scam?   174

How can you protect yourself from extortionist movers?   176

Can a homeowners' association really stop you from parking your company car in *your* driveway?   179

What do you need to know before hiring a contractor for your home?   180

If a natural disaster swallows your home, where do you start picking up the pieces?   181

Mold! *Mold!* There's mold everywhere! What do you do?   182

Is there any legal way to get your noisy neighbor to shut the hell up?   182

If your neighbor cuts branches off your tree (hanging over his property), who pays for the trim?   183

Your jackass neighbor just put up a fence on your lawn. What are your rights?   184

What happens if you apply for a loan, get it, and then can't pay it off?   185

After you lose your home in foreclosure, can the IRS come after you to tax "gains" made through your debt?   187

Chapter 7.   Your Pets
The Personal Petting Zoo   188

Can you really leave money to your pets?   189

Do you have any rights if the dog you recently purchased in a pet store croaks?   189

Insurance for pets—worth the price? 190

Who keeps the kitty when a marriage busts up? 191

What can you do if the bitch next door won't stop barking? 192

Can you get around the "no-pets" clause in a lease by hiding the animal in your apartment for three months? 193

Can a dog be guilty of trespassing? 194

What are you responsible for if your pet bites someone? 195

Why can some dogs shop in supermarkets and others need to stay outside? 198

Why aren't hunters arrested for "cruelty to animals"? 199

With post-9/11 flight regulations, can your dog still fly the "friendly" skies? 200

What do you do if the airline loses your pet? 200

What do the terms on pet food labels really mean? 201

It's legal to bury your pet in your backyard, right? 202

Chapter 8. Your Ride
Getting from Here to There 206

What are you supposed to do when you get into a car accident? 207

Who pays for damages if your friend crashes your car? 208

And who pays if the valet dents the vehicle? 209

Should you buy the supplemental insurance when you're renting a car or will your credit card cover you in the event of an accident? 210

How much can you drink before you're legally considered wasted? 210

Are there penalties for road rage? 214

How can you get out of a traffic ticket? 215

Can you really be arrested for tossing a cigarette butt out of your car window? 215

If your new car's a lemon, do you have any legal recourse? 216

How can all of these insurance companies advertise they'll save you 15 percent on your auto insurance? 217

Why is the job of repo man legal? Isn't he just stealing cars? 219

Do you get a Good Samaritan rebate for driving a hybrid and reducing your carbon tireprint? 220

Do airlines owe you anything if they cancel your flight and you lose your hotel deposit?   221

Is travel medical insurance worthwhile or is it another crappy tourist trap?   222

What can you do if the airline you bought tickets on folds before flight?   223

What's the worst that can happen to you if you leave your cell phone on in flight?   224

Chapter 9.   Your Health
Body Issues   226

Since health care is crazy expensive, can you and a friend share a health insurance policy?   227

What do you do if you need to go to the hospital but you're uninsured?   228

If you work freelance and get hurt on the job, who's responsible for paying your medical bills?   228

If you're an employee on the company health plan, they cover all your medical costs, right?   229

Say you are on the company health plan. Can your boss access your medical records?   230

If the government is going to tax smokers, why don't they give tax breaks to gym-goers?   231

How can you be sure the meds you're taking won't combine to kill you?   232

Does anyone regulate the cleanliness of tattoo parlors?   234

How can you learn if your boob job doc is a reputable surgeon or a dangerous boob himself?   235

Are there any laws to prevent a doctor from spilling your beans at the dinner table to entertain her friends?   237

Can you get your medical records back, or are they the property of the doctor who made them?   239

At what point is a health condition considered a disability?   240

On food labels is there a legal requirement for what "lean" must mean?   241

Are any food products exempt from the tyranny of nutritional labels?   246

For a product to be referred to as "natural," must it spring from the
earth fully formed?   247

Is there any standard for "pure spring" water, or is that just naïve
thinking?   248

Why are beverage companies forced to warn "phenylketonurics"
about their products?   249

Why aren't makers of "miracle" weight loss drugs punished for false
advertising?   250

Besides marijuana, are "herbal supplements" regulated at all?   251

Chapter 10.   Your Death
Or, if You Prefer, We Can Call It "Your Relocation to a Farm Upstate"   253

Can you sign a loved one into a nursing home against his or her will?   254

Does a power of attorney cover all decision-making aspects of a
person's life?   255

Once you get someone's power of attorney, are you responsible for all
financial obligations, too?   256

Can you face prosecution if you neglect your elderly relatives?   256

How can you make sure you don't get bilked out of your estate when
you're old and susceptible?   257

Is a will written on a napkin legal?   258

Who gets your stuff if you bow out before writing a will?   259

Assuming your partner doesn't murder you, can you disinherit your
spouse and kids?   260

How do you protect yourself from vultures who might pull your plug
to get their inheritance quicker?   261

What are your responsibilities if you're named the "executor" of
someone's will?   262

Say you want to contest a will. How do you do that?   263

If you've patented a world-changing device, once you die, does the
patent die with you?   264

Does dying get you out of your credit card debt?   265

Dying costs a lot of money. Is there anything you can do to cut costs
    in advance?   265

How difficult is it to switch life insurance beneficiaries if you later
    decide you hate the person you named?   267

Is there any way to cut health care costs as you're making your "final
    exit"?   268

Chapter 11.   Rights You *Don't* Have   270

You don't always have the right to speak to your lawyer.   271

You don't always have the right to say what you wish.   272

You don't have the right to get out of jury duty.   274

You don't always have the right to name your child exactly what
    you'd like.   275

You don't have the right to get a license plate telling cops to FCK
    OFF.   277

You don't have to be a Good Samaritan.   278

You don't always have a right to file a lawsuit.   279

Chapter 12.   Our Conclusion
The Actual Telephone Conversation . . .   281

Acknowledgments   282

Index   285

Introduction

- A man is secretly taped by his employer then fired for what he said about the boss in the lunchroom.
- A sweet, gray-haired bookkeeper, mother of four, grandmother of two, is arrested for drunk driving and wants to keep it a secret.
- A married man whose girlfriend gets pregnant isn't sure if the baby is his, or if there's really going to be a baby at all.
- A pretty twenty-something woman realizes when she's on a sales call in a client's office that the man with whom she's speaking is masturbating under his desk.

Amy

As a nationally syndicated legal columnist and general counsel of the Judge Group, Inc., a $200 million international placement firm, I hear it all—and frequently in graphic detail. I not only handle the firm's legal affairs, I'm also the person employees seek out to answer their private questions about the law, too. They come to me because I'm often the only lawyer they know personally. They come to me because I'm interested in solving their problems and helping to control the damage. And I'm pretty sure they also come to me because I don't charge them $200 per hour for personal consultations.

I get questions about speeding tickets, delinquent children, and nasty neighbor disputes. They ask about their office pools, prenuptial agreements, and household help. And while some are in real hot water and need independent counsel, others just want a better understanding of their rights and/or what to expect if they wind up in court. What I've seen in the fifteen years I've worked as an employment lawyer is that even the smartest, most self-reliant people have needlessly gotten themselves into trouble because they didn't know the law. So I've always viewed part of my job as an educator, and tried to drive home the notion that *what you don't know can get you sued.*

And I don't just get personal questions at the office. I get calls all the time—by friends, family members, and specifically by my sister, Robin—to give my $200 per hour two cents.

In the last year, Robin asked me to help her decipher a contract with a video game company in London. She asked me how to break her lease and get her security deposit back. She asked me what one friend should do about getting fined for a cell phone infraction on an airplane. She asked me what another should do about getting a restraining order against her mother.

Then one day, Robin asked me why I didn't put all of this information together and write a book. "You're the writer," I said. But she continued to hound me (she does that), saying that a book like this would be incredibly useful for people who have all sorts of legal questions but no sister-lawyer they could turn to and ask for free.

And then it dawned on both of us that what we should do is write this book together. You'll be hearing both of our voices from this point forward because we know very well that there are always two sides to a story. We also think that though legal issues can be scary, approaching them as a discussion in plain, easy to understand language can take away a lot of the anxiety these situations often cause. Finally, Robin and I just like to tell stories, and we find that if we can joke about topics even when they're difficult, the situation is already improving.

So we hope we can help you find the answers to your questions here, we hope you'll enjoy reading about some of the more outrageous cases that highlight and test the law, and we hope you never get caught going eighty-seven miles per hour in a forty-five zone while drinking hot coffee, chatting on your cell phone, and not wearing your seatbelt. (But if you do, you should turn to page 215 to see how to try to get out of that ticket.)

Robin

My sister and I are different: She has brown eyes, mine are blue. Amy's conservative. I'm liberal. She's a suburban home-owning minivan driver. I'm a subway-riding renter in New York City. Amy has a 401(k), a husband, and three children . . . I have some really good toys.

But despite the differences in our appearance, opinion, life-style, and politics, we're sisters and we chat with each other nonstop. This is particularly helpful since we both love to talk about everything, from news stories and family politics to gossip and pop culture. But one of our favorite topics of discussion is law and the incredible legal snafus regular people get tripped up in all the time. (For this we blame our childhood addictions to law-related television shows—that's right, Judge Wapner, we're looking at you.) Amy will even frequently joke that she became a lawyer because of *L.A. Law* (she's not joking). And I often say I became a television writer because I wanted to sleep with the actors. (Kidding, Mom!) But our mutual affection for conversations legal-eagle has been greatly enhanced by the fact that now Amy actually knows what she's talking about.

In fact, as an employment lawyer, one of the things Amy does in her daily work is to help her company's employees when they get themselves into a legal pickle. For me, as a comedy writer, pickles are my bread and butter, so I love to hear her talk about what she encounters. Amy indulges my morbid fascination by telling me stories of some of the funniest legal cases she's come across over the years, and has also dispensed to me a lot of excellent legal advice (for free!).

After countless conversations and e-mails, we collected all the relevant information and thought about how best to put it in some coherent order. Some people will presumably open this book looking for a specific answer to a specific question affecting them in daily life. Some might come looking to improve their general legal knowledge. Others might like our crazy stories and adorable author photo. Whatever your goal, we wanted to make this experience as user-friendly for you as possible. On this subject, Amy and I agree: life is hard enough.

That's why we've decided to arrange this book in a series of chapters that group together legal questions concerning various aspects of daily life—areas like work, home, and play. As in our relationship, I'll usually be asking the questions (some of which will be "heightened for dramatic effect"), and Amy will be providing the answers. But it's worth noting that although the questions I pose won't always be authentic reflections of my life, the responses Amy gives will be factually correct and will use true, real-life examples. We're also including some stories in "sidebars," that deal with some of the issues Amy and I have personally encountered over the years. Though they may not be universally applicable, we hope they'll help humanize some of the issues we're discussing.

Amy

And now for the legal disclaimer: **THIS BOOK IS NOT YOUR LAWYER.** We are not your lawyers. By reading this book, you do not become a lawyer. This book is intended to give you a general sense of the structure of the law and to teach the numerous pitfalls that people have learned the hard way. It is NOT meant to give you specific advice or act as a substitute for getting your own lawyer should you need one. When you are accused of a crime, need a will, have to go to court, or have a specific question about your personal situation, you should consult a real, live lawyer, not just a book. Despite what we like to think of as our enormous literary skill, just because you've read this book does not mean you should be emboldened to act as your own lawyer. Let the very first (and perhaps very best) piece of legal knowledge I bestow be this: *He who acts as his own lawyer has a jackass for a client.*

So Sue Me,
JACKASS!

Chapter 1

Your Job

*Hi Ho, Hi Ho, It's Off to Sell Your Soul
to the Devil You Go!*

Remember the days when you couldn't wait to get out of school so you could get a job and be your own boss? Ah, how young and stupid you were then! Turns out that old cliché "they call it 'work' for a reason" has an uncomfortable amount of truth to it. But though complaining about one's job has long been a great American pastime, these days just having a job seems like something to celebrate. This chapter will explore employment-related issues, from the things it's better to know before you go in for that big interview to the things you need to know if you want to keep your job to the things you should absolutely *not* do if you lose it.

Q: I just went for a job interview, but before they'd hire me, those assholes said I needed to take a personality test. Is that even legal?

A: Before Philadelphia Park Casino opened its doors, its management handed all job applicants—from bartenders to accountants—a blow-up guitar and told them to dance to the song "YMCA." Some applicants found the Guitar Hero portion of the interview fun; others, like the job seeker with the prosthetic leg, were not so amused. In explaining its rationale, the management argued that everyone who works at the casino is in the entertainment business and therefore needs to be outgoing. So is this interview request legal?

Young man, the answer is yes.

Why? Well, in order to understand what tests are legal and what questions can and can't be asked during an interview (or after you've been given a conditional job offer), you first need to know what "qualities" of yours it's legal for the employer to consider. There are many qualities that don't have to do with the job that an employer can still refuse to hire you over, like, say, poor grooming habits. While showering regularly might not have anything to do with how great you are at your job, if you stink, the company can say it doesn't want you around. It's a concept known as *employment at will* and it means that *an employer can hire you or not, and fire you, for any reason . . . or no reason at all—as long as it's not a discriminatory reason.* While there are certain public policy exceptions to that rule (like you can't be fired for blowing the whistle on illegal behavior, or for union organizing), for the most part, people can be fired for a myriad of unfair but completely legal reasons.

Candidates who argued that they didn't want to dance to

the Village People were told that they need not perform well, because they weren't being judged on the quality of their performance, rather on the enthusiasm they brought to the task. The casino said it put a premium on "character," and an unwillingness to form the letters *YMCA* with one's body apparently showed a lack of it. Refusing to hire someone for a "character issue" is not discriminatory. Of course a love of disco does not necessarily a great bookkeeper make, but if you're doing the hiring in the casino business, perhaps that's a gamble you're willing to take.

Q: So what are the "qualities" that it's illegal for an employer to consider? And what's considered a discriminatory hiring practice?

A: Well, there are certain aspects about a person that can't be changed—so-called immutable characteristics—and these are the traits that state and federal law say *must be ignored* when making a hiring decision.

Under federal law it is illegal for an employer to consider these traits when making employment decisions because they are immutable characteristics: *race, color, age, gender, marital status, disability, religion, and national origin*. In addition, many municipalities prevent discrimination on the basis of *sexual orientation*.

Because these characteristics are protected, each is referred to as a "protected class status." (Veteran status may not be held against you, although many employers do consider service to the country with favor.)

In other words, a discriminatory hiring practice is one in

which an employer rejects a candidate based on his age, race, color, national origin, marital status, disability, gender or the god he believes (or doesn't believe) in.

Q: **What about appearance? Can an employer refuse to hire me because I'm not pretty enough ... or too pretty (heh!) ... or because I just don't look a certain way?**

A: The answer to that is yes and no. As you now know, an employer can't refuse to hire you because of characteristics you were born with—like the shape of your eyes—but just because an employer makes a judgment based on your appearance, that doesn't mean it's illegal. For example, a former delicatessen worker at Costco sued the retailer after it fired her for not removing her facial piercings. The woman claimed that, as she was a member of the Church of Body Modification, Costco's dress code violated her religious beliefs. The gut reaction of many people upon seeing a food handler with a nose pierce is: "I don't care what church you belong to, don't you touch my food with the fingers that have changed that nose ring." How did it turn out?

Well, "Toro" wound up losing her case because the court felt that Costco was within its rights to limit the piercings on food handlers. You many not want to work for an employer that you feel squelches your individuality and that's your choice. But if you do choose to go for the job, remember the discussion about what is and what isn't a protected class: piercings, tattoos, and other appearance-related modifications are *not* characteristics you were born with. They therefore don't put you in a protected class, and as a result, the employer is within its rights to judge you on them.

Now let's compare that to the legal challenges faced by retailer Abercrombie & Fitch. When it was revealed that Abercrombie hired only "attractive people" for sales, the company faced so many suits by job applicants who didn't get the job because of the policy that the Equal Employment Opportunity Commission (EEOC) actually had a specific Abercrombie link on its Web site just for people who wanted to file a complaint. The EEOC beleived that Abercrombie's policy of hiring only the beautiful people in actuality translated to hiring only young, hip "un-ethnic" types.

Ultimately Abercrombie agreed that it had engaged in discriminatory hiring practices because the retailer was making decisions based on candidates' ages and races, not just on how dewy their skin or how radiant their smiles. Abercrombie & Fitch paid $50 million to resolve the EEOC lawsuit and agreed to ensure that minorities and women would be promoted into manager-in-training and manager positions without discrimination. The company also agreed to hire a vice president of diversity and to employ up to twenty-five diversity recruiters.

Q: **More and more I'm living my life on Facebook. But I've heard that employers are checking out people's profiles, and making hiring and firing decisions based on what they have posted. Isn't that corporate espionage or something?**

A: You're worried about espionage when you've willingly posted compromising photos of yourself online for the whole world to see? One of the frat boys featured in the movie *Borat* seemed to suffer a similar mental disconnect himself. He sued the producers of the film for trying to portray him in a false light. He claimed he's not really the drunken, misogynist numskull he appeared to be on-screen. But one of the hurdles he faced was that he'd posted a series of pictures of himself—virtually all with beer in hand—on his MySpace page.

The question is *not* whether employers look at MySpace and Facebook pages before hiring someone—obviously they do—but why it's legal for them to use something that has no bearing on job performance. Remember you're being hired as an employee at will. That means you can be hired and fired for any reason or no reason at all—just not a discriminatory reason. To the extent that you post the gospel of your church on your page, your prospective employer cannot judge you on your religion. But posting photos of yourself looking like a drunken moron does not put you in a protected class such that you can claim discrimination as a reason you don't get hired.

According to a recent survey by CareerBuilder.com, a full 63 percent of employers have decided against hiring someone after seeing the content of his or her online postings, for reasons including the candidate's reference to drinking and drug use, to pictures the person posted of him- or herself in a compromising position, and even because of the candidate's unprofessional screen name. (Hello, reeferlover1@aol.com!)

Q: So as long as I take down the "questionable" photos before I go for the job interview, I'm okay . . . right?

A: If you think you'll be saved by simply hitting the delete key, sorry to say it might already be too late. Just ask Miss New Jersey.

Amy Polumbo, Miss New Jersey 2007, posted some "not very

ladylike" pictures of herself on Facebook. She took them down before she took the crown, but years later they resurfaced anyway. You may believe that when you post pictures on the Web people can see them, and when you take them down they're gone. *Wrong!* Search engines like Google take snapshots of each page they examine as they crawl the Web and cache those pages as back up in case the original page is unavailable. When you do a search, you'll see not only the Web site you are looking for, but also a hot link to the cached page, which displays the history of the page at the time it was indexed. So even if you take a picture down, it still exists in cyberspace. And I'm sorry to say no amount of cash money will totally get rid of those naughty photos once they've been cached.

Q: **Yipes, so if I've already posted "incriminating" pictures of myself, am I done?**

A: Not necessarily. The reality is not every employer is so diligent; some don't check at all. For now, even those who do generally don't go all the way back to check your cached pages unless they really think there's more to uncover. So chances are good that if you take the naughty pictures down now, only the most resourceful of employers will go back in your history to dig up the dirt on you.

Just remember for the future that you don't really need the immediate world leering at the evidence you posted of your own "youthful indiscretions"—and don't do it again. There is some good news, though. I've heard they've created this great invention that lets you keep the memories of a fun vacation and even share them with friends but still maintain control over who sees

them. It's called a "photo album" and you can buy one now at
Rite Aid.

Q: Okay, I somehow managed to jump through the hoops, make
the photos disappear, and pass the personality test. Now I'm
being told the company wants to do a background check on
me. WTF? How is that relevant/legal?

A: You passed a personality test? Will wonders never cease! As it
turns out, more and more employers are delving into the back-
grounds of the candidates they are considering for employment
these days. If an employer is serious about your candidacy, it
can ask you to sign an authorization for background screening
if it hasn't already (many potential employers have you sign an
authorization at the time you submit your application). I know
you'll find this shocking, but people do lie every now and again
and employers want to make sure that what you've told them
about yourself is the truth. Of course it was especially ironic that
a chief financial officer of a company called Veritas was caught
lying on his resume, since *veritas* is the Latin word meaning
"truth."

What is your legal obligation to be truthful on a resume?
Most companies have a policy that lists lying on a resume or
job application as grounds for immediate termination, and there
are services that provide detailed checks of all the information
contained in a resume. Should you ever sue your employer after
you've been fired, and the company then discovers that you lied
on your application—even if it has fired you for an unrelated
reason—you may lose your claim if the company can prove it
would have fired you for resume fraud. For example, a com-

pany being sued for discrimination found out that the former employee lied on his application nineteen years earlier—and as a result the court eliminated his claim. This doesn't mean you can't polish your image to stand out from the crowd, but if you step over the line and lie, there are consequences. And that's the *veritas*.

Aside from your legal (and moral) obligation to be truthful, what are potential bosses who perform background checks allowed to find out about you if they choose to explore your past? More than you think. When you apply for jobs, most employers get your waiver to allow them to perform background checks and ask you to list references. While you expect them to call those people, you may not be aware that *before you're hired they are allowed to conduct education verifications; past employment verifications; county, state, and national criminal background checks; motor vehicle records checks; social security number verifications; and drug screening. If they notify you and tell you your rights, they can also check your credit history.* Though the brain trust at Veritas didn't think it necessary to use any of those screening tools, you may find that your potential employers will want to learn more about you than you'd like . . . and FYI, the first thing most employers check is your criminal record.

Q: My criminal record?! But it was just an open container . . . and I was in college . . . and, okay, yes, I might have been naked. . . . But ultimately I got off (so to speak). Can that really follow me around for the rest of my life?

A: Employers can ask if you have ever been *convicted* of a felony or a misdemeanor. However, in some states the law may prevent an employer from refusing employment on the basis of a conviction—even for a felony—unless the crime leading to conviction is related to the employment the candidate is seeking. (Example: if you've been convicted of stealing pharmaceuticals, you're probably not getting that job at CVS.) In making that determination, the nature of the offense, its severity, and the time that has elapsed since the offense are relevant considerations. Employers should therefore consider the ways the crime actually affects the candidate's qualification before rejecting him or her for employment.

In many jurisdictions, courts have programs for first-time nonviolent offenders that will "expunge" their conviction records if the person has complied with the terms of probation and stayed out of trouble. But be aware that *once a crime is expunged from your record it may still show up on your background screen.*

A Pennsylvania company that conducted preemployment background checks learned that an applicant had pled guilty to theft five years earlier—a crime of dishonesty. When they asked her about it, she provided paperwork showing that her record had been expunged. Prospective employers can find themselves not sure how to put the toothpaste back in the tube in a case like this: they stumble upon information that by law they cannot hold against a job seeker, but now they know something about a person they wish they didn't. Once a record is expunged, employers must treat the person as a court would: as someone with a clean record. What this means is that as a job seeker, if you know your background check is going to reveal information about you that you don't want to come as a surprise, you may want to consider coming clean up front. Either way, your employer is going to make a decision about your candidacy, based—whether a legal consideration or not—on your background. You may be better served by trying not to look like you are hiding something if your employer is going to find out the information anyway.

How far back can an employer check into your background? While most employers who perform background checks tend to go back seven years, *there's no legal limit on how far back into your history an employer can check.* The public transportation system in Pennsylvania has a regulation against hiring anyone who has been convicted for a violent crime. After starting his job as a driver for the division that transports the handicapped, one employee's background check showed that he had been convicted of second-degree murder following a fistfight when he was fifteen years old, forty-seven years earlier. He was fired for it, and he sued. He lost his case because the system argued successfully that it was a business necessity to prevent someone with violence in his past from transporting the handicapped.

Q: I'm supposed to sign a noncompete agreement before I start working. I get why they don't want me part-timing for a competitor while on the job, but this agreement bars me from going to a competitor even after I leave here. Isn't that a violation of the whole "life, liberty, and pursuit of happiness" thing?

A: No, ma'am. Except in a few states, like California, an employer can make it a requirement of employment that you sign a noncompete agreement in order to work for the company. More and more employees are handed noncompetes and told that if they want the job, they have to sign them. Assuming that you do want to take the job, try to negotiate the agreement before you start. First, ask that it be changed so it's only enforceable if you quit, not if you are let go. Second, ask to limit it only to certain clients or certain competitors.

When the former vice president of the EMC Corporation, a high-tech firm, was looking for a new job, he landed the chairman and CEO post at SANgate, one of EMC's major competitors. EMC, none too pleased with this development, contacted its former veep, reminding him that he'd signed a noncompete barring him from working with EMC's competitors or soliciting its clients after he left. Presumably the man thought what most people do when they're reminded of those agreements: "Whoa, you were serious about that?" Uh, yeah—EMC sued him and a judge ruled that he had to quit his new job until the noncompete period expired.

That's why it's important to remember that your best time to negotiate with your employers is at the start—when they want you for the job—not when you want to split and they have the power to stand in your way.

ROBIN: You're going to laugh.

AMY: Tell me.

ROBIN: *Gear* magazine published a piece I wrote.

AMY: Hey, that's awesome, congrats!

ROBIN: Yeah, I think you're going to like it. Has a lot to do with what we've been talking about. . . . In fact, it's all about another job interview I went on recently.

AMY: Really? Which one was that?

ROBIN: You know, might be better if you just read the piece. I'll forward it to you. . . .

Gear Magazine
RANCH DRESSING
By: Robin Epstein

The truth is I often dress like a whore. I mean, come on, what good girl-next-door doesn't? Yet when it came time to pick out an interview suit for an "adult entertainer" (read: whore) position at the Chicken Ranch, the world-famous legal brothel, I was suddenly at a loss. I was doing "undercover" research for a television pilot I'm writing, and my interview to hook was scheduled for 9:00 on a Tuesday morning.

I had no idea what to expect. Would I have to do a striptease, give free samples, shoot ping-pong balls from my crotch? When you're offering your body as an ATM—push buttons, stick card in slot, collect cash—nothing seems out of the question. But when I arrived at the Ranch, I was put at ease by the fifty-year-old woman in a bright green business suit who came to greet me. She had the short, efficient peroxide blond hair of a well-seasoned administrative assistant and told me to follow her into the parlor of the brothel.

I took a seat on a Victorian-style white velveteen couch encased in clear plastic covers—the kind generally favored by ethnic families in deepest Brooklyn. It seemed none of the furnishings had been purchased more recently than 1970, although I was not about to carbon-date any stains to be certain. One side of the parlor had a seating area; the other had glass cases containing T-shirts, mugs, and caps emblazoned with the Chicken Ranch logo—two sexy legs emerging from a cracked eggshell—to bring home to the wife and kids as a souvenir of your journey.

Eventually Vicki, the assistant manager, came out to meet me. She looked to be in her late forties, with frizzed brown hair and pockmarked skin. The phrase "rode hard and put away wet" came to mind. In a deep rasp Vicki explained she had a terrible cold, before she coughed into her hand then extended it to shake. "Oh, that's too bad," I replied, thinking a cold just might be the luckiest thing I'd catch here.

She sat down in the chair across from me and quickly took me in before lobbing the first question: "So, you ever done this before?"

I answered honestly that I hadn't, thinking this might be an asset. But she just coughed, cocked her head at an angle, and said, "But you've danced, right?"

"Oh, dancing, right. Sure." I smiled.

I waited for Vicki to ask me to stand up, twirl around, or do something provocative, but she didn't. Instead she simply asked where I lived and if I were planning to move to Nevada. So I asked her if the job required any special skills, like domination or the ability to pee on command. No, she said, most of the guys just like the normal stuff. They're businessmen, conventioneers, or foreigners, and it's a big enough thrill for them just to come here. She said the Ranch's business is directly linked to that of Vegas, so a post—September 11th downturn in tourism had hit them hard. Because of that, Vicki explained, and because of the competition presented by Sherri's Ranch, the recently renovated brothel next door, they did not want even one potential customer to walk away unsatisfied. She stared at me hard and I'm sure she was checking out my chest, which for the first time in a job interview seemed perfectly understandable.

Vicki then took me on a tour of the place to show me where the girls worked, lived, and ate. As we walked down a long hallway, I noticed several pairs of Lucite fuck-me pumps lined up outside the doors as if in a fine hotel, waiting to be shined. The girls were out that morning for their weekly gynecological exams, so we went into one of the bedrooms, a smallish gray room the most prominent feature of which was the bed. The bed didn't stand out because it was particularly large or unusually shaped, rather because it was jam-packed with stuffed animals. On the floor there were more stuffed animals, several pairs of aggressively designed shoes, as well as a brightly colored as-seen-on-TV Ab-Cruncher. There were no family photographs, yet the room still seemed as personally impersonal as the setting allowed. It was in this bedroom, which the girl rented from the brothel, that she lived and worked for the duration of her stay. Girls are required to work a minimum of seven consecutive days, but most opt to do two or three weeks in the house before taking time off.

In the large, mess hall–type kitchen we passed a pay phone and Vicki told me that this was the only phone the girls were allowed to use while they were at work; cell phones were confiscated until the girls left.

From the kitchen window, Vicki pointed to the cabanas outside, where if a girl got really lucky, a gentleman would take her for an entire weekend. The prostitutes get picked from a lineup, so I asked Vicki what happened if someone never got chosen. She nodded. "Happens sometimes," she said, "but generally a girl waits a few days then someone comes in who will want her. Takes all types, you know." And oddly, I found this reassuring.

Vicki then escorted me back to the parlor. "So why don't you give me a call to let me know what dates you can come back to work," she said. I smiled, thanked her, and realized this meant I could start writing "whore" on my 1040. Great!

Or at least, great material for a TV show.

AMY: Wow, Rob. I love the details—and I particularly liked your relief when you learned you wouldn't have to wait forever to be chosen (like a seventh grade girl at a middle school dance). But *ahh*! My eyes! My eyes! Shooting a ping-pong ball from your crotch? I get the whole "This is just for my TV show" thing, but I've now spent *waaay* more time than any sister should thinking about her sibling's special talents down there. And by the way, how proud Mom must be that your "career" has led to this!

I also liked when you wrote, "She was checking out my chest, which for the first time in a job interview seemed perfectly understandable." I think perhaps you interviewed for one of the only jobs where the size of your chest is the opposite of irrelevant—it's a bona fide occupational qualification.

You'd certainly have a hard time making a claim for sexual harassment, I can tell you that. So let's talk about sex—sex and the workplace, specifically—shall we?

Sexual harassment is a form of employment-based sex discrimination that violates Title VII of the Civil Rights Act of 1964. Because it's based on employment, sexual harassment must occur at your job to be considered actionable. That's why, despite how much he deserves it, you can't sue the jerk at the bar who tells you he'd like to use your thighs as earmuffs.

Q: In my last job, my boss and I had a conversation about how many dates people go on before they have sex. I said three seemed like the right number, he replied, "Oh yeah? Then what are you doing Monday, Tuesday, and Wednesday nights?" Made me laugh, but technically isn't that sexual harassment?

A: Okay, let's start with the basics: If your supervisor were serious about wanting to sleep with you Wednesday night, and your job depended on it, that would illustrate one of the two types of sexual harassment called "quid pro quo harassment." Quid pro quo harassment is when job action is premised on your acquiescence to sexual requests. In this case it seems pretty clear that your boss was joking, and you took it as a joke. He wasn't actually making a demand for favors, he was just kidding, so it wasn't quid pro quo harassment. *But* he was joking in a sexual manner, and that figures into a potential claim for the other type of sexual harassment known as "hostile work environment sexual harassment."

As a baseline, the first test to make out *any* claim for harassment is: *were you offended?* Since you weren't offended, it wasn't harassment. In fact, in this instance you were a full participant. You must be subjectively offended to file a claim for harassment. And that's true even if the banter would have shocked or surprised a reasonable person. Both prongs need to be met: you need to be subjectively offended, and a reasonable person would be offended by the comments (so someone on the other end of the taste spectrum—a superprickly and oversensitive person—can't necessarily file a claim just because she was offended, if it wasn't something that would offend a person with reasonable sensitivity).

Q: Then what's deemed a hostile work environment?

A: A hostile work environment is when the jokes, gestures, or other inappropriate conduct is not directed at any particular individual, but the workplace is so permeated by this hostility that it becomes impossible for a worker to do her job. A female worker can therefore be considered a victim of sexual harassment even if nothing is directed at her personally. But in order *to prove that a hostile work environment exists, a plaintiff must show both that the conduct was objectively offensive* (that a reasonable person would find it so—not a convent of nuns) *and that the conduct was subjectively offensive* (that the person filing the complaint was actually offended).

In a case in Florida, two less-than-gentlemen worked as supervisors together. They were the life of the office—telling dirty jokes to the entire office and hanging up naked photos. They were shocked when they were named as defendants in a sexual harassment complaint against the company by an older female employee. Could she make out a claim if she had never been the butt of their jokes and they had never once propositioned her? The answer is yes because she argued that the climate in the office was so offensive, it interfered with her ability to do her job.

Q: I heard about a case in a sitcom writing room (for the show *Friends*) where an assistant argued the same thing—that there was a constant stream of sexual jokes, gestures, and discussions. But she lost the sexual harassment claim. Why?

A: Well, it's much harder to prove that you are subjectively offended by sexual banter when it's your job to create sexual banter. The court found in favor of the sitcom's writers and refused to award the assistant damages because it found first that she was not subjectively offended. The court also found that while the comments she listed were crude, they were not regular or common enough to be considered sufficiently severe, or pervasive enough to create a hostile work environment. The initial verdict even required the assistant to pay the defense costs of the writers, in excess of $400,000, although that requirement was ultimately overturned.

Q: What if you just have a dirty mind and mouth? Can you protect yourself from claims of sexual harassment by letting people know in advance you're a little bit harass-y?

A: That's just what Dov Charney, chief executive officer (and underwear designer) for American Apparel, tried to claim. Dov thought it would be a good idea to conduct job interviews in his underwear. Guess he wanted the applicants to get an up-close and personal look at what he does for a living.

Unfortunately, though he may be an expert on the rules of fashion, he's less well versed in the rules of sexual harassment. No surprise, his ass got sued. But Charney's argument was an interesting one: he warns all applicants in word and deed that the environment fostered by the company is one of sexual openness, and if they don't like it, they shouldn't accept the job. So why—given the very full disclosure—does an employee later have a right to sue for sexual harassment?

Unwelcome sexual advances, requests for sexual favors, and other verbal or physical conduct of a sexual nature constitute harassment when the conduct explicitly or implicitly affects a person's employment or interferes with his or her work performance or creates an offensive environment. An offended employee does have a responsibility to follow the company's complaint procedure if he or she is offended, but under the law *simply telling an employee up front that the workplace is a sexually hostile work environment doesn't protect the company from a suit.*

Q: **What about porn on the job? Is it okay to look at it as long as I don't share it with others?**

A: Since most employers have a tendency to want you to work when you're at the office, it's *probably* against policy even if you're not trolling the nasty sites. But yes, you can still face harassment charges if you're looking at porn at your own desk. In a case in Illinois, a woman sued her boss for sexual harassment because he looked at pornography on his computer in his office even though he never sent the pictures to or discussed them with her.

She said she was so offended by the pornography her supervisor was viewing, she became afraid to enter his office at all. Despite the fact that he kept the porn to himself, he and the company were still liable for creating an intimidating environment that was sufficiently severe and pervasive enough to be considered harassing.

A court will consider whether all of the offensive incidents add up to "unreasonable interference" with the plaintiff's work performance by creating an offensive or intimidating work environment. But if you think it's hard explaining to your wife how the pornography got on your home computer, try explaining to your boss how the pornography and the lawsuit wound up on your desk at the office. Best advice—save the porn for a time when it will be for your eyes only.

Q: Let's say I get wrecked at the company Christmas party and get a little touchy-feely with an assistant. That's sort of like expected, right? I mean, nothing bad could happen to me, could it?

A: Well, Mrs. *Claws*, while a single instance of improper sexual conduct will rarely give rise to a finding of sexual harassment, the conduct of management and coworkers at Christmas parties is often used as evidence that management was aware of a sexually hostile work environment. That coupled with other incidents could lead to a jury verdict against the employer.

Now, can employers be held responsible for the improper behavior of their employees at a Christmas party? Yes, they can! But what if the party is off-site or if attendance is completely voluntary? It turns out that makes no difference—the company is still responsible for a party under its auspices when it's paying the tab. So employers should remind both employees and its managers before the party that they will be expected to behave professionally. I can imagine little more embarrassing than asking a manager in a Santa suit to explain why he's making employees sit on his lap while telling them what he'd like to stuff in their stockings.

AMY: Here's a story that happened to a colleague in my own office that I still find mind-boggling. A woman in my sales department is this very pretty, very cool twenty-something, and one day she walks into my office and asks if she can close the door—never a good sign. She sits down and tells me she's just been to see the procurement manager of a prospective client. He brought her into his office and told her to take the seat across the desk from him.

She starts her pitch by telling him about our company's offerings. But as she's talking, she notices that he's moving really close to the edge of his desk so she can't see his hands or anything below his waist. She keeps talking as she sees his arm begin moving up and down. He starts rocking back and forth right in front of her, the whole time keeping his eyes focused on her. She's not a dumb or naïve woman; she knows he's masturbating; but since she doesn't know what else to do, she keeps talking.

After a few minutes, he lets out a small moan, which he tries to disguise as a cough. Then he actually reaches over to grab a tissue and cleans himself off under his desk. When he's done, he ushers her out of his office. She was so shell-shocked she just walked out of his office, drove back to ours, and came straight to my office.

ROBIN: Holy shit.

AMY: I know. Just hearing the story shell-shocked me. After I tried to console her, I asked her what she wanted me—and the company—to do. She told me that she wanted justice: she wanted to sue him for sexual harassment and then get him fired.

ROBIN: Smart girl. So how much did she win?

AMY: See, that's the problem. She can't sue him for sexual harassment because sexual harassment is an employment-based discrimination claim and he's not our employee. He's the employee of a client, so no matter how extreme or outrageous or disgusting it was, she can't sue him for sexual harassment.

I told her that depending on the jurisdiction and what she saw, she could speak to the police to determine if a crime had been committed. But in the employment context on the civil side, she can't sue him for sexual harassment. Now what she could do would be to try to sue *us* for sexual harassment because as her employer, if we failed to protect her from that treatment, we could be liable. We'd be liable if, for example, we'd known that the procurement manager had a history of that and we still sent her over there anyway. (We didn't.)

An example of a case like that is Rena Lockard's. A waitress at a Pizza Hut, Lockard had complained several times about having to wait on a specific group of rowdy patrons when they came in, yet her manager forced her to continue serving them if they sat in her station. Every time those patrons came in, they patted her fanny, made catcalls, asked her out, and harassed her, so she quit—and sued Pizza Hut. Rena won, striking a blow against the protectors of cheese-stuffed-crust-eating fanny-patters everywhere. Feel free to insert your own "made off with the dough" joke here.

Employers can be held legally responsible for what's known as third-party harassment—the harassing acts of nonemployees—in circumstances where the employer knew or should have known of the conduct and failed to take action to stop it, in this case either by escorting out the patrons or allowing a male waiter to take over.

Companies should have a policy against harassment, one that forbids inappropriate conduct against its employees by people with whom they are, by nature of their employment, forced to interact. Managers are well served to protect their employees, even at the cost of losing some poorly behaved patrons.

ROBIN: Noted. So what happened with the woman in your office when she found out she couldn't sue the guy?

AMY: Well, she was furious (understandably) and asked me if she had any recourse. I told her I'd be happy to call the guy's boss for her, which I did. After I explained the situation to him, I then wrote up a memo to their human resources director. It's ultimately up to the management team of his company to decide how to handle the matter internally. But I also spoke to a manager in our office and told him what had happened. He then placed a note in the client record along with a Do Not Call message in the database, which we use once we've decided not to pursue the business of a particular client.

Finally I thanked the woman for telling me, so no one here would have to face the guy again, and I assured her she would never be put in that situation again, either. Though she said she was grossed out by the whole thing and wanted to go home and take a hundred showers, she also said she was grateful for the way we responded around here.

ROBIN: Strong work.

AMY: Thank you, but I'm just doing my job—trying to make one person slightly less grossed out each and every day.

ROBIN: It's a noble calling.

AMY: Which I take as high praise from a woman who almost wrote "whore" on her 1040. . . .

Q: Can a person go to jail for sexual harassment?

A: What we've been talking about is *sexual harassment as a civil claim—not a criminal offense.* Though you can be sued for monetary damages, it will not lead to jail time. (You might prefer to be put away than to face your wife if she finds out there's a claim against you, but let that be a lesson to you!)

However, a comedian in New York faced a criminal penalty when he decided to high-five an audience member's breast in the middle of his show. Apparently she didn't find this joke very funny, and she called the cops. The comic was charged with "forcible touching," and ultimately received a fifteen day suspended jail sentence. But the judge told him that if he "molests" another woman's breasts within the next year, he'll face those fifteen days in prison. The threat of jail looms because touching someone's private parts is the criminal offense of "sexual battery or other offensive touching." So in a situation like this, give yourself a hand by keeping your hands to yourself.

Q: My company's policy manual is less interesting than the translated instructions for my Humanure Compost Toilet System. I know how to do the job—do I *really* need to read this policy crap?

A: I know, I know, you *tried* to read that policy manual but your eyelids kept getting in the way, right? My suggestion is to pour yourself a big cup of coffee and try reading it again because the policies outlined in your procedure manual can be both helpful and potentially detrimental to you. In one case in New Jersey, a man who was suspected of stealing from his office sued the employer when he was fired because he never had an administrative hearing. Though this right doesn't exist under federal or state law, he claimed it was granted in the employment handbook.

Some policy manuals do make it sound like an employee is guaranteed a "termination procedure" before he or she can be let go, mandating that the company must first give a verbal warning, then a written warning, then a suspension, before a person can be fired. So the manual could obligate a company to follow certain procedures before canning you. But before you assume your employee handbook provides protections against swift dismissal, also look to see if your employer included an "Employment At Will" section. That's the part that says something to the effect of, "You know all this feel good nonsense about how happy we are to have you working for us and what a fair company we are? Yeah, well it's kinda baloney. You're still an employee at will, which means we reserve the right to fire you at any time for any reason—or for no reason at all!" It may also include an acknowl-edgment form for you to sign, stating that you understand that policies are subject to change and that the manual doesn't give you extra rights.

The bottom line is that the policy manual should help you to better understand what rights your employer is granting you, as well as what your rights and responsibilities are, to keep you gain-fully employed and/or to prevent the door from hitting you on the behind on your way out.

Q: **Say I've put on a couple—or twenty—pounds and can no lon-ger squeeze my ass into my uniform. As if this weren't a big enough blow to my self-esteem, my employer tells me he's going to fire me unless I lose the weight. He can't really do that . . . can he?**

A: Unfortunately "fat" isn't a protected class and therefore your boss isn't prevented under federal law from firing you based on your weight, unless it's as a result of pregnancy or a medical condi-tion. (For some reason the svelte framers of our Constitution didn't believe the need to "supersize it" constituted a medical condition.)

The Borgata Hotel Casino and Spa in Atlantic City set off a firestorm of criticism when it implemented a policy barring servers of a certain size from working at the bar. Servers and bartenders, both male and female, who gain more than 7 per-cent of their body weight for any reason other than pregnancy or a medical condition can be fired from the casino. Since the Borgata claims that people come there specifically to gawk at the servers—whom they believe are actually performers—they argue they are simply trying to maintain a certain look for those performers.

I'm sure you're wondering why this case came out differently than the one in which Abercrombie was cited for discrimination against "non-beautiful people." The reason is because there was no allegation that the Borgata only hired one ethnic group—and once hired, males, females, and all races alike had to abide by the same policy.

Q: Now say I have a friend who likes to take a toke of something every now and again to, you know, relax her. She'd never smoke up on the job, and her little habit doesn't affect her performance, so even if the company is given no reason to suspect there's a problem, can they drug-test her?

A: An employer is well within its rights to make employees take both medical tests *and* drug tests. And you can tell your friend, Puffy, that if she works for the government, she's screwed. The federal government has just made proposals to expand its drug testing of federal workers to include testing of hair, saliva, and sweat. Ew, right? But as a private worker, can your employer randomly drug-test you? In a word: yes.

Most state law allows an employer to conduct drug testing, with certain restrictions to protect employee privacy. Private employers generally may test employees both prior to giving an offer of employment and throughout employment. In general, the court tends to scrutinize more carefully random drug testing, as opposed to testing based on reasonable suspicion or after an on-the-job accident. In addition, courts may examine the procedures surrounding the implementation of all drug-testing programs, in-

cluding protections such as the integrity of the sample and the
employee's privacy. The best advice, of course, is just say no to
drugs. (The moral of that story brought to you by Mom, who
paid me to say it.)

And here's an interesting twist: although, as mentioned before, employers can generally refuse to hire for any reason short
of discrimination, it is illegal in twenty-nine states to fail to hire
a person for use of tobacco. But that leaves twenty-one states
where it's legal to do so, and many companies are moving to test
applicants for the presence of nicotine and other tobacco indica-
tors in the blood, along with the other drug tests they give. The
World Health Organization announced that it will begin asking
the following questions on its job applications: Do you smoke?
If so, if you were hired by WHO would you continue to smoke?
Like the question "Does this outfit make me look fat?" there is,
in fact, a right answer here—you will not be hired if you are a
smoker.

Both private companies and state and local governments
are getting into the smoker-punishment mode with a list
of penalties—up to and including refusal to hire employees
who smoke. In Georgia, laws have been passed that mandate
cigarette-smoking state employees and public school teachers to
pay a flat fee of forty extra dollars per month for health care. In
Alabama, smokers pay an extra twenty dollars. In Pennsylvania's
Montgomery County, the plan was to stop hiring smokers entirely (though the intention was announced, it never became the
policy). Keep in mind that under the law *your employer may le-*
gitimately take action against you for your off-duty conduct, particu-
larly where that conduct will negatively affect the employer. In this
case, the effect lies in the rising cost of health care benefits.

As for other medical testing, it is perfectly legal for an employer to demand that an employee comply as long as it is done to show that the employee can perform job duties (and not to use a disability as a basis to discriminate). This case was raised when a one-armed woman walked into an interview for a job as a paramedic, and she was eliminated "out of hand" (sorry, couldn't help myself) because it was assumed she could not provide services on the basis of a disability.

The Americans with Disabilities Act prohibits a company from conducting medical exams before extending an offer of employment. However, it does not prevent an employer from asking in an interview about an applicant's ability to perform—as long as the question is not designed to get to someone's disability, but only to his or her ability to do the job. Questions like "What's wrong with you?" are prohibited. The question "Is there anything that would prevent you from performing these job functions?" is perfectly appropriate. Once a job offer has been extended, the employer may also conduct medical tests to evaluate the employee's ability to perform. If you have more questions about what is and what isn't legal on that topic, visit the EEOC's Web site.

Q: **Now that I'm in my job and doing well in it, it doesn't matter what I post online . . . does it?**

A: From the "that's what picture frames are for, ya dumb-ass" department: a teacher in Austin was terminated after she posted topless photos of herself on MySpace.com. She called the pictures "art." Her students called them "Oh my *God*! My teacher's Tits Magee!" Though you and I (and, presumably, all of her students) find this hilarious, the school district had a distinctly different opinion.

People have the idea that once they get their job, they only have to perform it competently to keep it. They believe that what they post on the Web on their own time is their own business and that they can't be fired for it. *Wrong!* What you do off duty is up to you, but if you violate your employer's policy or the law, don't think you can't be punished for it. Employers are well within their rights to discipline workers who violate policy—even off duty—and particularly those stupid enough to publicize their bad acts.

It's just important to keep in mind that your employer may be less "cool" about these things than you think. So if you wouldn't post it on the walls of your cubicle, don't post it in cyberspace, where it may just as easily come to the attention of those who can fire you for it.

Q: The woman in the cube next to me must bathe in her perfume—her obsession with Obsession is killing me. What can I do about Pepé Le Pew?

A: Too bad your office isn't in Murfreesboro, Tennessee, because it's now illegal to stink there. In response to a city employee's body odor, the city council mandated a policy on good hygiene, including a limit on too much perfume.

In an office, it's in everyone's best interest for an employer to set a policy on good personal hygiene. Adding a dress code, requiring employees to dress neatly in profession-appropriate clothing, is generally a wise move, too. The policy is legally acceptable even where it includes examples of acceptable gender-related work garb: khakis and button-down shirts for men, skirts or slacks for women. It can't direct women to behave a certain way based on sexual stereotypes or impose unequal burdens on men and women. But adding a simple line to the dress code policy to include the requirement of good personal hygiene will make any later discussion easier to start.

Rather than taking an employee to task for not showering, it is much easier to tell him or her that he's not adhering to the personal dress and hygiene policy, and that he is required to look presentable and professional in a work environment. Obviously, you don't need to make a federal (or even city) case of this. Instead, if the discussion takes place in private and with sensitivity, it shouldn't happen again.

Q: Yeah, I complain about work every now and again, but there's a guy in my office who whines incessantly. Aside from a lobotomy, is there anything that can be done to make him stop?

A: Well, one German company has implemented a no-griping policy, which states employees must be in a good mood to keep their jobs. If they complain more than twice without also offering a suggestion for improving the source of the complaint, they risk losing their jobs. Those good-humored Germans!

In the wake of massive corporate meltdowns and malfeasance at companies like the Madoff Securities firm and Enron, complaining about financial or other improprieties in the workplace isn't necessarily a bad thing. So to the extent that a coworker voices a valid concern about an office practice, it may be illegal to take action against that person. But when the employee is merely a constant whiner, you do have a right to put an end to it.

If you work with someone who is hurting your morale, you

should feel free to tell the person that you prefer not to hear it. If you supervise such a person, you should have a discussion—and consider adding a memo to the personnel file—about office morale. Sadly, no such effective "stop whining!" options exist when you're taking your kids on a long car ride to Grandma's house.

Q: Do I have the right to see my personnel file?

A: Under most state laws, an employer must permit a current employee or an agent of an employee to view his or her own personnel file, and it must make the records available during regular business hours. The employer may require the employee to put the request in writing, along with the reasons for the inspection—employers know that happy employees generally don't ask to see their own files.

An inmate in the Pennsylvania prison system sued the state to view his inmate record, likening it to an employee's personnel file. (And perhaps it's apt for an employee to be compared to a prisoner.) But the court in that case denied his right to see the inmate file because he's not an employee of the state—he's a prisoner of it—and therefore isn't accorded the same rights.

Generally you, as an upstanding citizen and employee, will have this right but there are exceptions. In some states, *ex*-employees don't have a right to view the file. So once you get fired for what's in there, it's too late to see what it was.

Q: When I was told to stop hoarding and share my office supplies, I called my coworkers communists and made them Karl Marx beards out of *my* sticky notes. But my boss threatened to fire me if I kept it up! How is that not a violation of my First Amendment rights?

A: You're making the classic fourth grade mistake, the one that goes: it's a free country so I can do what I want! Yes, the First Amendment grants you the right to freedom of expression, but it only applies to the government, which must give you the right to free speech. *It doesn't apply to private entities,* which are within their legal rights to prevent you from freely expressing yourself on their time. In fact, a Wal-Mart greeter in Iowa was fired when he welcomed customers with a photo of himself, naked but for a strategically placed Wal-Mart bag. He told customers that Wal-Mart was cutting costs and that this was the new uniform. For whatever reason, fully-clothed Wal-Mart officials didn't find this terribly funny.

You need to remember that the First Amendment does not mean you are free to give anyone and everyone a piece of your mind or say anything you want, at any time, and expect to keep your job. If you want to complain about your employer, do it through the procedure it has set in its policy manual. And if you need to welcome people with a naked picture of yourself with your junk in a bag, do it at your own front door unless you're really ready to be sacked.

Q: My office is teeming with Republicans. They're everywhere (though mostly in management, go figure . . .), and when we start talking politics, things get heated and mean. Classic liberal's question, I know, but can the company do anything to help a girl out?

A: Talking politics can be rough stuff, cupcake—just ask former Vice President Dick Cheney, who might tell you to go "f***" yourself, as he did Senator Patrick Leahy on the Senate floor. But companies can, in fact, prevent employees from engaging in political discussions. Again, because your "right" to free speech is only a right when dealing with the government, the Constitution does not protect people from what they can and can't say to private entities like employers. Therefore, companies are well within their rights—and during a heated election may be advised—to create policies that require collegiality among coworkers.

While many states restrict an employer's right to terminate an employee for political associations outside the office, when an employee steps into the place of business, he may be required to act professionally and not verbally dress down a coworker for a difference of political opinion—even if that coworker really "f***ing" needs it.

Q: Burgerama fired me for wearing a PETA button on my uniform. That impinges on my freedom of association, doesn't it?

A: Well, if you had that right, you might have a case. But the claim didn't work for four corrections officers who joined the Outlaws

Motorcycle Club either. You may have heard of the Outlaws. They're the leather jacket–wearing no-goodnik archrivals of the Hells Angels, and in 1997, a U.S. Attorney indicted and convicted a number of its members for racketeering, murder, narcotics trafficking, and firebombings. Even though the officers in question were never accused of taking part in any crime, they were fired solely on the basis of their association with the club, so they bravely took justice into their own hands: they sued. Did they win?

No, they did not. The Outlaws Motorcycle Club corrections officers lost their lawsuit because the court found that their association with a club that promotes illegal activities reflected badly on the department of corrections, and their personal association could cause the public to fear for its safety. Keep in mind their employer is the government, which is bound to protect freedom of association (except in situations like this). And remember, your private employer has even more freedom to fire you if it doesn't like your peeps. The reality is, sometimes you do have to choose between your posse and your profession. So if you plan to choose the job, make sure your associations don't put it in any jeopardy.

Q: **I was just told I have to work Thanksgiving Day—a national holiday! It's so un-American, it has to be illegal, right?**

A: Unfortunately for you, the answer is no, it's not illegal for an employer to make an employee work on a national holiday. Mean, yes. Illegal, no. And as unfair as it may seem, under federal law it's also not required that your employer give you extra holiday or premium pay that day unless you've already worked more than forty hours that week. (In that case, you may be entitled to overtime if you're a nonexempt worker.)

Though it may be hard to swallow when you're punching the clock as your family's munching turkey, the bright side is that you still have an employer who wants you to work. In this economy, that's truly something to be thankful for.

Q: How much of a right to privacy do I have at my job?

A: Bradley Leedham, a manager at the Village Beach Market in Vero Beach, Florida, was told by the company's CEO that he wanted to inspect Leedham's briefcase to make sure he wasn't stealing anything as he was leaving the market. When Leedham refused to allow the search he was fired. You're wondering who died and made the CEO Columbo, aren't you? More importantly, you're probably also wondering if *your* boss has the right to search your briefcase or personal belongings.

Well, unlike the police, who need reasonable suspicion or a search warrant, when you're in your place of employment, your boss can search your personal items when he sees fit. While an employee may have an expectation of privacy in some aspects of the workplace—an employer can't conduct a strip search, for example—if it's stated in the policy manual that management reserves the right to inspect your personal property, those items can be searched.

In Leedham's case the boss argued exactly that: the company's handbook stated that the employer reserved the right to inspect belongings, and that failure to allow the search constituted insubordination, an offense punishable by firing. Peruse your policy book to recheck what your employer reserves the right to do. But the best advice is that whenever you enter the workplace you should only bring personal items that aren't too personal for inspection.

You should also keep in mind that if you work for a private employer, you do not have the right to privacy in your desk—and when I say "your desk," I mean the one that the employer provided for you to use. So if, say, you plan to commit armed robbery like one genius in Orlando, Florida, discovered, it's best not to leave the stickup gun in your desk drawer at work. But even if you're not suspected of stowing a firearm in your junk drawer, *your employer can look through your personal papers, pictures, or other items that are none of the company's (or the police's) business.*

It may be different if you get a locker and are given the only key to that locker—but in cases in which employers have searched a desk and found the contraband they were looking for, employees have not been able to show that the employers had no right to look for what they found.

Another note on privacy: Remember how cool you thought it was that your company gave you a BlackBerry or a company car to use? You might think it a smidge less sexy when you learn your company can use those devices to keep track of your movements. Though potentially very helpful to them, New York taxi drivers considered striking because they felt the GPS systems installed in their cabs could be used to pinpoint their whereabouts.

Cell phones are equipped with E911 technology, which can help the police locate you in the event of an emergency. The technology is, in essence, a global positioning system that can allow not just the police but your telecom company—and the employer who gave you that phone or the GPS in your car—the ability to monitor its location *and yours* when you're carrying it or driving with it. Currently there's no federal law that prevents employers from doing just that—with or without telling you they are doing so. In other words, if you have been given a phone by your employer, you should ask not just whom you can talk to but what that phone may be saying about you!

Q: New job ... killing me ... worked a hundred hours last week, and they just told me "no overtime pay." How can they do that?

A: Under the federal Fair Labor Standards Act (FLSA), employees must be paid at least the minimum wage for all hours worked (which, as of July 24, 2009, was $7.25 per hour nationally, but may be higher as mandated by state law). In cases in which there are labor laws on both the federal and the state level, the law that is more protective of employees will govern and employers must pay time and a half the regular rate of pay for all hours worked over forty hours in a week.

But there's a catch, and that is that the FLSA provides an exemption from both minimum wage and overtime pay for certain employees—so-called exempt employees—who are employed as bona fide executive, administrative, professional, and outside sales employees. To qualify as exempt, workers need to be paid a salary of at least $23,660 per year (or $455 per week) and meet certain tests designed to ensure that they act with discretion and independent judgment.

To qualify for the *executive exemption*, the employee must be salaried, primarily manage the business, regularly direct the work of two or more full-time employees, and have the authority to hire and fire.

Job titles don't necessarily determine if someone is exempt. Just because you're given a title like, say, "executive back scratcher," it's not necessarily going to make you an exempt employee. In general, an exempt executive is the owner or boss of the office, or a director or manager who has those responsibilities. It's not only the boss who is exempt, though.

To qualify for the *administrative exemption*, the employee must be salaried, primarily perform nonmanual work directly related to management or general operations, and exercise discretion and independent judgment.

The exempt administrator is someone who works in areas like budgeting, auditing, finance, quality control, personnel management, human resources, and the like and whose job entails matters of significance for the running of the business. The employee has the ability to affect or implement management policies or operating procedures and has the authority to make independent choices, even if those decisions are reviewed at a higher level. Insurance claims adjusters, employees in the financial services industry, human resource managers, and purchasing agents are all examples of the administrative exemption.

To qualify for the *professional exemption*, the employee must be salaried, perform work requiring advanced knowledge, do work that is primarily intellectual, and have acquired such knowledge by a prolonged course of specialized instruction.

As a writer, you're considered a "creative professional," which makes you a professionally exempt employee. As a lawyer, I also fall under the professional exemption as a "learned professional" (stop laughing). In addition to these major exemptions, employees can also be considered exempt if they fall into the "outside sales" exemption, where they make sales primarily away from the employer's place of business. Despite often being paid an hourly wage, computer professionals may also be exempt (as opposed to the salary test for the big three exemptions) as long as they make at least $27.63 per hour (higher in California) and are computer systems analysts, programmers, software engineers, or other highly skilled workers.

Finally, even if you don't fall into any of the above exemptions but make more than $100,000 per year, you won't get overtime. Why? Because that's the way it goes, Moneybags.

Q: Say I want to get time off instead of getting paid out for the overtime I've worked. Is that something I can demand?

A: Under labor laws, you are entitled to overtime (unless you are an exempt employee) so you'd get time and a half for all hours over forty that you worked. Comp time is essentially the same as giving you straight time, though—an hour off for an overtime hour—not time and a half. Employees in the private sector can only receive comp time in the same week that they accrue overtime. So if you work extra hours on Monday the employer can allow you to take off early on that Friday. But if you're in a time crunch and work long hours all week, you have to be paid for it in overtime—even if you'd rather have extra time than extra money.

Q: A friend is thinking of working on one of those fishing boats in Alaska, but he's grown attached to his fingers and wants them to remain on his hands. Are there any laws to protect him?

A: OSHA, the Occupational Safety and Health Administration, was established for reasons just as this: to regulate and monitor conditions that may harm workers. Though safety precautions were too late to help a chocolate factory worker who died when he fell into a vat of chocolate, OSHA investigated the death to prevent future accidents of the Augustus Gloop-ian variety. And though falling into a vat of chocolate might not sound like a bad way to go when your number's up, dying at work is not part of the job description.

When you work in a dangerous workplace—an asbestos mine, for instance—health and safety procedures are hopefully paramount and made abundantly clear to all workers. But most office workers don't think of the corporate park as a health haz-ard (unless we're counting being bored to death). Still, OSHA has regulations intended to protect the health and safety of all workers. In addition to classically dangerous workplaces, it also has regulations governing computer workstations, grocery ware-houses, nursing homes, etc. From ergonomics to mold and other building toxins, OSHA regulates the working conditions that may harm workers.

If you're concerned about safety standards in your workplace, visit www.osha.gov—even if the only chocolate around is in the break room.

Q: Ate some bad sushi the other day, and *blergh*, I lost more than my lunch, I think I threw up the gum I swallowed five years ago. I was out of work for two days. But you know what made me *really* sick? I was told the days I missed counted as my vacation time! How is that fair?

A: You may be surprised to learn that there is no U.S. law that requires employers to give you paid sick time. If you have a disability, the law requires an employer to reasonably accommodate it. And if you've been employed for more than a year you may be entitled to family and medical leave. But your run-of-the-mill virus doesn't entitle you to days off. So if your employer chooses to give you sick days, the requirements of when you may take them are based on the policy. In most cases, you are given vacation and personal days for precisely those reasons and sick time is meant for times you really are sick. In some cases, you may even be required to get a doctor's note to prove your illness.

Now let's consider the opposite scenario: can your boss make you go home if you are sick and she's worried you'll infect the rest of the office? Well, a private employer can't discriminate against a qualified individual with a disability (defined as a condition that substantially limits one or more major life activities), and can't let personal prejudice against the disabled or perceived disabled dictate personnel policies. *But* a cold or virus that will go away is not considered a disability. Not only can an employer send a germy employee home, it should have a policy that says that if you pose a danger of infection to coworkers, you should go home, get better, and then come back to work.

Q: A woman I work with needs back surgery and the doctor told her she'll be laid up for at least a month, which makes her worried she'll be laid off. Does she have any rights?

A: I'm sorry for your friend, no surgery is pleasant, but she may be entitled to up to twelve weeks of unpaid leave thanks to the Family and Medical Leave Act (FMLA). A Wisconsin woman wasn't as fortunate. Angie Arttus was diagnosed with breast cancer, and after telling her supervisor of her need for treatment, the supervisor told human resources. Four days later she was called into the human resources office and fired. The fact that the supervisor will likely go straight to hell was probably cold comfort.

Under the Family and Medical Leave Act, a person who has worked for more than a year at a company may be entitled to up to twelve weeks of unpaid leave for a serious health condition. But if an employee isn't eligible for FMLA leave and is out of vacation time, his or her job may be in jeopardy. (This was the case with Arttus, who had worked for her employer less than a year at the time of her diagnosis.) If an illness is considered a disability, an employer may be required to make reasonable accommodations, such as giving an employee an alternative work schedule so he or she can go to treatment. But where attendance at the job site is a bona fide occupational qualification, or an employee can't work at all, the law won't require what your morals might: time off to get well instead of termination.

Amy

When my daughter, Emma, was six years old, she was nominated VIP of her class—a proud moment for any parent. Of course if you're *this* parent, you're a little less excited when you learn that every child in the class gets to be the very important person for a week, which means the kid gets to wear a plastic VIP necklace and his or her parents get to do a lot of work to entertain the rest of the class.

The other parents had been very creative. The family of one girl, who liked gardening, brought in flowerpots that the kids decorated and filled with soil and seeds. To this day that adorable little flowerpot sits on my kitchen windowsill reminding me what a good mommy Olivia has.

I decided the activity for Emma's week would be to make play dough: 1 cup flour, ½ cup salt, 1 tablespoon alum, 1 tablespoon oil, a cup of boiling water, plus mint extract to make the whole thing smell a little less vomitous. The entire process was supposed to take all of five minutes, which was key because we were to start at 8:30 and I was due in the office by 9:00 to meet with my CEO. He and I needed to discuss an earnings press release before handing it to the board of directors at the 10:00 meeting.

8:30: Emma, my husband, Len, and I were at school and ready to roll. Teacher Karen smiled at us then said, "Okay, children. Let me see your backpacks so I can check to see if there are any notes from your parents." Shuffle. Pause. Line up.

8:40: Bags are checked. "Okay, children, have a seat."

8:44: Children are seated. One hour and sixteen minutes until the board meeting. I clear my throat to start and am immediately cut off. "Okay, Emma," Teacher Karen exclaims, shooting me a *shut up and wait your turn* look, "why don't you introduce your special guests."

"This is my mommy and daddy," Emma says, beaming at us.

"Okay, class, who wants to welcome Emma's special guests?" Teacher Karen asks. Thousands of tiny hands seem to shoot up in the air. "What do you want to say, Robbie?"

"Welcome to our class."

"Good! Ben?"

"I'm glad you're here."

"Good! Miriam?"

And so it went.

8:54: One hour and six minutes until the board meeting. Finally, we begin making the play dough. Everyone gets flour, which is immediately everywhere. And I can hear Teacher Karen, the bitch, sighing. Then salt. Then alum. Then oil.

9:04: Now the boiling water, which isn't. I stick my finger in the pot. It's warm. I pull out the mint extract and pass it around for everyone to smell.

9:08: I stick my finger back in the pot. Water is hot, no bubbles. We wait.

9:10: From the back of the room, I hear Daniella, a child I actively despise. "Waiting is boring," she says.

Screw it. I pour in the nonboiling water and make ooze. I decide to begin throwing more flour and salt into each bowl indiscriminately, hoping it will dry up well enough to resemble play dough. Next I throw plastic baggies at the children so they can take it home and show their parents what a bad mommy Emma has. My husband says, "Go. I'll clean up." And that's all the encouragement I need. I run over to hug Emma. "You're-a-very-special-kid-all-day-every-day-and-I-hope-this-was-special-for-you-love-you-gotta-go-bye!"

9:25: Traffic jam.

9:45: Office. Run to CEO's office, who, bless his soul, doesn't much care that I am now forty-five minutes late and thinks the press release looks fine. I give it to my secretary, who, bless *her* soul, has caught two typos and one huge issue (board member resignation) that I forgot to disclose in the press release. I rewrite. She types, prints, and hands the new release to me as I run into the boardroom at 10:00, picking hard chunks of play dough out of my fingernails. Just another day at the office . . .

Q: My friend just had a baby and is considering hiring a nanny so she can go back to work. Are there any rules or regulations she needs to know?

A: As a working mother myself, I can tell her two rules: (1) your once perky boobs will come to resemble deflated water balloons and (2) you will be so much happier if you start thinking of your stretch marks as racing stripes. As for child care, the rule is this: If you have a worker in your home and you control what work is done (child care, cleaning, etc.) and how it is done, that worker is your employee regardless of whether she is full- or part-time, or that you've hired her from an agency. Therefore, if you pay that employee cash wages of $1,300 or more a year, you generally must withhold social security and Medicare taxes from all cash wages you pay.

If, however, the worker controls how the work is done—like a lawn service that provides its own tools—then the worker is self-employed. You do not need to withhold the taxes but should fill out a 1099 for wages over $600 paid in a year—a form you can get on the IRS Web site.

Often people rely on grandparents or family members to help care for children, but be aware that this brings complications with it, too. A friend of mine found herself in just such a situation. When her mother was told that she needed an operation, my friend was doubly distraught: of course she was worried about her mother, but she was also worried because she paid her mother to look after her kids when she went to work. Even though you may be your parents' child, if you pay your mom to babysit your child, she's technically your employee, too.

Word to the wise here: arrange all conditions and terms of employment up front since it is much easier to establish salary, sick days, paid or unpaid vacation days, and the like when you're not over a barrel. And be sure to set a term when the job will end or be reassessed so it doesn't look like a termination or end with hard feelings. It may, in fact, be helpful to go through the personnel handbook you were given by your office to remind you of all the issues and rules so that you can discuss them before they become problems. You thought negotiating with Mom for your allowance was hard—now try negotiating with her for hers.

Q: My crazy, sleep-deprived friend, New Mommy, hired a new nanny, but like most young mothers, she's a paranoid wreck. Can she use a "nanny cam" to see what goes on when she's not around?

A: So with one new baby your friend is already thinking about bringing Big Brother into the house, eh? Under federal wiretap laws, it is illegal for a private individual to tap a telephone or bug a room without the permission of the person being recorded. (Many states also forbid audiotaping without permission.) In several states nanny cams are not just intrusive, they're actually illegal.

Videotaping without sound, however, though seemingly more intrusive, is not necessarily illegal. Still, taping must not be done in "private" areas like the bathroom or the nanny's bedroom. My opinion is that the best practice to ensure no privacy rights are violated is for the person considering a nanny cam to advise the nanny in advance that her actions will be monitored. The verbal scare tactic itself will likely be enough to keep the nanny minding her p's and q's.

The "My Sister Is Smarter than She Looks" Section: Pearls of Wisdom Amy Offered Me When I Needed Commonsense Advice

How to Complain at Work

Think you have a bad boss? Results of a study published in the fall 2007 issue of *The Leadership Quarterly* found that 39 percent of workers said their supervisor failed to keep promises; 37 percent said their supervisor failed to give credit when due; and 27 percent said their supervisor made negative comments about them to other employees or managers. What should you do—and what shouldn't you do—if you have an abominable boss?

- *Do* discuss expectations with your boss.
- *Do* ask for direction if you think you are not giving your boss what she's asking for.
- *Do* speak candidly (but not meanly) with your boss at your performance evaluation about how you can improve your performance.
- *Do* follow the company's policy if you feel you are being harassed.
- *Don't* go to your boss with every little problem.
- *Don't* whine to others about your boss.
- *Don't* post your complaints online.
- And most importantly, *do* remember that you have a right to walk out the door if you can't take it anymore.

Asking for a Raise

No one looks forward to asking the boss for a raise, but there are some simple steps to prepare you for your discussion.

1. Wait until the right time to do it. Don't think just because you had a great first month at the company it's time to demand your due. Wait until your six-month or yearly review.
2. Come prepared with a list of your accomplishments, including how you've saved the department time or money, or the ways you have successfully performed the tasks assigned.
3. To learn if you are actually being underpaid, do a search to find out what others in your position in your industry are paid.
4. Finally, set a good tone for the discussion without being whiny—be confident in your abilities.

Dress Code for Office Parties

Remember that what you wear to a company party is something which will be seen by your coworkers—people whose respect you probably want to keep. If you've ever witnessed the sixty-year-old bookkeeper in a spangly Spandex catsuit at the company Christmas party or the fat guy from accounting in a Speedo at the office Fourth of July pool party (or worse, if you *are* the fat guy in accounting and notice that no one will make eye contact with you the following day), you already have experience with the most important rule of office parties: it's still an *office* party. You may be in a different setting, but you are still with your coworkers. That doesn't mean you can't put on a bathing suit if you feel comfortable, but save the string bikini for a time you won't see the people with whom you sit in meetings, or generally need to have take you seriously come Monday morning.

If you are planning the party, you may wish to remind workers in advance that shorts are acceptable, but that obscene clothing isn't. Also refrain from making mean or harassing comments to an inappropriately dressed coworker, who still has sexual harassment protections outside the office. And in this as in other office party settings, if you're a woman, though they *may* be real and they *may* be spectacular, best to keep the boobs under wraps so the wonder twins don't go causing any trouble.

Responding to a Bad Review

A worker in Pennsylvania was told in her performance evaluation that she could never get to the point and wasted time. She strongly disagreed, and to rebut the claim, she attached a twenty-seven-page document, discussing every single project she'd ever completed, thus perfectly proving the criticism her employer was trying to make.

Unlike Chatty Cathy, I'll get right to the point: don't write a rebuttal. Generally an employer won't read your brilliant denial, slap his forehead, and say, "My God, he's right!" Instead he'll probably think, "That ass doesn't take criticism well, either." The person giving the evaluation isn't interested in conducting a therapy session about your feelings toward your evaluation and most certainly doesn't want to hear why he's an imbecile for saying such things about you. If your rebuttal is angry or mean, it could even possibly get you fired.

Instead, have a brief talk with your supervisor and explain that you've heard and understand the goals set for you, and you'll work to accomplish them.

Progressive Discipline

While employees tend to think that their boss only has the right to hire or fire them, employers have an arsenal of ways to correct the bad behavior or poor performance if they see fit. It's called progressive discipline, and it generally starts with a verbal warning (something like, "Please stop doing XYZ." Or even, "Hey, cut that out!"). Then it can move to a written warning in your personnel file. Then to a demotion or cut in pay or suspension for a limited period of time. Finally, for further infractions, it can lead to termination. But not every company has such a policy, and depending on your employer, your first infraction could be your last—something to keep in mind when you're tempted to send around that "hilarious" cartoon you drew of your soon-to-be ex-boss losing his shit.

Fear of Firing

When the economy's in trouble, no one's job is safe but the undertaker's. While it's not always obvious when the pink slips will be sent, there are some indications that your job could be at risk. Even if the company is doing well, if you have received poor performance evaluations it doesn't take a crystal ball to see the handwriting on the wall. Since it's much easier to find a job if you have a job than if you've already been let go, network even when you're fully employed. Keep your resume current, maintain certificates, and consider all opportunities rather than assuming that your job will be here forever.

Flat-Out Fired

While you are considered innocent until proven guilty of a criminal charge in a court of law, your employer has no such burden in order to judge you for your actions inside or outside the workplace. Guilt or innocence is not necessarily the determinative factor in employment-related issues; the bad publicity caused by the allegation of immoral or offensive conduct may be reason enough for an adverse employment decision.

What to Say/What *Not* to Say in an Exit Interview

As you leave your job, you may be asked about the projects you've worked on, your contacts, and most intriguingly, your reasons for leaving. While genuine and constructive criticism may be of help to your employer if done in a nondefamatory way, resist the urge to let loose with every grievance and grudge you carried with you as you sat seething at your desk.

If your goal is to be taken seriously, you don't want to look hateful and bitter. You can be honest but don't be nasty or juvenile; that's just stupid.

Deleting Computer Files as You Leave

You may be tempted to delete data from your computer before you leave your job. Getting rid of personal files is a good idea. Deleting company records or destroying its data in a final "screw you" gesture: not such a good idea. Under the Computer Fraud and Abuse Act—a law designed to protect against computer hacking—a person can face criminal penalties of up to ten years imprisonment on a first offense.

Employers need to know that data destruction has become

a common way for disgruntled ex-employees to express their anger, and they should create protections for backing up data. And angry ex-employees should know that if they absolutely feel the need to use a finger to express their rage, they're better off using the middle one instead of the one that hits the delete key.

Giving a Reference to a Departed Employee

Parents in a school district in Florida were horrified by charges of molestation against a teacher, and further outraged when they learned that the teacher had been under suspicion for similar behavior at his former school. When they discovered the previous school district had given him a glowing recommendation because the teacher otherwise threatened to sue for defamation, the parents were up in arms.

Often companies are so happy to get rid of a problem employee, they gladly write a great recommendation to speed his departure. But when it comes to references, issues of defamation and disclosure must also be considered. When giving a reference, keep this in mind:

1. Ask the former employee to request in writing that you give such information to a prospective employer.
2. Stick to the facts: dates of employment, job duties, salary if requested.

Finally, if you must discuss performance, keep it as objective as possible: the employee types x words per minute, the employee was given a satisfactory evaluation, and so on.

Getting a Reference if You've Been Fired

Not everyone who leaves a job does so under happy circumstances. If you've been fired what can you do to avoid getting smeared when a potential new employer calls for a reference? Well, even employers who are angry about the behavior that led to your termination understand that speaking badly about someone can lead to defamation claims. So after the dust has settled, call your former human resources department to discuss what you'd like the company to say about you. Most companies will agree to release only your dates of employment and salary and at your request may even agree with your version surrounding your departure.

Severance

Many people believe that if they've worked for a company for a certain number of years they are entitled to a severance package if they're laid off. Unfortunately that's not true. Under the law, unless you have an employment contract or are party to a collective bargaining agreement that provides for it, there is no right to receive severance even if you're laid off without cause.

But just because a company doesn't have to offer severance doesn't mean that they won't, or that they wouldn't negotiate. Often employers will make a bargain whereby they agree to provide a severance package in exchange for a promise that the employee will not sue. In this economic climate it's hard to predict how generous (or not) employers can afford to be with severance. But it's almost always worth making an inquiry because since you are the person most interested in your financial well being, you're the one who potentially has something to gain.

Two Weeks' Notice

Congratulations! You found a new job and you gave your employer the standard two weeks' notice. But your employer might not be so thrilled about your departure. In fact, he might tell you to pack your things and leave immediately, not letting you work and get paid for what you assumed would be your last two-week stretch.

Though you might find it unfair, it's perfectly legal for your employer to do this if she so chooses. Unless you are party to a collective bargaining agreement or signed an employment contract, you are an employee at will. Therefore you *can* quit at any time (as you have), *but* you can also be terminated at any time for any reason as long as it's not a discriminatory reason.

While an employer is obligated to pay you for all the time you actually work, there is no law that requires an employer to pay you for time you don't work. So your employer can legally tell you to skedaddle and refuse to pay your two weeks once you've announced your intention to leave. There is a bright side, though: now you don't have to work with that jerk for one minute longer.

Collecting Unemployment

If you think you can automatically collect unemployment compensation if you're fired from your job, I'm sorry to say this is not always the case. Just ask the prison investigator who was fired for selling drugs to an inmate. As he sat in jail awaiting trial, he actually applied for unemployment compensation, which was denied. Still, you've got to give it to the guy: *that* took balls.

You can lose your right to collect unemployment if you are fired for work-related willful misconduct, which is generally defined as "a deliberate violation of the employer's rules and a disregard of standards of behavior the employer has a right to expect from an employee." Employers are well advised to write and distribute policies they wish to enforce later—there is little that is more frustrating to an employer than firing someone for willful misconduct, only to have that person continue to collect money. As for employees, understand your employer's policies to avoid losing out on unemployment, or better yet, to avoid having to apply for it in the first place.

Chapter 2

Your Money

*Mo' Money, Mo' Problems . . . Unless It's No Money,
in Which Case It's All Problems*

Some say money makes the world go around. Others say money
is the root of all evil. Us personally? We kind of like it. And we
particularly like having more of it than less, since a shortage of
money can cause problems in virtually every aspect of life. For
people suffering from "too much money" issues, you'll have to
fend for yourselves here because in this chapter we intend to address financial concerns that are faced by the other 99.8 percent
of us. (But FYI, richies: we are happy to provide independent
counsel to you for a fee we're sure you'll be able to afford!)

Q: I'm a little short on cash right now, but I get paid in two weeks. If I postdate my checks, they can't be cashed until the date I write on them, right?

A: Wrong! Many people believe that a bank can't cash a check until the date written on it, but that is *not* true. So if you want to mail out bills before they're due but don't want it cashed until later, or if you're pressured by a debt collector to cut a check and told you can postdate it to payday so it will clear, *put down that pen*!

Under the Uniform Commercial Code, the guidelines that govern business transactions, banks can pay a postdated check immediately unless you, the customer, specifically alert the bank that you want to delay processing. You'll then need to give the bank specific information about the transaction such as check number and amount. If a bank does catch the fact that a check has been postdated, it has the option to pay it or not, but keep in mind most checks are processed electronically these days so discovery is rare. To be safe, don't give a postdated check to someone unless you call your bank first or you *really* trust the person to whom you're giving it.

Q: Alright, I get it that it doesn't help to postdate a check, but I don't have the money in my bank account to cover a bill. How bad is it if I just write the check now and send my apologies for bouncing it later?

A: Knowing the check will bounce and writing it anyway is not only ethically wrong, it's also illegal. Still, that didn't stop a man in Fort Worth, Texas, from doing it in a big, bold Texan way. He tried to pass a check in the amount of $360 billion. Would you like that in small bills, genius? Let me get the forklift. Luckily for him, his bail was only $3,700.

In tough times even smart people consider doing stupid things like writing checks they know they can't cover. But remember, every state has its own bad-check statute. In many states, a person commits a crime if he passes off a check when he knows it won't be honored by the bank. This is not to say that anyone who has ever bounced a check will be prosecuted, but when you intentionally pass off a check that you know you don't have the funds to pay, you *are* guilty of a crime. Also note the penalty increases as the amount of the bad check increases. Starting with a summary offense for a bad check, in some states you can be prosecuted for a *felony* for passing a bad check in excess of a certain dollar amount.

Q: How can I make calls from the collection agency stop?!

A: First answer: pay your bills. Second, know you do have some rights regarding the aggressive tactics of debt collectors. Take the example of Amanda Horkey, who owed a debt of $817 that was turned over to a collection agency. The agency called her at her place of employment. When Ms. Horkey told the agency worker that she couldn't talk at work, what did this clever collection agent do? He called her coworker and left a message asking why Amanda was acting like such a bitch. Nice.

Bitch gauntlet thrown, Amanda decided to sue the collection agency and won her case. The Fair Debt Collection Practices Act (FDCPA) has established rules regarding when debt collectors may call you. Know that it is illegal for a debt collector to call you at work if the collector knows that your employer prohibits you from receiving such calls. If you're being hounded by a collection agency, tell the collector that he can't call you at work, and ask for an address where you can send a letter stating that.

The FDCPA also requires collectors to cease all communications about a debt if you communicate in writing that you want all communication to stop. *Note that it doesn't prevent creditors from suing you for that debt*—so they can still take you to court to get a judgment and have your wages garnished or your assets sold—but it does prevent them from continuing to harass you over the phone or send dunning notices that harass you via the U.S. Postal Service.

Regarding debts owed, of course you are legally responsible to repay them. But there are some debts, called "time-barred debts," that are so old they're beyond the point a creditor could sue you to collect them. State law varies, but in most states the limit is between three and ten years. (Check with your state's attorney general at www.naag.org to see your state's limit.) The law also imposes limits on how a debt collector can collect time-barred debts. However, the law doesn't prohibit debt collectors from *trying* to collect debts that they know are too old, as long as they don't sue you or threaten to sue you while trying to collect. And, FYI, there is no law prohibiting them from trying to make your life so miserable you'll want to throw as much money as you can at the collectors so they'll shut up and go away.

Q: **Oh boy, a friend of mine is in real financial trouble. He owes money to *everyone*—his landlord, the IRS, his health care provider, and his auto mechanic. His plan to win the lottery hasn't quite worked out yet.... What should he do?**

A: I believe it was Benjamin Franklin who called lotteries a tax on the stupid. (This doesn't prevent me from buying lottery tickets; it just makes me sheepish when I do.) If your poor friend can't pay his bills, a smart first step for him to take is to call his creditors and explain that he's having financial trouble. He can tell them that he is working to fulfill all of his obligations and wants to pay in full. Then he should ask if together they can come up with a payment plan that both parties will find acceptable. In most cases creditors would rather work with someone who is making an earnest effort to pay off a debt than continue to be ignored until they feel obligated to pursue a lawsuit.

Q: **Bad news—my friend tried talking but no one was listening. Now several creditors have gotten judgments against him and plan to "garnish his wages." I'm guessing that doesn't mean they'll be putting parsley on his paycheck... but what does it mean?**

A: Uh, no. Garnishment is the process by which a part of your paycheck, before you even see it, is paid directly to someone who wins a judgment against you in court. This is to ensure that you don't wind up spending every dime of your wages before you pay what you owe others.

Q: **Whoa, so you could wind up working forty hours a week and get a paycheck of zero dollars once everyone who has a garnishment against you gets his piece?**

A: In general, the maximum amount of wages that may be garnished (withheld) from an employee's paycheck is 25 percent.

The one exception is that up to 50 percent of the employee's net may be withheld to repay back child support. And you don't get to choose which creditor you pay back first. Instead, if your payroll department receives multiple garnishment orders, it's required to pay them in the following order: The government always takes its money first—tax levies are satisfied before all other deductions (except child support orders received before the levy). Second are the child support orders. Third are the legal garnishments, and finally the student loan and other federal government agency garnishments. After that, keep your fingers crossed that your payroll department next chooses to repay the person wielding the biggest stick.

Q: **My roommate asked me to float her a loan through a rough patch and I'm going to help her out because I'm a softy/idiot. How can I make sure she'll pay me back?**

A: Fortunately for you, you know where she lives. . . . But if you lend someone money, you should not only get an agreement for repayment in writing, you should also get collateral on the loan (like a bank does). The collateral will be an item that goes to you if the money is not repaid. One case in Illinois between father and son, Jerome and Jim Rich, involved a very special collateral item: the pope's 1975 Ford Escort. As it happened, before young Mr. Rich started having financial trouble (and became Mr. Poor), he'd purchased Pope John Paul II's '75 Ford Escort GL at auction. The light-blue Escort was the car the pontiff had used prior to his ascension to popedom. But when Jim Rich was unable to repay his father for a loan he'd given him, Jerome Rich went after the pope's wheels as a collateral item. In other words, Rich Dad sued Poor Son.

Jerome Rich eventually did get his money back when the court ordered Jim Rich to put the car up for auction. (It sold for more than half a million dollars.) But to save yourself the hell of a potential court case, get your terms straight from the beginning: file financing documents with the secretary of state's office (in your home state) to "perfect" the loan, and consider hiring an attorney to help you make sure the paperwork is as bulletproof as the Popemobile.

Q: **What happens when a judge makes a ruling against you, but you *still* don't have the funds to repay the debt?**

A: Well, if a debtor can't or won't pay, the creditor needs to go back to the court from which the judgment was won. Depending on where the action was filed, he'll likely need to wait thirty days from the date of judgment, and then pay another fee and file an order of execution. At that point, the debtor will have his assets sold; a constable will go to the debtor's premises and tag items for levy at a sheriff's sale.

When Enron collapsed, its former CEO and his wife actually opened a thrift shop, hocking personal castoffs in an effort to pay their creditors. So while your creditor might not want to wind up with your used Enron stock or worn-out socks—he may well believe that it's better than nothing.

Q: Filing for bankruptcy seems like a pretty sweet deal. Sure, they cut up your credit cards, but then they also erase your debt. Other than bad credit, what's the downside?

A: If the debts you've accrued have become unmanageable and you're considering filing for bankruptcy, you've probably considered that the creditors who lent you money will be hurt by that decision. But you might not have realized that friends and family might also be affected by your actions.

When people or businesses decide to file for bankruptcy, before actually filing, with their remaining money they often pay off the accounts they like best first, not the debts they are most obligated to pay. To combat the problem of preferential transfers, the law requires that all payments made in the ninety days before bankruptcy must be returned to the bankrupt estate for fair distribution. In one case in Florida, a couple who had given money to their adult son and then filed for bankruptcy tried to revoke their filing when they realized that it meant their son would have to pay back the money. But the court found it would be harmful to the creditors and didn't allow them to do it. So before you file, consider all those to whom you gave money, because though your debts might get canceled in the process, so, too, might some of the more delicate relationships between friends and family.

Q: My cash-strapped friend's money has run out and winter's coming. Aside from layering sweaters, what can he do to get help with heating his home?

A: As the price of heating oil rises, many people struggle with the cost of heating their homes. If you find yourself in need of help, there are federal programs that can assist you. The Low Income Home Energy Assistance Program (LIHEAP) may be able to help your family stay warm. It operates in all fifty states and can help you with bill payment, energy crisis assistance, and weatherization and energy-related home repairs if you qualify. You don't need to have an unpaid bill to receive energy assistance, and you don't need to be on welfare to qualify. To find out if you are eligible and how to apply, you can go on the Internet and type LIHEAP into your search engine or call 866-674-6327 to speak to someone about how to apply.

Q: I ignored my credit card bills for a little while after college (just like everyone else I knew!), and it killed my credit rating. Will that stupid youthful mistake haunt my credit report forever?

A: Okay big spender/little repayer, here's what you need to know: negative information on your credit report can generally be reported for *seven years*. Tax liens remain on there for seven years from the date they are *paid*. Bankruptcy information can remain on your report for ten years. Information reported because of an application for more than $50,000 of credit or life insurance has no time limit.

As you may or may not realize, bad credit can bleed into a variety of aspects of your life, even prospects for future employment. You are afforded certain protections concerning your credit rating, though, because credit scores aren't always accurate. (If your accounts have ever been hacked, for instance, your credit could have been affected, and that shouldn't be held against you.)

There's also a second prong to bad credit: while it seems obvious that a record of bad credit will affect how likely it is that you'll get future credit from a bank or credit card company, most people don't realize that some employers—particularly if you're applying for a job with a financial institution—often do a credit check before deciding whether or not to hire you. But the good news is that the Fair Credit Reporting Act (FCRA) does offer some protection in the ways a bad credit report can be used when it affects your employment. Two casinos in Las Vegas were charged by the Federal Trade Commission with violating the rights of applicants under the FCRA. The casinos obtained applicants' credit ratings and then used them to rate the job seekers as "poor," "fair," or "good" candidates. Based on that rating, the casinos' human resources department would then recommend the applicant as either favorable or unfavorable. Kind of ironic that institutions that do more than their fair share of credit wrecking would care so much about one's credit report, no?

Though it's true that the casinos were well within their rights not to hire someone with poor credit, here's where they went wrong: the FCRA requires that before taking adverse action against a job applicant based on his credit report, the future employer must give that person a copy of the report and a written description of his rights under the act. After taking the adverse action it must (among other protections) provide the job seeker with notice of the action, the name and address of the credit bureau, and a notice that alerts the job seeker that he has the right to dispute the accuracy of the information with the credit bureau. The casinos wound up paying out $325,000 in civil penalties for the violation—certainly one of the few times the odds went against the house.

Q: Hard to believe, but my boyfriend's credit is even worse than mine. If he asks me to become "Mrs. Sucky Credit," does joining in holy matrimony mean I'll be saddled with his debts as well?

A: Ah, romance. Though taking on his debt would be a real sign of true love, luckily for you, debts that were individually incurred before marriage don't become part of your credit history. If you get joint credit cards or joint bank accounts, though, keep in mind that debts accrued during marriage will have your name on them even if you weren't the one who made the purchase. Credit reports are individual, so debt that was brought into the marriage stays on the report of the one who accrued it. But remember, you can, even after marriage, continue to get credit cards in your name alone.

At some point you two might want to buy a home or make a big purchase like a car together. To make joint loans possible, you should encourage your mate to regain good credit by paying bills on time and establishing a better record. After all, it would be a shame after getting married to find out that it's till *debt* do you part.

Q: Shiiiiittttt! I lost my ATM card! What happens if someone finds it, cracks my insanely easy PIN code, and withdraws all my money?

A: It's okay, the good news is that as long as you report the missing card, your assets are protected. Under the Electronic Fund Transfer Act (EFTA), if you notify your financial institution within two business days of realizing your card is missing, your losses are limited to $50 or the amount of the unauthorized transfers, whichever is less.

If you wait more than two business days to report a lost or stolen ATM or debit card, though, you could be liable for losses up to $500. And if you wait more than sixty days after receiving a bank statement that includes an unauthorized transfer, your bank doesn't have to reimburse you at all. Don't let a thief clean you out: keep your bank cards in a safe spot. But if your card does go missing, don't crack up, just call your financial institution and let them know.

Q: After my fantastic trip to Buenos Aires, I started finding charges on my Visa for things I couldn't even pronounce. No way am I paying for this stuff, but how can I prove I didn't make the purchases?

A: First consider yourself lucky that you're not the New York businessman who was sued by American Express for refusing to pay a bill he allegedly racked up one night. The man and his three business associates spent a rather long evening at a "gentlemen's" club. At the end of the night their bill came to $241,000. Yes, that's right: $241,000. At a strip club. In one night. As I'm sure you can imagine, the man was incredibly angry—especially since he said only about $20,000 of the bill was legitimate. (No doubt that fact made his wife feel much better: "Honey, I swear, I only spent twenty grand of the kids' college fund on plastic boobs and watered-down booze.")

But Husband-of-the-Year *really* blew it when he failed to respond to the credit card company's investigation asking him to explain why he thought the charges were fraudulent. Under the Fair Credit Billing Act, if you have a disputed charge on your credit card, your credit card company must acknowledge it and conduct a reasonable investigation, resolve the inquiry, and communicate the results to you and to the merchant within ninety days.

If you see a fraudulent charge on your credit card bill, you should absolutely dispute it. Then, be smart and cooperate with the investigation or you will risk losing that dispute, and if you lose, the credit card pays the merchant and you owe the credit card company. That's something you need to know even if you didn't spend your dollars on empanadas ... or in one of those not-so-gentlemanly gentlemen's clubs.

Q: Uh-oh, after buying that set of fancy cookware I remembered something very important: I can't cook. Now it's sitting there in my kitchen mocking me. Can I just cancel payment and send it back?

A: Anyone who's ever watched late-night infomercials knows there's no shortage of truly useless products. And anyone who's ever watched late-night infomercials also knows that the later it gets, the better idea these products seem—until you wake up the next day wondering if you really bought it or if it was just a bad dream. While there are protections for consumers against unauthorized charges on your credit card, most people assume you can't dispute a credit card purchase you actually made.

Turns out that's not true. You *can* dispute a credit card purchase even if you did make it, but before you buy something find out the return policy. Contact the merchant first and put your complaint in writing. If the merchant refuses to take the product back and reverse the charge, then call your credit card company. Often the charge will be removed during the investigation. But if the credit card company ultimately sides with the merchant, you will have to pay the cost and the finance charge.

What you must keep in mind is that there is no legal obligation for a store to take back items you purchased except pursuant to the return policy it has stated. There are, however, a few types of retail contracts that by law you have the right to rescind. If a salesperson comes to your door to sell you a product for more than twenty-five dollars, under federal law you can automatically return it for up to three days after purchase. In many states you also have three days to rescind a health club membership when you realize there's no way you're hauling tail to that gym, and under the law of many states, you have five days to cancel the purchase of a time-share. These are all things to weigh when you're considering making your next purchase, either for that crock of cookery or that unused ab machine now doubling as a towel rack.

Q: I was about to buy my boyfriend a video game console because, well, because I am the best girlfriend ever. Then the clerk at Best Buy suggested I buy him an extended warranty with that. Is an extended warranty *really* a best buy, or is it a really stupid waste of money?

A: An extended warranty is a contract to perform services related to the maintenance or repair of a product, and it can be sold under many names—extended warranty, service contract, or maintenance agreement. By law, service contracts must be written in simple and understandable language and must contain a description of your cancellation rights.

You should try to better understand the warranty by asking the salesperson the following questions: When does the contract begin and when does it end? What does it cover and what is excluded? Does the product you're buying come with a free warranty, and if so, what does the extended warranty give you that the product's warranty doesn't? What's the total cost? Must you buy it at the time of purchase? (You may be able to think about it before buying.)

Finally, here's maybe your most important question to ask when considering the purchase of that extended warranty: for the money I'm spending, is the service contract going to outlast the boyfriend to whom I'm giving it?

Q: I feel like I never get back as much money as promised by ads that offer rebates on products. They lure me into the stores with the great prices, and then shaft me. How is that legal?

A: Yeah, you buy it because the price touts:

$100 SAVINGS!!*

*after mail-in rebate

So you spend more than you would up front with the promise of a refund on the back end. But under the Fair Trading Act and other consumer-oriented laws, it's false advertising if manufacturers or retailers get you to buy something by promising a rebate if they aren't going to give you one.

As you've no doubt realized, though, that doesn't mean that manufacturers have to make it easy for you to collect your due. If you still haven't sent back a rebate that's set to expire, you should do the following: Hang on to your receipt and all the packaging until you've made sure you have all the required proofs of purchase to collect the rebate cash. Make copies of all the documents before you mail them in. Then put a note on your calendar around the time the company promises you the rebate so you remember to follow up in case you don't receive it; report it to the state attorney general's office if you don't. Remember, like your interest in the product itself, the rebate offer will expire, so make sure you turn it in if you haven't already.

Q: Hey, thanks again for that great gift certificate to the spa you gave me two years ago . . . it just resurfaced from the bottom of my desk. Can I still get the massage even though the gift certificate expired a year ago?

A: I recently found a twenty-five-dollar gift certificate that someone gave me as a wedding gift in 1992! I can't find the scrap of paper on which I wrote today's To Do list, but a twenty-five-dollar gift certificate from 1992 I still have. I haven't managed to go ask Williams Sonoma if they'll honor it yet—partly out of embarrassment, partly because I know that it will barely cover a single muffin tin at this point.

But like many people, if you'd heard that gift certificates cannot expire, you are right—*if* you live in California, which has a law preventing gift certificates from expiring. In Hawaii and Massachusetts, gift certificates can't expire for at least two years. If you live elsewhere, you are in a state that doesn't have laws preventing gift certificates from expiring and are most likely out of luck.

Some business owners will honor gift certificates in the name of good customer relations even after the expiration date, so it doesn't hurt to ask if the certificate will be honored. Of course, the best advice is to get someone a certificate that she can't wait to use and leaves in plain sight so she won't forget about it.

Q: I just made a ton of money selling my ex-boyfriend's clothes, stereo, TV, and almost-brand-new video game console on eBay! I don't have to pay taxes on the money I earned, do I? (And please keep in mind, having dated that jerk for a year I really do believe I earned the money.)

A: Interesting question, and it's one that a lot of "creative entrepreneurs" find themselves pondering. As you can well imagine, the IRS is not likely to say, "Oh, you made money on your old junk? Good for you and enjoy your pocket change!" Rather, all income—including gambling earnings; lottery, raffle, and horse and dog race winnings; church bingo payouts; profits from illegal activities (recall Al Capone was put away for tax evasion); and small business profits—is taxable. Your first move is to figure out if you're actually making a profit. If you're just looking to clean out your garage, you are likely selling the items for less than you bought them and so would not be making a profit. But if you are buying goods from a wholesaler and reselling, or if you are producing the goods and selling them like a business for more than the cost of manufacturing, then you are running a profitable business. On eBay, one man's trash may be another man's treasure, but to the IRS, that treasure can and will be taxed.

Q: Looking for some new action, I went to Atlantic City with my friends and we all won big! We don't have to pay taxes on our blackjack booty, do we?

A: That depends on what your definition of "big booty" is. The law requires that the casino (or whoever the payer of the winnings happens to be) is required to issue you a form W-2G if you win $600 or more. If you win more than $5,000, the casino is generally required to withhold 25 percent for federal withholding. So yes, the government will take its cut, but if you're a betting woman, you'd have already put odds on that.

Q: Beyond giving away all of my ex's stuff, I'm a very charitable person.... So how much money can I get back for donating things come tax time?

A: Many people view tax deductions as another opportunity for creative accounting practices. And those who make charitable contributions should feel good as they put down that deduction on their 1040s. But let's be honest . . . sometimes the contribution you make to a nonprofit entity is not *entirely* done out of the goodness of your heart. Sometimes you also give to get something in return. So what happens when you make a charitable contribution from which you benefit, like paying a church or synagogue for religious school for your kids? Or what if you buy a basket full of goodies they're selling as a fund-raiser? Can you deduct the whole sum every time you write a check to a nonprofit?

The answer is that if you receive a benefit as a result of making a contribution to a qualified organization, you can deduct only the amount of your contribution that is more than the benefit you receive. For example, if you go to a charity auction and win a week's stay at a beach house for $1,000, if that amount is not more than the fair market value for the rental, you haven't made a deductible contribution, even though the money is going to charity rather than to a landlord. Still, while you can't deduct the amount you're paying, knowing that you are helping a worthy cause can be priceless. . . .

Gifts "in kind" are a slightly different matter. For instance, though many people think of the IRS as bloodsuckers, you can't actually deduct the value of the blood you give. The reason is that you can only deduct contributions if you itemize your return and if the contribution is made to a qualified organization. For instance, you can deduct contributions made to religious organizations, nonprofit schools and hospitals, and organizations like the Red Cross or the United Way, and war veterans groups. But you *cannot* deduct contributions to social and sports clubs, labor unions, most foreign organizations, for-profit groups, homeowners' associations, or political groups, or the cost of raffle, bingo, or lottery tickets. And while some nonmonetary contributions (like a car) are deductible, you can't deduct the value of your time or the value of the blood you donate—so if you're giving to the Red Cross because it's the right thing to do, by all means do it; they can certainly use the blood. If you're doing it for the tax deduction, though, save the cost of the Band-Aid and make a monetary contribution instead.

You *can* also deduct gambling losses, but only if you itemize deductions. Those losses also can't be greater than what you've reported as gains, so you can't actually make money on your losses. To deduct losses you have to be able to provide receipts, tickets, or other statements that show both your winnings and your losses. Though no one likes to remember the big losses at the casino, if you do start hemorrhaging cash, in order to write it off later at least make sure you get some sort of written statement that details the massacre.

Q: Speaking of charities, I'm constantly getting calls from organizations with shady-sounding telemarketers. I keep thinking if I give money it'll go straight into that person's wallet. How can I check on that?

A: Solicitations from police organizations are particularly rough, aren't they? It's the nagging feeling that, if you're not going to contribute, you better not have a busted taillight. But frequently it's so difficult to tell who you're speaking to when you get those calls that the Federal Trade Commission initiated a campaign entitled "Operation *Phoney* Philanthropy," designed to stop scam telemarketing companies from passing themselves off as charitable organizations. Various states have also filed twenty-four separate law enforcement actions designed to prosecute phony telemarketers. In one of those cases, the individual defendant created sham nonprofit corporations with names like "Firefighters' Assistance Foundation" and "Police and Sheriffs' Support Fund." He used those entities to collect millions of dollars in donations from unwitting, generous consumers. The attorney general of Tennessee discovered that of the $11 million raised by telemarketers on behalf of charitable operations, the telemarketers kept $8 million for themselves.

So follow these tips before deciding whether or not to give to Officer Krupke, or the telemarketer who seems to be acting on his behalf:

- Ask for identification. That is, ask if you are speaking with a police officer (the answer will be no). Then ask the name of the company the person on the phone actually works for.
- Ask how the money you give will be distributed and what percent of your gift will actually go to the charity on whose behalf you are being solicited.
- Be skeptical if someone thanks you for a pledge you don't remember making. It's a common ploy used by telemarketers to make you think you've given money in the past.
- Know the difference between tax exempt and tax deductible. Even if the organization is tax exempt, it doesn't mean that the dollars you give to the telemarketer will be tax deductible. If you choose to give, ask if your donation will be tax deductible and ask to get a receipt so you can deduct it.
- Finally, if you're still uncertain if the charity is on the up-and-up, two helpful watchdog Web sites are www.give.org and www.guidestar.org, and you can check these resources to see where organizations are spending your donation dollars.

Q: I work from home, so I know I get to write off some of my rent, electric bill, and Internet service. Now I'm thinking I should also deduct the gorgeous new wet-bar I put in my living room because it helps my workflow and improves workplace morale. What do you think?

A: Oh brother, sister, let's just say this is not one of your more inspired ideas. The IRS is pretty clued in when it comes to stuff like this, and I'm guessing they particularly love catching people who think they're going to outsmart them. A Mary Kay cosmetics saleswoman was shown "her colors" when the IRS busted her for deducting several thousand dollars in losses. No doubt selling cosmetics out of the trunk of a pink Cadillac is a tough business, but this woman still tried to write off her "losses" on her tax return despite the fact that she'd never earned a dime. The tax court found that she lacked an honest profit motive, based on the facts that (1) she had no experience selling cosmetics; (2) all of her travel expenses for visiting so-called customers happened to be to family or friends who lived out of state; and (3) her family had other substantial income that her losses helped shelter.

The bottom line is that you can't deduct the whole cost and operation of a personal residence. You may deduct the "home office" part, yes. But simply putting a calendar, desk, file cabinet, or some other business-related item in each room and saying it's an extension of that office doesn't increase the amount that can be deducted. Additionally, you generally can't deduct travel, meals, or entertainment under the guise that everyone is a potential client. Trust me, the IRS has your number on this one—and as that Mary Kay rep will tell you, getting busted for phony shelters isn't pretty.

Q: I'm not sure I get how some tax prep firms can offer instant refunds. Can you explain that to me?

A: Don't feel bad for not understanding; you're not alone. In fact, a class action lawsuit has been brought against tax preparation firms because experts believe the fees people will pay to get their refunds "instantly" aren't being properly explained. That was the case for single mother Canieva Hood, who walked into a Jackson Hewitt Tax Service office in 2002 hoping to receive an instant tax refund so she could pay her rent.

But that "instant refund" cost her $135, in addition to the $155 tax preparation fee, which represented more than an eighth of the total refund she was entitled to. "Instant refunds" are actually refund anticipation loans (RALs). That means they're a loan given by the tax preparer (like Jackson Hewitt or H&R Block) that are secured against your anticipated refund. But they frequently involve fees that can eat up half of the total refund you'd get if you filed your own taxes electronically, which you can do for free. Before you fall into the trap that bagged Ms. Hood, you want to understand the cost you'll actually be paying to get the money that you are already due.

Q: If the Constitution grants me the right to plead the Fifth and not incriminate myself in a government proceeding, can't I refuse to tell the IRS what I earned? And say I object to the government's policies, can't I conscientiously object and refuse to pay for them with my tax dollars?

A: You should ask the actor Wesley Snipes if it's a good idea to stop paying taxes. Apparently he thought that he was exempt from paying money to the government because he'd already given America *To Wong Foo.* . . . Needless to say, the IRS hears plenty of reasons why people don't believe they should pay taxes; as you can imagine, it strongly disagrees.

In a document called "The Truth about Frivolous Tax Arguments," the IRS categorizes all the arguments it has received over the years on why taxes are illegal, immoral, or inapplicable and then knocks them down. Some of the more common arguments tax protestors have made include:

1. The filing of a tax return is voluntary.
2. The United States is only the District of Columbia.
3. The IRS is not a U.S. agency.
4. There are "untaxing" trusts that can legally eliminate the need to pay taxes or file returns.
5. The Sixteenth Amendment was not properly ratified and therefore the federal income tax laws are unconstitutional!
6. And, a favorite of smarty-pants like you everywhere: the Fifth Amendment prevents me from incriminating myself.

The final part of the IRS document is on the penalties you can receive for making a frivolous claim, including a penalty of up to $25,000 if the court finds you instituted a proceeding for delay, that the position you took is groundless, or that you failed to pursue administrative remedies. To view the brilliant and not so brilliant arguments on taxes, go to www.irs.gov to see for yourself. And then make sure you file those taxes by April 15.

Q: **When you get married, what are you supposed to do about your tax returns?**

A: When you're newly married, there are a lot of new experiences in store for you. Some will be fun, others less so (like doing someone else's laundry). At the top of the "not-really-fun newlywed experiences" list is tax planning. Taking a few simple steps now, though, will help you avoid having taxes ruin your wedded bliss later.

First, you must provide correct names to claim personal exemptions on your tax return, so if you changed your name, let the Social Security Administration know and update your social security card so it matches your new name. If you have a new address, notify the postal service so your mail can be forwarded. Seems obvious, I know, but each year the IRS gets back thousands of refund checks as undeliverable because the addressee has moved. Newly married taxpayers may also find that they now have enough deductions together to begin itemizing their tax returns. Medical care, mortgage interest, and charitable contributions can all be deducted if you itemize. Believe me, encouraging you to attend to these matters when you're first married is *not* an attempt by this long-married woman to end the honeymoon prematurely. But as you'll learn, marriage is about the fine art of compromise, and rather than being compromised later, best to start planning now.

Q: I'm between gigs and looking to pick up some extra work. I keep seeing ads for those work-at-home opportunities where you can supposedly make good cash "right from your kitchen table!" Are these things on the up-and-up?

A: Here's the deal: many "work-from-home opportunities" are really ads telling you that for a small fee, they'll teach you how to earn money stuffing envelopes. But look closely—the ads aren't actually offering you a job. Once you pay the money, the way you make cash is by placing the same envelope-stuffing opportunity ad that you responded to and getting money from the people who, like you, fall for the ad that tells them to pay to learn how to make money. Before responding, ask: Who's really going to pay me? When do I get my first check? What is the total cost? And what am I going to have to do to earn the money? If you don't like the answers, you should tell the promoters to take this so-called opportunity and stuff it.

Q: My friend opened a java shop and asked me to help him write his ads. He can't pay me for my work but offered to trade coffee for copy. The government doesn't really expect me to list on my tax return how many cups of joe I drink, does it?

A: If I were your friend, I'd give you the coffee before you started writing to make the job go faster. But barter is an ancient form of commerce—cash-strapped businesses frequently trade products or services for the goods they need rather than paying cash. From babysitting services to the sale of computers, the value of products and services bartered is estimated to be more than

$8 billion. Just because cash doesn't change hands doesn't mean Uncle Sam doesn't get a cut of the action, though. Under the law, you must report as income the fair market value of the property or services you receive. You don't have to open your wallet when you get your goods; just when you get the tax bill.

Q: A magazine I freelanced for went under and filed for bankruptcy. Will I ever see the money they owe me?

A: Keep your fingers crossed, but yes, you should eventually collect that money because in bankruptcy, a company is required to pay employees and other labor first. That said, you should keep following up if you don't get the check. During a company's "financial restructuring" in Chapter 11, it's always better to be the squeaky wheel that gets the oil than the quiet, dirt-poor cog.

A company's bankruptcy filing can have broad implications for an employee's benefits, from pensions to 401(k)s to health care plans, so as soon as you're aware that your employer is about to declare bankruptcy, consult the Department of Labor's Web site: www.dol.gov/ebsa/newsroom/fsbankruptcy.html.

You might also find yourself involved in bankruptcy scenarios in which you're not the employee, but merely have dealings with a company that's having serious financial woes. This was the case for frantic brides in four states who were horrified when they learned that the gowns they'd paid for were behind locked doors when the bridal chain they used went bankrupt. The problem (aside from the creation of multiple angry and dressless Bridezillas) was that when a store files bankruptcy, all of the assets—including the inventory—are immediately frozen and may not be distributed, to protect the creditors. That means that you, the consumer, may be out of luck when you try to collect your purchase.

To protect yourself, pay for goods by credit card so you can dispute the charge. Keep your receipt until you've gotten your merchandise and only purchase items on layaway from stores you know to be reputable. If the company files bankruptcy, you can contact your state's attorney general's office and file a proof of claim form with the bankruptcy court. There are plenty of good reasons to cry at a wedding, but bawling about your missing gown shouldn't be one of them.

Q: **Did you know that between tuition, fees, and room and board, it can cost almost $50,000 a year for a student to attend a private university? How are families supposed to afford this without selling their kid's organs first?**

A: Way back in the dark ages (1987), a young man named Mike Hayes had a great idea to help him finance his college education. Mike wrote to *Chicago Tribune* columnist Bob Greene and asked him to ask all of his readers to "send Mike a single penny." In less than a month he collected more than 2.3 million pennies and eventually ended up with the $28,000 he needed.

Unfortunately, with tuition costs continuing to skyrocket, casting around for pennies might not do the trick anymore. But there are other ways to help students swing the cost. The Department of Education provides more than $78 billion—about 60 percent of all student aid—to help students and their families finance postsecondary education. Getting your share might not be as difficult as you think. The Free Application for Federal Student Aid is available and may be completed online at www.

ed.gov. The site also contains information on other federal grants that are available. The key for college kids to keep in mind is that if they're smart enough to get into college—they just need to do their homework on finding the help to get them there.

Q: I almost got the shit scammed out of me when I was apartment hunting online. Now I'm hyperaware of con artists looking to get my money and personal information. But how do I know who I can really trust with my credit card and social security numbers?

A: Virtually every business, hospital, and credit card solicitation asks for a social security number. But only a few have the legal right to demand it. Federal law requires the use of social security numbers for welfare agencies and motor vehicle departments. Transactions involving taxes also require social security numbers, so your employer, bank, and brokerage also have a legitimate interest in receiving it.

For anyone else who requests it, you should ask if an alternative piece of identification will do. If it won't, seriously consider whether you need to do business with that company. In many cases there are no repercussions to simply leaving blank the line for social security number on a form you fill out. Even if there's no reason to suspect that identity theft is the motivation for asking, you still don't always have an obligation to give it.

Remember, too, that scammers are very good about keeping up with the advances in technology, and every day they devise new and clever ways to part you from your money. A man in England, for example, bid on a motorcycle on eBay but ultimately didn't win the auction. Three days later, however, he received an e-mail from the seller. The person said he was writing to let him know that the winner had backed out. Now he had a second chance to get the motorcycle if he wired the money ASAP! If he didn't wire the cash, the bike would go to the third runner-up. Luckily, the buyer had the phone number of the original seller and when he called to verify, he found out that he was the target of what is known as a "second-chance scam."

Second-chance scams occur when the bidder who didn't win an auction is contacted by a thief posing as the seller. The thief tells the losing bidder that the sale fell through and the item is once again for sale. Generally the losing bidders are so happy, they immediately send a check or wire money . . . and then it disappears. It is therefore important for you to remember that an internet service provider has no legal obligation to check the truthfulness of content posted on its site by third parties. That means it's *your* responsibility to ensure the person to whom you are sending money is who he claims to be. To prevent this second-chance scam from happening to you, check the eBay ID of the sender and beware if it's different from the original seller. Be extremely careful if the e-mail suggests wiring the money through Western Union, which is untraceable once the scammer collects your cash. Finally, if the message seems urgent, be suspicious. It's always better to ask questions first than wish you had later as you're staring at your empty wallet.

This is the actual transcript of e-mail correspondence between Robin and a person advertising a rental apartment on Craigslist. Robin was initially concerned that the advertiser wrote that the apartment was on the Upper East Side of Manhattan when the address indicated it was located in the East Village, but she was so excited by the prospect, she contacted the advertiser anyway. When things got a little more suspicious, though, she brought in the big guns. . . .

----- Original Message -----
From: katapalinger@aol.com
To: ROBIN EPSTEIN
Sent: 2/26/2008 5:23:51 AM
Subject: Re: $2100 / 1br - East 12th Street Apartment For Rent on East of Manhattan (Upper East Side)

Hi Robin,

Thank you for your interest. I'm a 36 years old woman and i have available the apartment located in 407 East 12th Street, with 1 bedroom and 1 bathroom, 880 square feet, because I moved with my job in United Kingdom, London and I need money to pay the rent here, that is the reason I want to rent at this price and to find a trustworthy person for my apartment. The apt is located on the 4th floor, with hardwood floors, there are full laundry facilities in the unit—The kitchen features top-quality appliances including microwave, dishwasher and washer/dryer. I can rent you the apt for max. 5 years because I have signed a working contract here for this period. I'm the owner of the apt and its like in the pics. The rent for 1 month is $ 2,100.00 USD (the whole price—not per person) you can have access to all utilities (water, electricity, Internet, cable, parking, air conditioning, fireplace, dishwasher, garbage disposal, microwave, refrigerator). You can move in the apt in the same day when you receive the keys. The only problem is that i'm the only person who have the keys but I hope that we will find a compromise.

Thank you for your interest and wait news from you,

Best Regards!

Katalina Palinger

----- Original Message -----
To: katapalinger@aol.com
Sent: Tue, 26 Feb 2008 3:55 pm
Subject: Re: $2100 / 1br - East 12th Street Apartment For Rent on East of
Manhattan (Upper East Side)

Hi Katalina,

Thanks so much for getting back to me! I'd love to be able to get
into the apartment to see it. Might there be some way of mailing
the keys to a neighbor? Or, if you'd feel comfortable doing this, you
could mail the keys to me and I could mail them back?

I'm on Skype if you'd like to chat that way. Looking forward to
hearing from you!

All the best,

Robin

----- Original Message -----
From: katapalinger@aol.com
To: ROBIN EPSTEIN
Sent: 2/28/2008 8:31:31 AM
Subject: Re: $2100 / 1br - East 12th Street Apartment For Rent on
East of Manhattan (Upper East Side)

Hi again Robin,

**Thank you for your reply. I'm in London/UK already. Like
I informed you before, the price you shall pay for one
month of rent will be $2,100 US, with no extra taxes to
pay. The money I want to receive it monthly to my bank
account, I hope will be no problem for you to wire the
money to my bank account. The apartment is ready for
you, you will need only to receive the keys and the contract to check it, and see if you like it.**

Obviously we need a way to complete this deal that will allow us to make sure we receive what we are after. I have found a way for us to complete the deal safely and fast, and in this way you will receive the Keys in less than 2 days, if you move fast as well. The solution is provided by a company which is similar to FedEx, DHL or UPS, which will handle the payment and delivery of the Keys.

I have found a procedure that will allow you to pay for the rent of the apt only after you will receive the keys it and through this way you will see it and decide if you will stay in the apt or not before I receive my payment.

Let me know if you are interested please because I really need to take care of this matter by the end of this week.

Thank you for your interest and wait news from you,

Best Regards!

----- Original Message -----
From: ROBIN EPSTEIN
Sent: Thursday, February 28, 2008 9:08 AM
To: Amy E. Feldman
Subject: FW: Re: $2100 / 1br - East 12th Street Apartment For Rent on East of Manhattan (Upper East Side)

Hey Amy!

Guess what? I have a legal question for you.... Okay, so I've been searching Craigslist for any possible apartment boondoggle— people tell me they do occasionally exist—and I found this ad for a place in the East Village. I emailed the person to learn more and this is the string of our responses....

Does this sound like a scam to you? Is there any way of making sure it isn't??? I went to a Web site called "property shark" to

check on the ownership, and though I'm not 100 percent sure
it lists all titles and owners in the building, this woman's name
is not on it at all. Needless to say, that's a concern. How do you
think I should proceed? I mean it's EXACTLY the deal I'm looking
for—but smells kinda funny to me. Whaddya think?

My gut screams: SCAM!!! what say you?

~R

----- Original Message -----
From: Amy E. Feldman
To: ROBIN EPSTEIN
Sent: 2/28/2008 9:34:04 AM
Subject: RE: Re: $2100 / 1br - East 12th Street Apartment For Rent
on East of Manhattan (Upper East Side)

**I am ALWAYS concerned about sending money to a
foreign country—it's impossible to get back. And a lot of
foreign scams involve not putting out any money until it
all checks out—and the scam only catches up with the
person after money has been sent. The problem here is
that for all you know, she knows the owner is out of town,
sends you the keys, you send money, and then the real
owner comes in—or that she's renting it to four other
people simultaneously. Additionally, there are linguistic
clues that make me think that English is not "her" native
language ("signed a working contract" and "I'm the only
person who have the keys").**

**Before going any further, I would say that you (1) need a
tour of the apartment and (2) want to see a copy of the
lease you'd be required to sign. She makes reference to your
paying only after receiving the keys—but I still worry. Tell
her to send the keys and the lease and then when you get in
there, see for yourself. Also, tell her you are uncomfortable
sending money through a service and ask if you can either**

pay by credit card or by pay pal. Ask her to mail (not email) the lease (tell her you need two originals so she should sign it and you will sign both and return a fully-executed copy to her which will require her to list her actual address) so you can see where the postmark comes from—many of these scams start in Nigeria and not England. Probably worth a site visit before even going any further.

I agree with your instincts. This seems fishy, but if it is a scam it's well done. I did look up the name Katalina Palinger on Google and found that there is a relatively famous female sports star in Zagreb (former Yugoslavia) by that name, which makes me wonder if it's akin to an American scamster going to Yugoslavia and posting an ad that reads: I am renting an apartment. Sincerely, Michael Jordan.

I still think it's worth a trip there (to the East Village, not to Zagreb).

----- Original Message -----
From: ROBIN EPSTEIN
To: katapalinger@aol.com
Sent: Thu, 28 Feb 2008 9:46 am
Subject: Re: $2100 / 1br - East 12th Street Apartment For Rent on East of Manhattan (Upper East Side)

Hi Katalina,

Can you tell me which unit in the building is yours and when you purchased it? Before I'd feel comfortable wiring any money, I just want to make sure I've done all my research, and I can't seem to find a record of ownership. Having lived in the city for a very long time, I've become a rather wary consumer as I'm sure you can understand!

Thanks,

Robin

----- Original Message -----
From: katapalinger@aol.com
To: Robin Epstein
Sent: 2/28/2008 4:53:13 PM
Subject: Re: $2100 / 1br - East 12th Street Apartment For Rent on East of Manhattan (Upper East Side)

Robin,

I want to inform you that the service will hold the money until you will confirm to them that you like the apt and keep the keys. If you don't like it, you only have to return the keys to them after they will refund the money to you and they will deliver the keys back to me on my expense.

Now i must know for sure if you agree because here are a lot of peoples interested to have this apartment rented and i want to know for sure what i must tell them. If you agree what i suggested i will tell them that my apartment is already rented and i will keep it for you. If you agree then i must have all the shipping details so i will be able to make all the arrangements for delivery.

Thank you for your interest and wait news from you.

Best Regards!

Katalina Palinger

UPDATE

With Katalina's command of English disintegrating with each subsequent e-mail, Robin decided against responding to this final note. She did, however, decide to forward the chain to the Craigslist fraud department. The ad was quickly removed from the Manhattan apartment listings, and Robin found a great place in Brooklyn instead.

Amy, however, did not escape this experience entirely unscathed: the site she visited to check up on Katalina Palinger had evidently installed a tracking cookie on her computer and it *still* continues to send her approximately five spam e-mails—in Russian—every day.

Q: On the subject of things that seem too good to be true, what about all that fax spam offering great vacation packages? I'd really like to vacation in the Caribbean this Christmas—any chance those are real?

A: When a woman in Florida received a fax at work for a "fabulous $200 vacation package!" she called to get details and was talked into buying a thousand-dollar package instead. After thinking better of it, she asked for a refund and was told she could get it. . . . Eight months later, she's still waiting for her money back.

Especially come holiday time, you may find yourself receiving more unsolicited faxes for travel offers that seem too good to be true. I won't say that great deals don't exist. I will say they are very, very, very rare. So the first thing to do when deciding whether to book a trip like this is to understand who you're dealing with. Contact the attorney general or the Better Business Bureau in your state. Then get the details of the offer in writing. (If it's a charter flight, you can investigate by calling the U.S. Department of Transportation's public charter office at 202-366-2396 to see if there actually is such a charter leaving at that time from that city.) Finally, if you decide to book the trip, pay by credit card. In these situations, a good rule of thumb is to examine the obvious: if it sounds too good to be true it probably is, and it's better to do some advance checking than learn too late that you'll be vacationing at the Heartbreak Hotel.

Q: **In a rare fit of cleanliness, I'm trying to de-clutter my apartment. Can I toss all those old bank statements and tax documents, or do I need to keep them?**

A: There are some documents with which you should never part— your birth certificate and social security card, your marriage certificate and divorce decree, as appropriate—all of which should be kept in a secure location. Some recommend you keep tax returns forever; at the very least you should be safe if you've kept them for seven years. Some documents you should keep for as long as you own the property—the deed to your house and title to your car—and it is a good idea to keep warranty information about products for as long as the warranty (and the product) lasts. Insurance information should be kept for the life of the policy (and life of the person if it's for life insurance).

It is possible to take the document collecting to the extreme, though. The brothers Homer and Langley Collyer were eventually found dead in the Harlem brownstone they shared, surrounded by one hundred tons of papers and trash that they couldn't bear to part with. In 2007, an eighty-six-year-old man named George Butcher was required to vacate his home after inspectors found it stacked floor to ceiling with approximately fifteen thousand books and countless newspapers and manuscripts that filled every room and spilled into his hallways. He argued that the collection was imperative to the research he has been conducting since 1949 for a book he plans to write (but has not yet begun). Though I can't tell you how long to keep the research you're collecting to write the Great American Novel—that's between you, your publisher, and your trash collector—the items I mentioned above are critical for your personal story.

Q: Okay, I'm done—I want to retire. How do I do that?

A: You sound like the forty-year-old lottery winner who, when asked several days after his big win how he planned to spend his time, responded, "Well, I've been retired for about four days now." As soon as he matched his numbers, he shuttered his business and called it a day.

But there's more to closing a business than simply locking the doors behind you. You must file forms with federal, state, and local governments. You have to file an annual tax return for the year you go out of business, and if you have employees, you have to file the final employment tax returns in addition to making the final federal tax deposit of those taxes. The good news is that you can get virtually all the forms you need online at the

IRS Web site, www.irs.gov. No, it's not as good as winning the lottery, but it does make the task a little easier.

Now, if you're still some years off from retirement, you'll want to explore options for saving the money that will become your retirement income. The 401(k) plans employees contribute to each month have largely supplanted pension plans to become the major source of expected retirement income. Despite this, after making an initial choice of funds, many employees' sole continuing involvement is to exclaim "yay" or "doh!" when they receive their semiannual statements. They then do nothing else until the next statement arrives. A series of recent lawsuits may make you rethink that strategy, though.

The lawsuits filings have alleged all kinds of bad dealings on the part of 401(k) plans, from biased consultants to exorbitant and bad-faith fees charged to participants' fund accounts. 401(k) plan earnings will make a huge difference in your retirement, so before you put in your hard-earned money ask what you're being charged for to see who else's retirement your money may be funding.

Something else to keep in mind as you look toward retirement is the security of your benefits. Can a company legally cut health care benefits to retirees?

The answer is yes. Private employers are not legally required to promise retiree health benefits. Even when they do offer them, nothing in federal law prevents the company from cutting or eliminating those benefits later unless they have made a specific promise to maintain the benefits. So, in order to understand what your company has obligated itself to provide, read the summary plan description to see if it is required to maintain the benefits. Look for language like "the company reserves the right to modify or revoke the program at any time," which gives it the right to take away benefits. If you're considering early retirement, review all the agreements from your employer with the guarantee of future benefits in mind. If you have questions, you may call the Department of Labor's Employee Benefits Security Administration at 866-444-3272 for more information. And of course, congratulations. I hope you'll have fun during your hard-earned time off!

Q: **What happens if the company I retire from folds? Does my pension vanish in its bankruptcy?**

A: Fortunately in most cases, if your employer goes bankrupt, your retirement assets should not be at risk. This is because according to federal law, retirement plan assets must be kept separate from the employer's business assets. According to the DOL's Employee Benefits Security Administration, "The funds must be held in trust or invested in an insurance contract. The employers' creditors cannot make a claim on retirement plan funds. However, it is a good idea to confirm that any contributions your employer deducts from your paycheck are forwarded to the plan's trust or insurance contract in a timely manner."

It becomes especially tricky when bankruptcies, mergers, and acquisitions result in employers abandoning their individual account plans (e.g., 401(k) plans). This makes it difficult for participants to know how to access the benefits they've earned or even whom they can contact to discuss it. Your best bet in this situation is to explore the department's Web site at www.dol.gov/ebsa or call its toll free number, 866.444.EBSA (3272), with questions.

Chapter 3

Your "Love" Life

*Bad Lovin', or, Breaking Up Is Hard to Do,
Particularly if Your Partner's an Asshole*

It's said that marriage requires a person to prepare four types of "rings": an engagement ring, a wedding ring, suffering, and enduring. We don't entirely believe that. Or at least not necessarily the last one. Though we are both big fans of "happily ever after" romances and firmly believe that marriage can be a wonderful thing, generally it's not the people involved in happy marriages who seek legal advice on the subject. So in this chapter we'll discuss what happens when love goes bad, which can occur at any point from mere minutes after the question is popped, as well as issues that can persist long after the marriage has gone bust.

Q: When my ex-fiancé broke our engagement, Señor Shitface told me he'd be needing his grandmother's ring back. I told him the only way he'd see that ring again was when my fist connected with his nose. He claims the engagement ring is his. I say it's mine. Who's right . . . and who gets to keep the rock?

A: While common courtesy dictates that the ring should remain with the dumpee, the law in most jurisdictions dictates that if a ring is given in contemplation of marriage, the woman doesn't take title to the ring until the marriage takes place. That means if the marriage doesn't take place, the ring goes back to the giver. If the ring was not given in anticipation of marriage, however, but as a gift—or in one actual case to reimburse the woman for cash and labor she'd invested in her fiancé's property—the ring is hers to keep. Of course, when you get a proposal like, "I can't pay you for gardening, but here's a diamond ring," one more question should be going through your mind: "Do I really want to marry this putz?"

Q: So now that the wedding to Dickbreath is off, who has to pony up the down payments for the hotel, caterer, and florist?

A: Ah, young love! Well, at least your engagement didn't end like Stephen Mujerm's, of York, Pennsylvania. Mujerm was at a New Year's party when he proposed to his girlfriend, Victorine Taboh. Shortly after accepting the proposal, Taboh stepped right into her new role as "nagging wife" when she began criticizing her future husband's driving on their way home from the party. Mujerm stopped the car and the couple got out to continue their argument on the side of the road. At this point the blushing bride-to-be found Mujerm's steering wheel lock and began smashing the car windows with it. Mujerm responded by grabbing the lock out of his fiancée's hands and conking her on the head with it, knocking her out. I think that's what you call a "broken engagement."

You may be surprised to hear this, but it's not necessarily the jerk who broke the engagement who's on the hook for the cost of various wedding details (the invites, down payments on the food, band, minister, etc.)—it's the jerk who signed the various contracts.

If you find that your name is all over the payment schedules and your beloved's is nowhere to be seen, it might be time for an unromantic discussion. It's better to find out sooner than later if you're going to wind up getting dumped and *then* hit with the bill to pay the piper. One dumped groom sued his fiancée for the thousands of dollars he'd spent on vacations, jewelry, and the *vasectomy* he'd had at her behest. Ultimately the court ruled against him on all of his claims, saying the money he spent on things during the relationship was a gift to his poorly chosen bride-to-be. However the ring, which had been given in anticipation of the canceled wedding, had to be given back. No such luck with the rest of the man's junk . . .

Q: Speaking of the joystick, I heard about a case where a man sued his girlfriend for breaking his penis during sex. Two questions: (1) Can you really sue someone for damages incurred during sex? (2) There's a breakable bone in the penis?

A: Though it sounds like the stuff of urban legend, a man really did sue his long-term girlfriend for fracturing his penis during sex. The case—"Doe v. Moe" (to protect the privacy of two people who went to court over *really* bad sex)—turned on whether or not you have to exercise reasonable care when copulating. Here are the facts of the actual case: Boyfriend and girlfriend are in "the act." She's on top with her legs wrapped around him. To increase her stimulation, she "unilaterally" decided to change positions, moving her feet near his abdomen without consulting him first. The woman then somehow "landed awkwardly" on her lover, breaking his dick.

Doe did what any red-blooded American who got his pee-pee broke would do: *he sued his girlfriend.* Classy. Now generally, as the plaintiff claimed, the law requires that reasonable care must be exercised to avoid injury to others. But since the court determined that because it's not "workable" to establish guidelines for sexual behavior, adults must take care not to engage in "wanton or reckless conduct" while doing the nasty. What was the verdict? The court concluded that in this case changing position midnookie did not constitute wanton or reckless conduct. (Phew!)

Q: I had the best time at a wedding last weekend! I just wish I knew the bride or groom's name so I could thank them as I was escorted out. Okay, no, I wasn't technically "invited," but since the party was at a public hotel, did they even have a right to toss me like the bouquet?

A: I find it pretty funny that people are now dressing up and going to hotels to crash weddings, particularly since you have to drag most men to weddings when they actually *do* receive the cream-colored envelope. But showing up to any party that you're not invited to makes you a trespasser, and eating the food or drink paid for by another is akin to dining and dashing at a restaurant when the bill comes—you're effectively stealing food.

Although hotels are public accommodations that can't discriminate against any protected class, "the Uninvited" isn't a protected class. Private parties are just that—private—and therefore can be limited to those who have been invited. If you're planning a wedding and don't want to risk having a crasher catch the bouquet, ask the hotel to station an employee to check names as people arrive—or simply walk over and talk to anyone who looks unfamiliar.

Q: Prenup: I do or I don't?

A: When fifty-eight-year-old Donald Trump married thirty-four-year-old Melania Knauss, his third wife, he naturally asked her to sign a prenuptial agreement. Apparently she wasn't put off by the idea that marriage to the Donald is forever—or at least until he divorces you. For many, it is difficult to explain why in the midst of pledging undying love for each other, you also need to pledge not to ask for any of his stuff if the love goes south. But it is a discussion worth having.

First let me explain exactly what a prenuptial agreement is: it's a document most often used to keep finances and debts separate, particularly if one party comes into the marriage with huge assets or liabilities (by which I mean debts—not bad hair). Additionally, these agreements are helpful if one party comes to the marriage with children and wishes to protect their inheritance and support in the event the marriage ends or the parent dies. A prenuptial agreement can also define what each party will get if the marriage ends. Without it, state law governs how property is divided.

But there are some things a prenuptial agreement can't legally control. Most state courts will not enforce provisions giving up custody, visitation, or child support rights in a prenuptial agreement even if you both agreed ahead of time. Michael Jackson's ex-wife Debbie Rowe, for instance, signed a prenup giving up custody of the children she bore for him. However, her later suit for visitation was still considered by the court in spite of this agreement.

Additionally, courts won't honor prenuptial agreements that bind parties to do something illegal, nor will they enforce mari- the number of times per week a couple must copu- wants Judge Judy in the bedroom mediating that tates also won't honor agreements to give up the ony. Most importantly, nonmonetary agreements trol the spouse's conduct during the marriage—like onsibility for household chores or who has to walk n't be binding in court. (Who has to walk the pet something apparently Michael and Debbie didn't contest.)

By their very existence, prenuptial agreements presuppose the possibility of divorce, which is a bummer. But keep in mind, the only difference between a married couple and a cohabiting couple (other than a mother nagging about when he's going to pop the question) is a contract called a marriage license. In that vein, a prenuptial agreement is just a different type of contract. And like any kind of contract, it is only intended to set expectations ahead of time when couples are happy and in a rational state of mind and never needs to be considered again—except if the marriage ends. In that event, couples can save the money fighting over what constitutes "equitable distribution" by already having the piece of paper with the details. If you have assets you care about protecting from the person you'll soon be marrying, explain to your sweetheart that you're just following Trump's example (though promise you won't end the relationship by telling your mate, "You're fie-uhed!").

Be aware that there's also a document called a "postnup," a postnuptial agreement, that's signed after the wedding, not before. A postnup usually lists the couple's assets and liabilities and discusses who would retain what should the marriage end. Couples who sign postnups are usually those who already have a prenup and have had a substantial change in fortune while married (say in a case like Michael Jordan and his now ex-wife, Juanita). Or when one spouse enters a family business he or she wants to protect. Or where one party who had been working agrees to stay home to raise kids, but wants to maintain financial status in the event of divorce.

For a postnup to be valid, both sides need to give consideration, which means both need to give something up in return for the other spouse's signature. And, no, giving up one's sanity doesn't count. . . .

Q: What if, drunk and in Vegas, my boyfriend and I accidentally say "I do" before we come to our senses and realize what we're doing? Shouldn't that be counted as "temporary insanity" and therefore not legal?

A: Well, villagers in India shooed a groom away from his own wedding because they determined that he was too drunk to get married. While many Americans may now be wondering where those villagers were on their wedding day, it raises an interesting question: under the law, are you considered incompetent to marry if you are drunk at the time of your vows, and if so, is your marriage void?

Ha! Nice try.

While state laws differ, many do prevent people who are visibly intoxicated from getting a marriage license. Once the vows are said, a person may later claim that the marriage was voidable because of incompetence. But in most states the Britney Spears fifty-five-hour marriage of the *I got drunk last night and did what, now?* variety is not automatically void. You still need a divorce or annulment to end the marriage. If you thought you needed a drink before you said "I do"—imagine what it will take to say "Uh, on second thought. . . ."

If you genuinely *do* want to get married, you first need to show that you are eligible to do so, which means that you have reached the age of consent, you are capable of entering the partnership, and you are not already married to someone else. Once you get married, you remain married until your divorce is official. All those people who renew their vows don't become more married with every ceremony. Marriage is marriage, divorce is divorce, and everyone knows renewing your vows is just another way to get more gifts off your registry.

So even if your husband romantically tells you he wants you to have a wedding ceremony in every baseball stadium in the country, no subsequent ceremony performed between the same couple is of legal impact. It instills no more rights, responsibilities, or obligations than it did the first time around. This also means that if you're ready to divorce the lout and his beer hat after you've been forced to smooch him on JumboTron #43, you'll only need to end it once and for all.

Q: **My best friend and her boyfriend, let's call him "Peter Pan," have been living together for ten years, but he won't propose because (1) commitment scares him and (2) he's a yutz who won't grow up. But my friend says she doesn't mind because they've lived together for seven years so now they're "common law married" anyway. Is that right?**

A: Um, no. But it's a good question because it turns out "common law marriage" is not what most people think. To enter a common law marriage, you must first be eligible to be married—that is, neither party is a minor or married to someone else. You must express words in the present tense—"we are husband and wife"—not "we'll be together in the future" or even "someday, baby, this will all be yours!" Beyond that you need constant cohabitation and a "reputation for marriage," meaning you have held yourselves out to the community as husband and wife. Even with these things in place, only a handful of states recognize common law marriages. So though you may think it's hard to get him to say "I do," absent all that proof, it's probably even harder to get the state to say "you did."

Amy

I make no claim to be a wedding planner, but I'm pretty sure "violence" is a bad theme for the big day. My father-in-law, Ray, told me a story about a wedding he attended that went a long way toward proving my theory, when an altercation broke out at the reception of his friend's son. Ray explained that the two families had bickered before the event, but it wasn't until the wedding day itself that their fists started doing the talking for them. . . .

The groom's parents' guests were a spirited crowd, and that was a good thing considering the bride's parents seated them next to the blaring band and swinging kitchen doors, a.k.a. the worst table in the room. Theirs was also the last table to be served dinner and the groom's guests grew hungry listening to waiters repeatedly asking guests at the other tables, "Chicken, fish, or steak?"

At long last, when a waiter made his way over to Ray's table, before he even asked the question my father-in-law raised his hand and said, "I'll save you the trouble—I'll take the steak." The waiter shook his head. "Sorry, sir," he said, "your choice is chicken or fish." "You ran out of the steak?" Ray asked. "No," the waiter replied, "the steak is only for the bride's family's tables."

Upon hearing this, the groom's father went mental. Observing the brouhaha from across the room, the bride's father and brothers ran toward his table. Ray, all five feet eight of him, wanted to stop the looming train wreck and stepped between the two furious fathers. He was rewarded for his peacekeeping efforts by being shoved into the band's drum set.

Now, my father-in-law is no dummy, so at that point he grabbed my mother-in-law's hand and the two escaped from the wedding/melee. He later learned that though there was little physical damage to the ballroom or guests' faces, the union between the bride and groom did not fare so well. The couple filed for divorce six months later.

Q: How can a divorce be "no fault"—isn't it *always* someone's fault?

A: Yes, it's the fault of the minister who married you. Divorce laws differ based on state law, but almost all states now allow for "no-fault" divorces, which means neither spouse has to prove the other is guilty of cruelty, adultery, or abandonment of one kind or another. In fact, fifteen states don't even allow fault grounds for divorce, perhaps because the courts just don't want to smell all that dirty laundry or engage in what's generally an ugly trial of "he said/she said/he did *what* to whom?"

All you need to prove in a no-fault divorce is just that the two people are incompatible and have been separated for a set period of time. *This means that the divorce will happen if they have been separated long enough, even if only one person wants to be divorced.* In other words, in no-fault states, you can be divorced even over the objections of the objectionable spouse.

Q: A friend is divorcing and found himself the best lawyer in town. Then his wife called the same shark, wanting him to represent her, too. Can one lawyer represent both sides in a divorce proceeding?

A: Not under the codes of legal ethics, no. (Stop laughing, a legal code of ethics is not an oxymoron.) There are many uncontested divorces in which the parties simply want a lawyer to file the papers on their behalf. While they don't like giving each other money, they *really* hate the thought of paying two lawyers' fees. Often couples ask a lawyer to represent them both. But under the codes of legal ethics, a lawyer can't represent both the hus-

band and the wife, because one person can't zealously advocate on behalf of two litigants in the same dispute.

Q: I love reading about the disgusting details of celebrity divorces, but if I were getting divorced, I wouldn't want anyone to see *my* disgusting details. Is there any way to keep that stuff private?

A: Most states allow both fault divorce and no-fault divorce. So if you and your future ex-husband really want to keep all personal details unspoken, you can simply agree to a no-fault divorce. In that case, all you have to show is that you have irreconcilable differences and that the marriage has become irretrievably broken. Coupled with proof that you have lived separately for some amount of time (depending on state law), you can then get divorced.

But despite the fact that no-fault divorce exists, many people still choose to show that the other party was at fault in the marriage. While vengeance is certainly one rationale for providing the specifics, the reason why others lay out all the "disgusting details" is because in some states, the judge may consider fault when determining alimony payments or "equitable distribution" (how the joint property is to be divided).

Those revelations may also go into consideration when determining custody. This was the hope of actress Jeri Ryan (best known as *Star Trek: The Voyager*'s ex-Borg, Seven of Nine) when she spilled the beans on her husband, the investment banker and future Illinois politician Jack Ryan. When, in 1999, the ex-Borg sought to become the ex-Mrs. Ryan, she pled fault, claiming that her husband had taken her to sex clubs in New York, New

Orleans, and Paris and tried to coerce her into publicly having sex with him and with other people. Those custody records were initially sealed, but when Jack Ryan ran for the Illinois senate in 2004, reporters sought to have the records released. And because documents filed with a courthouse are considered public, a judge agreed to do so. Needless to say, once accusations of sex club attendance came out, Ryan was forced to pull out of the race, too.

For the most part, courts do try to maintain the privacy of divorce papers by requiring anyone who wishes to see them to come to the courthouse and (generally) register with the court as well. In some jurisdictions, all courthouse records are available online, making it even easier to get your "sensitive" details. In others, papers may be sealed upon a judge's order, so if you know your records contain information that's embarrassing to you, ask your divorce lawyer how to petition the judge to have those papers sealed. Hopefully that should prevent your legions of adoring fans from learning about all about your "funny" little habits.

Q: *Holy cow!* Leslie Blum's ex-husband posted the sickest pictures of her on Exwifepicture.com. Though I don't know Leslie personally (although now I sort of feel like I do), I can't imagine she's happy her cooter is flapping across the Net for all to see. Is there any way to stop an ex from spreading your nasty bits across the Web after spreading 'em for his camera?

A: If you type the words "I hate my ex" into a Web browser, you will come up with more than eight hundred thousand entries of people all too happy to wax poetic on the subject of the scumbag former love of their lives. In the course of a divorce, exes will write agreements detailing the end of the relationship down to the last salad fork. Yet those rarely contain confidentiality or nondisparagement clauses. Not smart in this day and age. When writing up your final divorce papers, consider including a clause that would preclude the other from writing nasty things about you and posting them in cyberspace where a future employer— or your own child—might someday find it. If you need to say something nasty, get one of those old-fashioned diaries, say what you need to say in it—and then throw away the key.

Q: **If you haven't canceled the joint credit card with your ex, and he or she flies to Paris and spends $100,000 on the card, you can't be held liable for that once you're divorced, can you?**

A: Well, in the case of Hogg vs. Hogg (seriously: Hogg v. Hogg, you know sometimes you can't make this stuff up) the former Mrs. Hogg sued Mr. Hogg because he had racked up so much debt after their divorce; he filed bankruptcy and wouldn't pay her the percentage of the marital estate granted to her under the divorce decree. Many people believe that once debt incurred jointly during a marriage is divided, they're responsible only for the part apportioned to them. But here's the thing: while the decree sets up an agreement between former husband and wife, it doesn't bind the creditors.

Do you know what that means? It means that if your former spouse fails to pay his portion of the debt on a jointly held credit card, the credit card company can still come after *you*. Your recourse is that you can then sue your ex, but you stay on the hook with the creditor. Once your debts are split, it's best to transfer the balance of each joint card to one you hold individually. Then close any joint accounts to prevent your spouse from going hog wild with your credit.

Q: **What if you have to pay alimony to your former spouse? Do you have to shell out for taxes on that money, too?**

A: Fortunately alimony is generally deductible for the person who pays it. If you receive alimony from your ex, you must pay taxes on it. Child support is never deductible. But if your divorce decree calls for alimony and child support, and you pay less than you are required, the payments apply first to child support (which is not deductible) and the remainder is considered alimony (and is deductible).

If you have questions about how to pay your taxes, go to the IRS Web site at www.irs.gov. For questions about how not to despise your ex-spouse, call your therapist.

Q: **How do divorced spouses work out issues of financial aid when their kids go to college? And what happens if a wicked stepmother refuses to pay for Cinderella's campus cash?**

A: There is a specific formula for calculating the amount of federal financial aid you are eligible to receive when you complete the Free Application for Federal Student Aid (FAFSA). But what's surprising to many is that only the household income of the custodial parent is considered in the FAFSA calculation. And if the custodial parent has remarried, the income of the stepparent in the custodial household goes into the calculation. This means the assets and income of the stepparent who is married to the custodial parent must be included on any financial aid form, including the federal forms, even if the custodial stepparent refuses to pay any money toward the stepchild's education. That said, many private universities also ask about the finances of the noncustodial parent when making decisions about need-based scholarships. And keep in mind, prenuptial agreements don't shelter the assets from the calculation of parent contribution.

When buying a wedding ring, the terms used by jewelers may sound the same but mean very different things. Here's what you need to know about the terms that are legally defined:

- Pure gold is 24 karat. But because it is so soft, it is usually mixed with other metals. The karat marking tells you in what proportion the gold is mixed with these metals, so 14-karat gold, for example, contains 14 parts of gold mixed throughout with 10 parts of metal.
- Gold-plated, gold overlay, or rolled gold plate jewelry has a layer of gold bonded to a base metal. Caveat emptor: "gold bonded" layers will wear away over time.
- Natural gemstones are found in nature, but "lab-created" stones are man-made. They are referred to as laboratory grown, created, or synthetic, and while you can't see the difference between man-made and natural, the distinction affects the price.
- Some natural gems can be treated to improve the appearance, but the treatments may affect the price so a jeweler must tell you if the gem has been treated.

But of all the big decisions you make, it's the quality of the spouse—*not the jewelry*—that should be your biggest concern.

Chapter 4

Your Kids

Yes, Sir, That's My Baby . . . and Other Things You Might Not Want to Admit to Your Child's Arresting Officer

There are only two things a child will share willingly: communicable diseases and its mother's age.

—Dr. Benjamin Spock

Noted pediatrician and parenting advocate Dr. Benjamin Spock encouraged parents to be more affectionate and permissive with their children, and his writings on child rearing influenced a generation of baby boomers. His message to mothers was clear and comforting: "You know more than you think you do." It's just a shame no one told this to their children. In this chapter we'll explore the legal snafus your little darlings can get into and what this means for you, the legal guardian, a.k.a. the patsy, a.k.a. the ATM machine.

Q: Parenting seems like a lot of work . . . and a lot of money. Are there any rebates for having kids?

A: It's true, when you've got kids, the fun—and costs associated with that fun—never seem to end. Not even during summer vacation. These days parents can send their fancy kids to the Canyon Ranch summer camp, which provides health food, facials, and pedicures for kids for the bargain price of about $3,000 for two weeks! The simple pleasures of youth, my eye . . .

But because many working parents must arrange for the care of young children during the summer when school is out, they often turn to day camps to fill the void. The IRS recognizes this as a *valid expense* toward the child and dependent care credit. You get credit for up to $3,000 of expenses, or $6,000 for two or more kids, and the credit rate ranges from 20 to 35 percent of expenses, depending on your income. Parents who send their children to overnight camp don't qualify for the credit because, really, that would just be too awesome, wouldn't it?

To learn more, visit the IRS Web site, www.irs.gov. Though getting a tax credit might not be as satisfying as a facial, it might help relieve some of those ugly worry lines on that face of yours.

Q: Joe Camel, the penis-shaped cartoon character, was banned from Camel cigarette ads because it was intended to appeal to kids. Why doesn't the law equally apply to beer commercials, which seem geared to eight-year-old boys?

A: Parents in Michigan asked the same question and decided to file suit against beer manufacturers whose advertising, they claimed, was responsible for the illegal underage purchase of alcohol by minor children. The parents were alleging both economic injury and injury to their parental rights.

As it turned out, the court ruled against the parents and refused to restrict the manufacturers' freedom of speech. The court instead found that if the parents were convinced that alcohol advertising—and not parental controls or minors' actions—caused underage drinking, they should take it up with the legislature, not the court. What damage the parents did to their kids' high school popularity was apparently not a matter before the court, either.

In general my children refuse to eat anything that hasn't danced on television.

—Erma Bombeck

Q: **I thought it was pretty funny that when we went to the supermarket with your kids, they already knew exactly what brands of food they wanted. Are there any laws governing what, when, and where you can shill to kids?**

A: Anyone who's ever heard a three-year-old ask, "Can I have a Happy Meal?" has probably thought: jeez, is there no end to commercials on kids' programming? The answer is yes—there are legal limits on commercials that run during children's programming.

During shows primarily geared to kids under twelve, both broadcasters and cable operators must abide by certain advertising time limits and restrictions. In an hour-long program, ads may not exceed ten and a half minutes on the weekend or twelve minutes during the week. If an ad for a product is aired during a program associated with that product, then the entire program is considered a program-length commercial. In other words, if the commercial is for dolls based on the characters featured in the TV show, the whole show is considered a commercial. And character endorsements that make it difficult for a child to distinguish between program and nonprogram material is also prohibited. The limits won't prevent your kids from asking for a Happy Meal, but parents can be a little happier knowing that there are some limits after all.

Q: **In Japan they have "monster parent" insurance that teachers use as protection against lawsuit-happy parents. Does that exist here? Should it?**

A: "Monster parent" insurance isn't yet a reality in the United States, though it might not be a bad idea considering the litigious nature of many American parents. Consider the case in which one father sued his son's softball coach because the team didn't have a winning season. The father sought $2,000 in damages, claiming his kid lost the opportunity to compete in a championship tournament. Apparently good sportsmanship was not seen as its own reward. . . .

When he threw out the claim, the judge stated, "In life as in sports you will try and sometimes fail. There will be no apparent reward except to know that you did your best." To paraphrase: "Suck it up and deal, loser." Don't let a parent with potentially litigious sideline rage stop you from coaching (or discourage you from trying to educate today's youth). But there are precautions you can take to minimize your potential liability. First, look at

safety issues. If you're a coach, inspect the field for dangers before the kids start playing. Implement procedures like keeping
kids away from a swinging bat to prevent injuries. You can also
ask parents to sign a waiver, which can be as simple as one line
that reads: "I understand that there are risks associated with any
sport and I hereby agree to assume the risk of injury on behalf
of myself and my child." The risk of a lawsuit should not prevent
you from engaging in an activity that will create memories last-
ing a lot longer than who actually won the season.

Q: **I've heard kids are no longer allowed to keep their medication
with them at school. What are the rules for when a child can
and can't carry her meds?**

A: Though there is no national regulation on this issue, based on
zero-tolerance policies for drug use, many state and local ordinances have prevented children from carrying any drugs—
prescription or otherwise—in school. Ironically, the idea of
zero tolerance was to protect students from the harms of drug
use, but these policies have also yielded unintentionally negative (and expensive) results. For example, a $2.3 million verdict
was awarded to the family of a fifth grader who died during an
asthma attack because the school staff couldn't put together his
nebulizer.

With the increase in diabetes among school-aged kids and
the growing understanding that "fast-acting inhalers" must be
used "fast" to be effective, states have finally begun to change
some of these policies, particularly in regard to insulin pumps,
asthma medication, EpiPens, and other emergency treatments. In
Pennsylvania, for instance, a new law requires schools to develop

a written policy that allows a child to carry and use his asthma medication as needed if the child can "demonstrate the ability to use the inhaler, behave responsibly when using it, and notify the school nurse immediately following each use." However, a school has the right to deny "the privilege" of carrying an inhaler, or to restrict its use, if school policies are abused or ignored.

If your child is on medication for what could be an imminent health crisis, like an asthma attack or a severe allergic reaction, make sure you check with your district to see if your child can carry the emergency dose of medication with him. In fact, for all medications, it's best to find out ahead of time what the policy is. The school may be educating your child on reading and writing, but it's up to you to educate your child on the procedure with his medicine when he needs it.

Q: A little girl and her dad were seated in the row in front of me on my flight back to New York. She screamed the whole way and the beastly man ignored her (and ignored me kicking his seat). I kept thinking "Where is the mother?!" ... which then made me think, "Huh, where *is* the mother? Maybe the man's a kidnapper!" Are there any rules about traveling with children to prevent that sort of thing?

A: If you are a single parent planning an international vacation with your kids (and yes, Mexico and Canada are considered foreign countries), in addition to luggage, toys, passports, food, entertainment, DVDs, CDs, and various other sundries, there's one more thing you can't forget to take with you: evidence that you are allowed to travel alone with the child and that you are not abducting him or her.

Some countries require a notarized letter of consent. So before you travel, call the consulate of your planned destination to find out what is required. Various Web sites exist on tips for traveling as a single parent, such as www.singleparenttravel.net, which includes a sample consent document. If you visit those sites before visiting your planned site, at least you know one part of your vacation will be hassle free.

Q: **Let's talk child labor: I want to hire a chimney sweep, but I know kids under a certain age aren't supposed to work. What are the rules on that?**

A: Have you ever seen any of those *Oprah* episodes where she profiles amazing kids? I caught one recently that told the story of Gurbaksh Chalal, a young man who came to the United States with his parents when he was four years old. G, as he now calls himself, said that when his family arrived here from India, his parents had only twenty-five dollars to their name and were forced to take menial jobs to survive. Fortunately they had a son who was not only smart, he was also a budding entrepreneur, and at age sixteen, he dropped out of school to build an Internet business called Click Agents. Two years later G sold the company for $40 million. Amazing, right? Want to know what's more amazing? Had anyone ever reported the sixteen-year-old G's activities, it's possible that he could have been severely penalized for violating child labor laws.

Under federal law, you can't work—except in agriculture—if you're under fourteen. Fourteen- and fifteen-year-olds may only work during nonschool hours, for three hours on a school day, eighteen hours total in a school week or forty hours on a vacation week. They are also only allowed to work between the hours of 7:00 A.M. and 7:00 P.M. from Labor Day through June 1. Federal law does not limit hours or times of day for workers sixteen years of age and older, but some states have enacted their own child labor laws as well. Why would they do this? Precisely to prevent cases like G's, in which the child drops out of school in order to work. Though the Department of Labor isn't exactly out investigating every entrepreneurial kid with a lemonade stand, they may become involved when truancy becomes an issue. The DOL also gets involved when it learns of companies that hire young employees to perform dangerous tasks, and has sued deli owners for allowing minors to operate the meat slicers (so be careful when slicing the lemons for the lemonade stand). If you have a child who wants to work (or a child *you* want to work), no matter how successful you know he or she will be, child labor laws must be adhered to, even if that kid's destined to become the next G or Bill Gates.

Amy

I'm convinced that sometimes being a responsible parent means beating a kid at his own game. Still, I'm not sure who learned this lesson best that rainy Saturday morning when my husband, Len, and I took our kids to temple. Sheets of rain were coming down so hard all I could pray for was that the storm would let up before we needed to build an ark to get home. After the service ended, I was chatting with some of the other parents when William, my four-year-old son, wandered out into the hallway. A few minutes later, some big kids came into the room and said, "Mrs. Feldman, William's outside." I said, "Yeah, I know." They replied,

"Not outside the room, outside the building." And sure enough, when I glanced out the window there was my little pride and joy leading the charge into knee-deep puddles with two other small children in tow.

When I stepped outside and yelled to the boys to come inside *right now*, of course the three took off in the other direction as fast as their slick little legs could carry them. Mere moments later, with three sopping-wet, adrenaline-pumped four-year-olds sprinting away from me, and me giving chase in my skirt and high heels, I was struck with divine inspiration. As the entire congregation watched us from the window, I yelled, "Last one in's a rotten egg!" then I turned tail and started running back toward the door. Miraculously the Three Mud-sketeers suddenly reversed their direction and began running after me.

Back inside we were met by the scowling dad of the other two boys, who was clearly mentally calculating how to explain his soggy offspring to his pissed-off wife. He grabbed each boy by the hand as he led them away from William and me. "I have one question," he asked sternly. "Are you crazy?" By this point I was soaking wet myself and laughing so hard that, to be honest, I couldn't be sure if that mad dad was talking to his kids or to me.

Q: When I was in high school some parents (a.k.a. the cool ones) let their kids drink beer at their parties because they thought it was better for their children to drink under their "watchful eye" than have them drink elsewhere. Serving minors in a bar is illegal, but can parents get into trouble for serving them in the privacy of their own homes?

A: Many states have begun to implement strict laws to combat underage drinking. In New Jersey, for instance, adults who provide alcohol may be charged with a misdemeanor. In Kansas, the state senate passed a bill that makes it a crime punishable by six months in jail for adults to allow underage drinking in their homes even if they don't provide the alcohol. One permissive papa was arrested under this law for hosting an underage drinking party at his home in Lenexa, Kansas; twenty-one juveniles were also taken into custody. And in August 2007, Nassau County, New York, resident Karen Dittmer had the distinct displeasure of becoming New York's first parental bustee under the state's new social host law, which targets adults who permit underage drinking in their homes. She pled guilty to the charge and was fined $250.

There are also likely to be additional penalties from the crimes that happen as a result of the alcohol. A mother in Bangor, Pennsylvania, was sentenced to one to four and a half years in prison for involuntary manslaughter after hosting a party that led to the drunk-driving deaths of three teenagers. As a parent you must keep in mind that it's okay to say "It's not okay to break the law. And I'm not going to break the law by letting you."

Q: I saw on the news that girls were banned from their proms because their dresses were judged "too sexy." How is that fair? And how are they supposed to lose their virginity that night if they can't flaunt the goods?

A: The parents of twenty-five New Orleans teens whose daughters were barred from the prom because their attire was "too revealing" argued a *slightly* different point. They said the practice of barring their daughters was discriminatory because the only girls who were bounced from the prom were those who were well-endowed; they argued that since flatter-chested classmates were given a pass, that constituted discrimination. Now, while my gut reaction might have been, "Oh, boo hoo, you're young, attractive, and have enormous knockers," it does raise some legal questions: namely, can a school have a dress code at an off-site prom, and is it discrimination if only the big-chested are barred?

Legally, schools are allowed to create dress codes for regular daily activities and are more than entitled to do so for off-campus extracurricular activities, too. For those New Orleans teens, while being turned away was unfortunate it was not discrimination. (No doubt many of their concave classmates would have gladly traded places with them just to walk a mile in Chesty McPopular's pumps.) In the New Orleans case, the code was too vaguely worded and therefore left people confused about what constituted "inappropriate attire" (read: "slut gear"). But if you're ever concerned about a dress code, ask for clarification before spending the money on a dress better suited for a sex club in Amsterdam than a formal dance at the local country club.

Never raise your hands to your kids. It leaves your groin
unprotected.

—Red Buttons

Q: **In Los Angeles the city government is trying to fine parents the cost of removing graffiti sprayed by their kids. Isn't that equivalent to punishing someone for another person's crime?**

A: Yeah, changing diapers is also a good example of that. . . . I can tell you that as a parent, there are days when you look at your precious children and you think: good grief, what happened? There is really no end to the amount of trouble kids can cause, from the annoyingly mischievous to the downright criminal. As a parent you should know that when kids engage in criminal behavior, it is the individual who perpetrates the crime who is arrested for it. (If it's shown that the parent was an accessory to the crime or if the parent obstructs justice by hiding evidence, that's a different story.) But for property damage that results in civil penalties—meaning it costs money—*the parents may be responsible to pay the debts created by their minor.*

Michigan parents Susan and Anthony Provenzino learned this lesson the hard way. After their sixteen-year-old son burglarized homes and churches and committed random assaults, *they* were charged under the local parental liability ordinance for the damage caused by his bad behavior. Ultimately, they were each assessed a $100 fine and $1,000 dollars in court costs (not including the tab their attorney cost them). They were also forced to pony up $13,000 for the residential detention center their son entered. Happy Mother's Day!

Q: **What if your kid does damage of a different sort and goes on a shopping spree? As a parent, are you responsible for the debts your idiot child rings up on your credit card?**

A: Many parents consider sending the kids off to college with an "emergency" credit card. They are then often surprised to discover that while their definition of "emergency" includes the words "life endangering" and "natural disaster," their kids' include words like "beer," "Scooby snacks," and "low price on new releases!" If you thought your parental responsibility ended when you got the kid out of the house, think again, Mom and Dad! Turns out you, proud parent, are almost always responsible financially for the debts incurred by your minor children. Even for college-age kids who have reached the age of maturity, if a parent hands a daughter a credit card, adding her as a "permissive user," the parent is still responsible for the charges the daughter racks up.

If an adult child applies for her own credit card and the parents are not cosigners, the debt she accrues is her own responsibility. Stored-value cards (like prepaid phone cards) are a compromise—they look like credit cards but are actually a prepaid account—and once the money is spent, it's gone.

But before you buy a prepaid phone card, understand how much you are actually paying for a minute of conversation time. There are almost always extra charges, including activation and access fees, as well as additional charges for calling from a pay phone. Many of these cards expire, too, so take a look at the expiration date to see if you'll really use all the time before the card expires. Finally, buy the cards in small denominations in case one doesn't work or gets lost. If it doesn't work, call the customer service number on the card and if that doesn't work you can call the Federal Trade Commission to file a complaint at 877-FTC-HELP.

For the first eighteen years, they were your responsibility—now make sure the financial decisions they're making are their own responsibility.

Q: **When a parent drops a kid off at college, is the school legally responsible for him at that point?**

A: The term *in loco parentis*, meaning "in place of parent," refers to the legal burden of the college to take on the responsibilities of the parent. Though this concept fell out of favor in the 1960s, and it was briefly believed that once kids got to college they became men and women responsible for their own decision making, those days now seem as prehistoric as the era before e-mail. *In loco parentis* made a big comeback shortly after the drinking age was raised to twenty-one and college kids, who either didn't get the memo or chose to ignore it, kept drinking anyway. But what the law did was provide litigation attorneys looking to pin responsibility for stupid behavior on a new, deep-pocketed target.

In general, private colleges have the right to govern the conduct of students and do so to prevent drinking on campus, "sharing" answers on exams, and other behavior it considers inconsistent with the educational mission. But while colleges must take reasonable action to prevent known harms (like making sure the fire alarms in the dorms work), case law is inconsistent about how far they have to go to prevent students from doing the stupid, crazy things that students, when given the time and opportunity, will do.

Interestingly, wrongful death lawsuits filed at MIT show how far the pendulum has swung in both directions regarding the doctrine of *in loco parentis*. In the late 1990s, two different cases were brought against MIT alleging wrongful death by the families of students. The first was the case of Richard Guy, Jr. Guy died of suffocation resulting from nitrous oxide intoxication during orientation. His parents sued MIT, claiming that MIT failed to provide reasonable care, supervision, and oversight of students in its dormitories, contributing to Guy's death. The university settled the Guys' claim by setting up a fund for preorientation programs. MIT likewise settled another claim, in 2000, brought by the family of Scott Krueger, who died of alcohol poisoning. But the university fought the parents of Elizabeth Shin, who died of self-inflicted immolation. Shin had been in counseling with the university health system for depression but MIT had not notified her parents of her ongoing psychological issues. As a result, the family claimed MIT breached its duty to exercise reasonable care in protecting her by failing to provide for her security or to notify them so they could take action. MIT disagreed, stating the parents' request would lead to a loss of confidentiality between adults in need of counseling and the university providers. Ultimately the Shins' claims against MIT were dismissed after evidence surrounding the circumstances of her death pointed to an accidental cause rather than suicide.

The bottom line is that *in loco parentis* is a doctrine argued in court about who has to pay after a tragedy happens. It's far better to encourage your kids to act as intelligently as possible because ultimately their best chance to stay safe is when they act as if they're adult themselves.

Robin

Though no one I knew was entirely certain of its origins, the annual event called the Nude Olympics had become one of the most eagerly anticipated and beloved traditions on the Princeton campus. At midnight on the evening of the first snowfall of the school year, members of the sophomore class would gather in one of the campus's beautiful gothic courtyards, strip naked, and run around in circles until they became thoroughly exhausted and/ or their buzzes wore off.

After viewing the event as a freshman, I decided hell would freeze over before I took off all my clothes and ran around in the snow—stark naked for all to see. My roommate, Jamie, had the opposite reaction and immediately declared her intention to run the following year. Brave woman that she was, Jamie also planned to do it totally sober. When the day of reckoning came the following year, Jamie, true to her word, was ready to run and did not lift even one ceremonial shot of Jaeger to her lips. I, on the other hand, inspired by the fear that I'd miss out on this quintessential college experience, changed my mind. I was completely sober when I made the decision to participate, and then I soberly decided I would need to drink as much as possible before the event began.

When we arrived at the designated Olympic stadium, the pristine Rockefeller Courtyard, Jamie and I tossed off our coats, followed by every last piece of clothing we wore but our sneakers. And then with a few hundred other naked classmates, at the crack of the starter pistol, we took off running around that courtyard to the great adulation (cheers, jeers, and occasional snowballs) of our schoolmates.

Once Jamie and I felt we'd satisfied our Olympic ambitions, we located our coats so we could head back to our dorm. But it's a funny thing about snow and ice. Turns out it can be rather slippery underfoot, and as we approached the courtyard's archway, Jamie started to skid. In what I can only imagine was a boozily heightened sense of gallantry, I reached for my roommate's arm to brace her. Heroic? Possibly. Effective? Not remotely. In the blink of an eye, we both went crashing to the ground.

The fall itself probably wouldn't have been terribly traumatic had not a breakaway group of Olympians come running through the slippery archway at exactly that moment. And then down they fell, one on top of the other on top of the other on top of me. Jamie somehow managed to escape the dogpile, but I was literally at the bottom of the heap, nude beneath my overcoat and fearing I was going to die in the scrum. But worse than that thought was envisioning the headline in the next day's paper: NAKED PRINCETON STUDENT, ROBIN EPSTEIN, DEAD IN NUDE OLYMPICS DEBACLE.

Fortunately I made it out from under the pile alive, with only a very muddy overcoat and a body full of black-and-blue marks as my battle scars. But perhaps not surprisingly, a few years after I graduated, the administration officially banned the Nude Olympics because it was decided the event posed "intolerable risks" to the student body. Now, as one of those student bodies who risked life, limb, and ass to participate in the event, it is hard to deny the university's logic on this one. But as a proud former Nude Olympian, I must confess it was one of the most memorable experiences of my college career.

Q: They sure don't make it cheap to own a kid these days—tuition payments alone can put you in the dog house. Are there any legal ways to defray a child's education?

A: One of the most generous gifts that a parent or grandparent can give a child is the gift of an education, and you may be surprised to hear the IRS has just made it a little easier to do this.

In general, when a donor makes a gift to someone, the person who receives the gift takes it tax free. The donor, however, must complete a gift tax form if the gift is in excess of $12,000. (This will later reduce the amount that person can leave to his or her heirs tax free.) The IRS ruling states that prepaid tuition by a donor is not considered a taxable gift. But you need to make sure you're giving "correctly" to avoid gift tax implications: if you want to give money to pay for the child's education, don't give the money directly to the child. Even setting up a trust to pay for tuition will not cause the money to be exempted from gift tax. Rather, the money must be paid by the donor directly to the institution. To become better schooled on this issue, visit www.irs.gov.

Now, when the time comes to send your child to school, you'll likely be solicited by businesses (both legitimate and fraudulent) to help shepherd you through the process. Oftentimes firms will try to lure people with the prospect of finding scholarship dollars or seminars that promise solutions and matching grants. Operators of financial aid scams generally promise that their services will ensure that students receive either a scholarship or increased financial aid. The scams usually fall into the following categories:

- Scholarships for profit, whereby they get an application fee from you and you never get the scholarship.
- A "money-back" guarantee offering to match you with scholarships but which will neither give you the money they promise to match for you nor return to you the money you give them.
- Seminars featuring consultants who pressure you to sign up for expensive services that will ultimately bear no fruit.

For information about real loans and scholarships and how to get them, visit www.ed.gov to avoid a costly lesson before school even starts.

Q: Speaking of writing kids off, I know parents can claim dependent children on their taxes. But when parents get divorced, does the child get written off twice?

A: You know how when your kid is behaving badly, you turn to your spouse and say, "Your son is behaving horribly!"? Well, when tax season comes around, suddenly most divorced spouses both want to claim that kid as their own. In addition to parental pride, someone is going to get a dependency exemption for that adorable little menace.

A child can be claimed as a dependent on only one tax form. If you are married and filing jointly, there's no problem. But in order to figure out which divorced spouse gets to claim him, the IRS has a test: If only one person is the biological parent, that parent gets to claim him. If, however, both are the biological parents, it's the parent with whom the child has lived for the longer period of time who gets the exemption.

If the child has lived with each parent for the same amount of time, then the child will be treated as a dependent of the parent with the higher adjusted gross income. Too bad that's not the test when the question is "Who gets to change the diaper?"

Q: What happens if, for whatever reason, a parent can no longer afford to pay child support?

A: Frequently a parent who can no longer afford the designated amount of child support simply stops paying it. That's what you call a boneheaded move. Andre "Bad Moon" Rison, a five-time Pro Bowl–playing football star, was one such bonehead. He was dragged off to jail for failing to pay child support totaling $127,000. Though it may be difficult to believe the Super Bowl champ was having a hard time finding the money, if you find that your circumstances have changed since your support order was entered, what can you do?

Well, in an effort to encourage the stability of support arrangements and to prevent frequent modification requests, the court will generally only change support obligations if the spouses can show changed circumstances (like the end of a football career). Depending on the change, the modification can be temporary (like for a child's medical emergency or a parent's temporary inability to pay because of a job loss or his or her own medical emergency) or permanent (such as when one parent becomes disabled, the child develops a permanent medical condition, or one parent receives additional income from a remarriage).

In any event, what you should never do is simply stop paying what you owe. Doing that not only makes you a loser, it might also make you the personal cheerleader of some burly "player" in lockup. Go to court and get a modification.

Q: In the Kanye West song "Gold Digger," he describes the plight of a football player who pays child support for eighteen years, and then, on her eighteenth birthday, he finds out she isn't his! Can an ex stop paying support if he suspects he's not the baby daddy?

A: In a Florida case, when a couple divorced, the ex-husband was required to pay child support, which he failed to do. Two years later, when his ex-wife sued for unpaid child support, the man decided to conduct a paternity test. That's when he learned the child was not biologically his. The Florida court ruled that even so, he still had to pay child support. Why? Because the man waited too long to claim the "Billy Jean" defense—*She says I am the one, but the kid is not my son. . . .*

During a marriage, the husband is presumed to be the father of a child born to his wife. While state laws differ, in many states paternity may be questioned during a divorce proceeding. If it's proven at that time that the ex-husband is not the biological father, he won't be required to pay child support. But since the man in Florida waited years before he made the claim, he was time-barred. The lesson is that paternity can be disavowed, but only for a limited time, after which you lose your right to make the argument.

Ultimately, what is in the best interests of the child, and not the feuding parents, is paramount—both during and after the marriage.

Q: **I've heard that in the case of some ugly divorces, a judge will mandate that the bickering spouses come up with a parenting plan. Beyond "pray it ain't ugly," what is a parenting plan?**

A: You've been reading *Us Weekly* again, haven't you? In many celebrity divorces that get played out in the media, you'll often see judges requiring these famous combatants to create a parenting plan, like in the awful proceedings of Britney Spears and Kevin Federline. Certainly enough ink has been wasted on these two, who are clearly in need of babysitters themselves. But what Britney did wrong, causing her to lose custody of the kids, is actually an important lesson.

Lesson one: when a judge tells you to take drug tests, get a driver's license, go to parenting classes, and create a parenting plan, you're best served to do so, even if you can't plan to wear underwear that day.

Lesson two: a parenting plan is a document created to set forth each of the parent's responsibilities. It can be a long and detailed list of duties or a general summary of the ways each parent will be involved in the lives of the children. It should also lay out an overview of the schedule and reflect the types of involvement each parent will have, from overnight visits to sports spectating.

You don't necessarily need the court's intervention to come to an agreement that you both understand; you just need to be civil long enough to put the kids' needs ahead of the parents' unhappiness.

Q: Do grandparents get visitation rights in the case of divorce?

A: Yes, they do. The Ohio Supreme Court ruled recently that grandparents have rights to see their grandkids, even against the wishes of the parents. Every state has third-party visitation statutes that define the rights of people other than parents—such as grandparents or stepparents—who can go to court to maintain their relationship. Some states have what's called "restrictive visitation" statutes, where grandparents can get court-ordered visitation, but only if the parents have divorced or died.

"Permissive visitation" statutes allow court-ordered visitation even if the parents are together, if it's in the best interest of the child. But obviously the most desirable scenario is for parents and grandparents to be able to work out visitation with the grandkids without having to resort to court or rely on statutes.

Amy

Think you're a good negotiator? You can't hold a candle to a seven-year-old who has the determination to win every argument and all the time of yours to waste in the world.

Actual conversation:

Emma: Can I have some ice cream?

Me: No.

Emma: Please? Just a little?

Me: No, you already had dessert.

Emma: Please? *Pleeeeeeeeease!* Just a teeny-weeny eeny-weeny bit?

Me: No.

Emma: But please?

Me: No means no.

Emma: Please, Mommy. Mommy, please. Please can I have some ice cream?

Me: Okay, okay! Just a little.

Emma: Can I have a lot?

Chapter 5

Your Online Profile

A.k.a. What the Whole Wide World Knows About You!

Does such a thing as privacy even exist in the age of the Internet? Do you have any rights concerning your image, your name, or what gets posted about you with or without your knowledge? We'll talk about ways of protecting your identity online and off in this chapter, and how best to avoid becoming the latest greatest viral cautionary tale.

Q: A "friend" of mine posted the most embarrassing picture of me online! (We're not talking "spinach in the teeth" embarrassing, we're talking *oh my God, Mom will murder me if she ever sees this* embarrassing. . . .) It's my image, do I have any rights to prevent it from appearing on the site?

A: Well, I'd say if you have equally compromising photos of your friend, you could encourage her to delete the pictures by using the old "e-tit for e-tat" ploy. But what are your options if acting mature is important to you? You can sue a Web site to take down an unauthorized picture of you if the photo is defamatory (say, for instance, it implies you were engaged in a crime when none was committed). You can also sue if your photo is being used for a commercial purpose, making it look like you're endorsing a product when you're not. (This one primarily applies to celebrities.) You also have a claim if you are portrayed falsely in a highly offensive manner—if, for example, someone has Photoshopped your head onto a nude body, or for an invasion of privacy if it's a picture of you in a situation where you had an expectation of privacy—like a locker room.

On Facebook you have the option to remove the tag that identifies you by name in the photo (this will prevent the picture from popping up when people search for you by name). But currently there are no regulations that allow you to demand the photo be taken down, something to keep in mind when you're three sheets to the wind and posing with your pants down.

Q: What happens if I'm photographed or videotaped without my knowledge or consent, and I only find out about it once the images have been posted online?

A: It's a tricky issue in the age of ubiquitous camera phones and web-cams because technology evolves much more quickly than our legal system. But the Video Voyeurism Prevention Act prohibits the photographing or videotaping of a naked person without his permission in a gym, tanning salon, dressing room, or anywhere else he has a reasonable expectation of privacy. If you're on the street and someone snaps your picture, however, it's not illegal because the courts have found that there is no reasonable expectation of privacy when you are in public places. That's the lesson Olympic swimmer Michael Phelps learned when he was photographed at a party with his lips wrapped around a bong: even if you're at a "private party," when you're in a living room surrounded by other people, any argument for "the expectation of privacy" goes up in smoke.

A junior at the University of Pennsylvania faced disciplinary charges for posting pictures online that he took of two naked students who could be seen through a dorm window in a compromising position. That's right, Mom and Dad, there are your tuition dollars at work! But the junior Fellini argued that when the people made a public spectacle of themselves, they took the risk of being caught on tape. The naked folk argued they were only making a spectacle of themselves *in private*. . . .

The best advice I can give is to be aware of your surroundings and anyone who looks suspicious while holding a cell phone. And, for God's sake, close your drapes!

Q: My friend found out he'd been listed on a Web site called DontDateHimGirl.com. Er, not the most flattering profile and he wants to sue the person who wrote "his dick is as small as a Munchkin's whisker." (Paints a picture, doesn't it?) The problem is, it was posted anonymously. What can he do?

A: You mean aside from showing evidence to the contrary? Unfortunately there are a lot of very angry people trolling cyberspace, and postings to message boards are frequently defamatory. In fact, many companies are now trying to take action against their defamers, but most often the people making those nasty, nasty comments are doing so anonymously. The ESPC, a trade union of embroidery software companies, filed a lawsuit when it stumbled on an online hobbyist forum and found some rather *unseemly* postings about the ESPC. Since the posters were anonymous, the ESPC subpoenaed the Internet service provider's records to get the identities of the posters.

Different courts have come out differently on the issue of whether or not an ISP must identify an anonymous poster. What anonymous posters need to know is that eventually they may well be unmasked, and that if they fight to remain anonymous it will be a costly undertaking. You may be best served by the message your grandmother no doubt embroidered on a pillow: if you don't have something nice to say, don't say anything at all.

Still, some people just can't seem to hold their electronic tongues. Here's one from the "are you out of your mind?" category. John Mackey, the chairman and CEO of Whole Foods, posted a series of anonymous (*and bitchy*) comments about Wild Oats Markets, a Whole Foods competitor. Critics said Mackey was trying to diminish the value of Wild Oats stock while simultaneously pumping up Whole Food's image in addition to his own—in one post he even referred to himself and his new haircut as "cute." Aside from being slightly ridiculous and stunningly adolescent, did Mackey break any laws with his anonymous postings?

Well, if Mackey's comments contained inside information (that's information known by the company's board of directors, management, and/or employees but not by the general public) then he could be breaching securities laws. Same is true if his posts were designed to manipulate stock prices for the purposes of a more favorable acquisition (Whole Foods was trying to purchase Wild Oats Markets at the time). The SEC ultimately cleared Mackey of wrongdoing in May 2008, but beyond legality is the question of advisability. Understand that you can't assume you will remain anonymous. Don't ever post anything that would embarrass you if your identity came to light—no matter how cute you believe your own haircut to be.

Now let's consider the case of a defamed plastic surgeon. He claimed a Web site that advocated against breast implants posted messages that slandered him. He sued both the writers of the messages as well as the administrator of the Web site, whom he had e-mailed to request their removal (which the site chose to ignore). But lawyers for the Web site claimed it should not be liable for the acts of the people who wrote the postings. Ultimately the California Supreme Court ruled that the defamed doc could pursue his claims against the individual authors of the defamatory postings but could not sue the Web site that published them.

The best option for someone who feels slandered by a posting is to ask the Web site to remove the malicious comment. If he learns the identity of the poster, he can then take legal action against that person. So memo to the angry trolls out there: keep in mind that just because someone can't see your face, that doesn't mean you can't be held responsible.

Q: I just got back from an Internet date with a guy who claimed to be "Mr. Tall, Dark, and Handsome." Turned out he was more like "Mr. Fat, Bald, and Living in His Mother's Basement." I'm sick of dating sites that promise to find me my perfect match then deliver duds. Shouldn't that be considered fraud?

A: Under the law, an Internet provider cannot be held liable for the lies told by third parties. In other words, sorry, Charlie! But consumer protection statutes do require that a site cannot mislead the public into thinking it is doing more to protect them from liars and predators than it really does. Check the terms of use for every dating site to see what the site is obligating itself to do. You will see that most sites specifically state they *don't* conduct background checks on their members and therefore your safety is your own responsibility.

When you're using dating sites it's also important not to fool yourself into thinking you know the person just because he or she has typed you a message. You really don't know if what he's typing is true or not so don't let your guard down when you meet. Arrange the date in a public space or consider bringing along a friend for safety. Don't believe everything you read about Mr. Right or about the site's ability to find him for you.

Additionally you also want to be careful when considering what type of information you're giving out to potential "personal encounters." A thirty-year-old male network administrator in Washington State posted a graphic ad on Craigslist claiming to be a female who was into kinky encounters. He received many responses, including those from men who sent pictures of themselves . . . and their private parts. Some gave out their phone numbers, provided their real names, and used their work e-mail addresses. The network administrator then posted all of the responses online, including the pictures.

I'm guessing the thing those responders probably found most frustrating was *not* that Lola was a man—but that they'd let their small heads do the thinking when they used their work e-mail addresses and gave out personal information to a stranger online. And while it is possible that the poster may have broken the law by posting personal information about others, the bottom line is that even if the network administrator were convicted of a crime, the law won't give these guys their jobs back or free them from the embarrassment of the sting.

Q: Buying stuff online and sending my credit card and personal info through the ether makes me nervous. How do I *really* know if a site is secure?

A: You're right to be cautious because rarely can you be 100 percent certain of that fact. Unfortunately even sites that assured customers they were safe have been hacked. This was obviously an unpleasant surprise to the T. J. Maxx shoppers who learned that in 2005 and 2006 more than 45 million credit and debit card numbers were lifted from the store's "secure" server.

Every online merchant has a privacy policy, explaining to what lengths the company goes to protect you. Click on the policy and make sure it obligates the company to treat your information as confidential. If it does and the company breaches that policy, those assurances are false and misleading to the public, which is a violation of the Federal Trade Commission Act. But note that while the FTC will sanction companies that don't live up to their privacy policies, it will only do so after there's been a breach. Your smartest move is to use only credit cards with Internet fraud protection when buying online.

Additionally, if you're thinking of shopping on a site with which you are not familiar, do some research before you buy: Call the seller's phone number to make sure it is a working number. If there isn't one, walk away. Type the name into a search engine and read reviews. Don't respond to an unsolicited e-mail. Instead of replying, type the Web address into your browser to make sure it's a real site. It's also a good idea to log off and shut down when you're ready to walk away from your computer to prevent scammers from installing software to control it remotely.

One final note of caution: There is often publicity surrounding a security breach as the company scurries to reach out to those whose privacy has been compromised. Frequently, opportunistic scammers—not necessarily those who perpetrated the original scam—realize that there are still suckers to be had and begin randomly calling people to tell them they may have been the victim of fraud. It's ingenious because if you've read about the security breach, you might have reason to believe that the scam exists and that the caller is actually investigating the underlying crime.

The caller (who has identified himself as an investigator) asks you, the "possible victim," for your credit card number to verify if fraud has occurred on your card. If you give this guy your information, you're no longer a "possible victim," you're now an actual victim. *Never, never, never* give a credit card number or other identifying information to a random stranger who has called you—even if that person says he's an officer or investigator. Instead, ask the "investigator" to send you information in the mail (*and don't give your address—a legitimate investigator will already have it*). Finally, double-check by then calling your own credit card company to ask if there was a security breach involving your card.

Q: What happens if a hacker gets my information and suddenly I'm Sandra Bullock in that forgettable movie—the name of which I've forgotten—where her identity is stolen?

A: Something similar happened to a Philadelphia man who was perplexed when he got a bill for jewelry purchased at a local mall. His confusion turned to horror when it became clear that someone posing as him had opened store credits at many stores in the mall and racked up more than $30,000 in charges all in his name. If you are the victim of identity theft, what's the first thing you should do? And then what? And *then* what?

As soon as you discover you've been the victim of identity theft, contact one of the three credit reporting agencies (Equifax: 800-685-1111; Experian: 888-397-3742; TransUnion: 800-888-4213) and put a fraud alert on your file. Get a copy of your credit report and read it carefully to see what accounts exist that you didn't create. Close all the accounts you know or think may have been tampered with. Make sure you keep a list of all the people to whom you speak at the credit card companies and follow up in writing. File a police report and file a report with the Federal Trade Commission. For more information, go to the commission's Web site at www.ftc.gov or contact its identity theft hotline at 877-IDTHEFT.

At this point, thirty-eight states and the District of Columbia now have laws allowing you to lock up credit reports through what's called a credit freeze. A credit freeze prevents all the credit bureaus from issuing reports in your name, so credit card companies will not allow new credit cards to be issued. This means that no one—not even you—can open a new account in your name unless you specifically lift the credit freeze by using the PIN that each credit reporting agency sent you when you placed it.

Unlike fraud alerts, which are free but can expire, there is a minimal fee to set up a credit freeze. But considering the time and money you'll spend correcting a fraud, setting up a freeze, if one seems warranted, is priceless.

In addition to the financial implications of identity theft, hackers can wreck havoc on personal information, too. Pro golfer Fuzzy Zoeller realized this when he found that someone had hacked his Wikipedia entry. Posing as Fuzzy, the hacker embellished the entry by stating that "after popping a handful of Vicodin," he had just "polished off a fifth of Jack Daniels." Also added to the page was the "fact" that he beat his wife and kids. Fuzzy hunted down the anonymous hacker and sued, contending that "the false and defamatory statements damaged his reputation and caused 'mental anguish' and loss of income."

In one way, Fuzzy was lucky: at least he realized he'd been the victim of a hack. An unknown number of job seekers on Monster.com still might not yet know they've been victimized. When they clicked on a posting for a phony job, a trojan was deployed into their hard drive that stole sensitive, personal identifying information. By the time the job seekers realized that the ad was not for a real job, their information had already been lifted.

There are good ways to protect yourself from most of these invasions, but you need to remain vigilant. Up-to-date antivirus software puts a wall up in front of most malicious trojans, preventing them from blasting into your hard drive. But many home users get a trial version of Norton or another antivirus program, then fail to renew it when the trial time expires. That leaves you open to a breach, which is dangerous and potentially very costly in the long run. There are plenty of high-tech anti-identity-theft techniques that require firewalls and other complicated solutions. But much of the malware that invades the computers of hundreds of thousands of unwary users is easily and cheaply blocked with even the most basic level of regularly updated antivirus software.

Q: **Is there any way to stop a Web site from monitoring my purchasing history or movements online?**

A: Yes, throw out your computer. The reality is many Web sites require that you accept a "tracking cookie" in order to use the site. A cookie isn't a virus or spyware—technically it's just data—but it does track your preferences and browsing history. Most people unwittingly wind up blabbing their predilections across the Web by agreeing to a site's terms and conditions without ever bothering to read its privacy policy.

In a public relations debacle, AOL released the searches of 650,000 subscribers. Even though no names were listed, people could be identified by the searches they conducted. AOL apologized and took down the list but what the company did wasn't illegal. Why not? Because AOL subscribers had already given permission to the company to release information about their searches to whomever it wanted.

Why would anyone be so dumb as to give AOL this permission? you snicker. Well, how many times have you instinctively hit a Web site's "I agree" button without first reading exactly what you were agreeing to? Probably a lot. And therein lies the problem because therein lies the company's privacy policy. If you don't want a site to have particular information about you, find another place to do your browsing and buying. But just keep in mind that the next time you push the "I agree" button without actually reading that long, boring block of text, you may be giving away your right to remain e-nonymous.

Q: What about regular old brick-and-mortar stores? If they have my basic info, they can potentially sell it to advertisers, too, no?

A: You better believe they can! People give away their private information all the time. Remember all that data you filled in in those boxes when you wanted that new credit card? How about the details you happily gave up when you ordered those airline tickets? What about medical records or bank information—are there *any* laws that prevent institutions from selling your stats to the highest bidder? Uh-uh.

While banks are regulated against the disclosure of financial information, and new laws prevent health care institutions from releasing privileged patient information, private retailers are bound only by their concerns for customer loyalty—*not* by law—to protect the privacy of their consumers.

Think of the schmuck who learned that lesson when he tried sending flowers to his girlfriend. His problem started when the florist, 1-800-FLOWERS.COM, sent the man a thank-you note for the order . . . and his wife happened to see it first. The wife, who hadn't received flowers, was understandably confused. So she called to find out about the order, at which point the company faxed her a copy of the receipt, her husband and his girlfriend's identifying information, and the card, which read "I Love You!" You may not be surprised to hear the wife was mighty, mighty pissed. Fortunately her husband, chastened by his cheating, owned up to his mistake and resolved to make amends. Kidding! He actually sued the florist instead. (What a prize he is, huh?)

In his suit, Cheater Von Shouldhavekeptitinhispants claimed that 1-800-FLOWERS.COM led consumers to believe that their transactions were confidential. Now, now, no tears when you hear he lost the case. Why? Well, as it turns out, companies are not bound by law to maintain the confidentiality of your transactions unless they specifically say they will keep your confidential information confidential. Evidently the guy should have read the vendor's privacy statement before he placed his order. Even more obvious is the fact that he shouldn't have cheated on his wife in the first place—I'm just saying. . . .

Information you give a private retailer—like your address, e-mail, spending habits, income level, etc.—is information it may just as freely sell or give to other entities that collect such information. Consider that the next time you sign up for a department store card in exchange for 10 percent off your first purchase or a supermarket club card to get that ninety-nine-cent can of tuna. You better believe that even if you're not watching how or what information you disclose about yourself, others are!

Q: Speaking of spying, I keep hearing about all of these federal wiretapping issues. No one's listening in on my conversations . . . are they?

A: It's like an old psychology joke: you're not paranoid if people *really are* spying on you. In 2007, the number of secret wiretaps across the country surged by 14 percent. According to *Wired* magazine, "State police applied for 27 percent more wiretaps in 2007 than in 2006, with 94 percent of them targeting cell phones, according to figures released by the U.S. Courts' administrator." Just look at the scandals that took down the governors of New York and Illinois. Both men were busted thanks to what they were caught discussing on their "private" telephone lines.

Now, under federal law it's illegal for an individual to record a conversation without the permission of one or both parties to the conversation. That means if you suspect your spouse is cheating, you can't tap the phone to record her conversations with her potential lover because neither she nor the suspected lover is aware that the recording is taking place. However, in certain states, as long as one party involved in the conversation gives permission for the taping, then it's legal to do so. In these so-called one party states, if, say, you are trying to get your sister to admit on tape that she took your favorite shirt, you can record the conversation because one party (you) is aware of the taping even if she is not.

But the government may tap a phone pursuant to a criminal investigation as long as it complies with "stringent" rules. It must first draw up an affidavit spelling out why authorities believe they have probable cause to assume you're committing a crime. They must then make an application for a court order, which is presented to a judge for approval.

When the FBI wants to conduct a wiretap, its own procedures are even more extensive. The truth is, it's a huge expense and allocation of resources to conduct a wiretap, so if you hear clicking on your phone, it's much more likely because you have a cut-rate phone service than because the government is listening to your late night conversations.

Q: I just got a ticket—in the mail!—that showed my car sliding through a red light. I might have been chasing the yellow, but this whole Big Brother, "take my photo and don't tell me till later" thing is creepy. Why isn't that considered spying?

A: The answer is it's because you were in a public place and therefore had no reasonable expectation of privacy. Though the thought of being taped without your knowledge may be disconcerting, it's not illegal. In fact, there has been a huge upsurge in surveillance video from places like department stores to intersections. Police in New York City have installed over four hundred new cameras in various neighborhoods. The cameras aren't monitored, but they do record the action on the street on digital tape and will be reviewed if a crime occurs. That said, although "red light cameras" cannot be challenged on privacy grounds, other legal arguments have been made against them with great success, including challenges to their accuracy and an increased likelihood for rear-end collisions. The state of Mississippi recently ruled that such cameras are illegal and must be uninstalled.

Still, if you're out in public, it's very possible (and completely legal) for you to be taped. It's just something to keep in mind if you're considering perpetrating a crime . . . or leaving your home without applying your lipstick first.

Q: I have sensitive info on my computer, but I need to bring it in for repair. How can I be sure Johnny Geeksquad won't snoop through my personal files and make them public?

A: By "sensitive" I assume you mean something like your social security number or embarrassing pictures of yourself from your high school days instead of, say, something related to an issue of national security. This was not the case in New Jersey, when two men went to Circuit City wanting a videotape that showed them praising jihad and firing guns transferred to a DVD. The employee assigned to make the transfer decided to bring it to the attention of the police and was hailed as a hero because it was believed his actions helped thwart a terror plot on Fort Bragg.

Thankfully most people won't have that sort of information on their hard drives, but there are plenty of files and pieces of data that the average computer user wants to keep private. And while most would probably commend that Circuit City employee for being so vigilant with the jihadists' tape, when it's *your* personal property that's being monitored, it might feel like a violation.

If a company puts out a privacy policy advising consumers that their information will be held in confidence, then the company must abide by it or it risks violating the law. But if a company doesn't make any promise about your privacy, you take the risk that your information won't be held in confidence. It's certainly uncomfortable to think that someone could be viewing your "private" files, but it's not illegal.

So the next time you bring in a computer for repair (or resell it, recycle it, or throw it away) clean the hard drive of any information you wouldn't want others to see.

Q: **I read on the Internet that the world's most prolific spammer was arrested and sentenced to ten thousand hours of community service teaching senior citizens how to use computers. Is that true?**

A: You've hit on two of the great scourges of the modern age: spam and compu-hoaxes. You're right about the arrest of the great spammer: in May 2007, Robert Alan Soloway was busted for allegedly using networks of compromised "zombie" computers to send out millions of spam e-mails. Soloway was charged with e-mail fraud and identity theft and was sentenced to forty-seven months in federal prison. He was also forced to repay over $700,000. There are now regulations in place to "stop the spamness," as ineffective as they may be.

The Controlling the Assault of Non-Solicited Pornography and Marketing Act (CAN-SPAM) requires that unsolicited commercial e-mail messages be labeled, that they include opt-out instructions, and that they contain the sender's physical address. It also prohibits deceptive subject lines and false headers in the messages. So if you receive spam that is in violation of this act, you can make a complaint to the Federal Trade Commission at www.ftc.gov.

As for all that false information that friends "helpfully" e-mail you, the perpetuation of electronic hoaxes has become so common, it's virtually impossible to open your in-box without being advised about the "most dangerous computer virus ever!!!" or where to call "so your cell phone number isn't sold to telemarketers."

The reality is you will not be getting telemarketing calls on your cell phone. And all those virus warnings you receive from some well-intentioned friend or coworker are most often electronic versions of the urban legend. Last year, a warning hoax instructed people to look for a file and then destroy it. The problem was, the alleged virus was actually a necessary file, and if you destroyed it you had to reimage your PC.

To check on the veracity of a warning message, you can go to www.snopes.com. The site provides an age-old lesson for the modern age: don't believe everything you read—and don't forward warnings until you know they're true.

Another word on spam: people are often tempted by mail they get online offering various prescription drugs at a greatly reduced price. If you have a legitimate prescription, there are no legal prohibitions against buying medicine from an online pharmacy. Legitimate pharmacy sites are convenient, private, and cost-effective, but if you're uncertain whether a site is licensed, check with the National Association of Boards of Pharmacy at www.nabp.net to learn more.

What you should not do is buy a drug from a site that doesn't provide access to a licensed pharmacist, but still includes claims of amazing results or offers a new cure for a serious disease. Also keep in mind that prescription drugs that have not been approved by the FDA—or products not made, labeled, stored, or distributed according to U.S. requirements—are illegal and can't be sold over the Internet. Finally, though magic cures are tempting, you can be pretty sure that if a site or mailing misspells the name of, for instance, a weight loss drug, the only thing that will "lose inches!" is your wallet.

Q: When I Googled myself I found another Robin Epstein (also a writer) who's got some great credentials. Is it wrong to refer people to the Internet and let them just assume Robin and I are one in the same?

A: Wrong and illegal, Robin—if that's who you really are. Everyone's seen knockoff fast-food joints that try to pass themselves off as the real deal, but despite cosmetic similarities, the product isn't going to taste the same. With the Internet, it's even easier for posers to try to co-opt identity. That's why the Anticybersquatting Consumer Protection Act (ACPA) was created. Cybersquatting is the practice of registering a domain name close to the name of an actual company for the purpose of creating confusion by directing people to a site that they believe is actually the company's. For instance, there was a time when, if you typed www.ernestandjuliogallo.com into your computer, you may have been surprised to find that that Web site was not the company's site but a link to a page discussing the dangers of alcohol. It was actually owned by a cybersquatter who registered more than two thousand other domain names and then tried selling them over eBay to the highest bidder. The ACPA now prevents people from registering a domain name with the intent to profit from it by selling it back to its proper user.

However, the law does *not* protect anyone from registering domain names critical of a company's product, such as the actual site www.ballysucks.com. As you might have deduced, Ballysucks.com is devoted to criticism of Bally Total Fitness. Why is that legal? Well, because no user is likely to mistake that as Bally's official site. The lesson to companies or individuals with sites who fear cybersquatting is that you should register yourname.com, Ihateyourname.com, and any other name that a user might type when trying to locate you.

In addition to cybersquatting, there's also a practice known as "typosquatting." That's when people register domain names similar to popular sites but with common misspellings of the real company's domain name. Instead of wallstreetjournal.com, for example, they register wallsreetjournal.com. They then redirect the traffic to a site that pays them per hit. Under the law, it's illegal to register a domain name identical to or confusingly similar to a trademarked name and used in bad faith to misdirect someone who believes he's going to the company's actual site. If you find your customers are getting redirected to a typosquatter, you can file an action, but to head it off at the pass, don't overestimate the intelligence of the visitors to your site. Register both your name.com and also your misspelledname.com.

The thing to remember when you're building your own Web

site is that you never actually own your URL (a.k.a. the Web address), you're merely renting it when you register your domain name. Web site registration is akin to having a billboard—while you may have rights to the content, the billboard itself will become available to others if you fail to pay the rent.

Once you have registered the domain name, you have right of first refusal when it's time to reregister. But if you fail to reregister, the domain name will be up for grabs. There are companies that monitor domain name registrations and seek out domains that are set to expire—that's where "drop catchers" come in. Residents of one Pennsylvania township learned about drop catchers when they went to their county's Web site (whose domain name had expired) and they were redirected to a porn site. If your domain expires and you have failed to reregister it, drop catchers snap up the site name and either use it themselves or sell it to the highest bidder.

Therefore, before it's too late, make sure that someone in your company is accountable for ensuring that you remain master of your domain (name).

Robin

When I first decided to become a writer, I set a series of goals for myself to serve as a marker of my advancement in the field. Though I knew it wouldn't guarantee my financial success, I thought seeing my name appear in *The New York Times* should be one of those milestones. It seemed like a worthy goal, and it was one I became hell-bent on achieving.

But as I was browsing through the *Times*'s Arts and Leisure section one weekend, I had what can only be described as a "someone up there has a sense of humor" moment, which quickly morphed into a "careful what you wish for" reminder. Yes, there was my name, Robin Epstein, in bold letters at the bottom of this (abridged) letter to the editor:

> To the Editor:
> . . . Dorothy Cantwell and I founded More Fire! Productions in 1979. . . . Yet whether through ignorance, self-interest, or deliberate self-aggrandizement, the small world of lesbian theater artists is seeking to benefit by writing me and Dorothy . . . out of our rightful place in lesbian theater history.
> Robin Epstein
> New York

My initial joy at seeing my name in the paper of record dissipated almost immediately when I realized it was one of the other Robin Epsteins who had written to *The New York Times*. And I'll confess it upset me a little. Why was I agitated? Was it because Robin Epstein just told Gray Lady readers of her gayness? Of course not. Many of my girlfriends are lesbians. But the woman was making us sound frickin' ancient! I mean was it really necessary to say that she started her theater company in 1979? (Good Lord, Robin, how is anyone ever going to buy that we're still twenty-five if you keep doing math like that?!)

In fairness I knew I had little right to be upset since I was sure this serious dramatist probably had a beef with me, too, since my novel, *Shaking Her Assets,* was the first thing to come up when you Googled our name. But it also made me wonder what serious journalist Robin Epstein, who wrote *Citizen Power* (blurbed by Jesse Jackson), thought about this. Or for that matter, what whole food nutritionist Robin Epstein, who wrote recipes about latkes and discussed baby topics on the Web, would make of it.

Ultimately I realized I'm very fortunate to share a name with these distinguished women because I'm genuinely impressed by the work of my namesakes. In fact one day I hope we can all gather in a room where we can chat about our work and discuss the effects of the mean-spirited taunts and nicknames we suffered as children (Robin Red Breast, Robin Laid an Egg, etc.).

Of course it'd be only fair to include all the Amy Feldmans running around, too . . . especially because one of them is a writer at *BusinessWeek* magazine and I have a feeling she could give us all some good advice on how to improve our portfolios.

Q: I love me my eBay, but I have a sneaking suspicion the Fat Elvis jumpsuit I spent my rent money on isn't the real deal. How do I know something's authentic, and how can I protect myself from getting conned in the future?

A: A man from Cape Cod sold what he claimed was a piece of Plymouth Rock where the Pilgrims landed for $609. Unfortunately the executive director of the Pilgrim Society cried poppycock, noting that it would be pretty darned difficult to verify that a piece of rock had been touched by the bottom of any Pilgrim's shoe.

The fact is the issue of fake goods sold on eBay is no small matter. In May 2008, a French court ruled that eBay had to reimburse the luxury goods maker LVMH $63 million because its French site didn't do enough to prevent scammers from selling knockoff products. Interestingly, when luxury goods manufacturer Tiffany sued eBay for virtually the same claim in the Southern District of New York, it was eBay that came out the victor. In both cases, the loser—eBay in the French case, Tiffany in the American—plans to appeal. But whatever the ultimate outcome of those trials, as a buyer you should always be wary, and the first tip for making purchases on an online auction site is to know your seller. Go to a reputable company with a Web site or check out any unfamiliar sellers either with the Better Business Bureau or from an online auction site's feedback forum. Also, be sure to get the physical address of the seller, not just the Web address. Finally, pay by a credit card that will allow you to dispute a purchase if it doesn't arrive or turns out to be just a rock instead of the gem you thought.

There's also another issue that buyers need to consider when making these types of online purchases: vendors could be trying to sell you stolen goods. A now former employee of the New York Department of Education was arrested for allegedly stealing hundreds of historical documents—including a letter written by John Calhoun, the vice president under Andrew Jackson—then selling them on eBay. Bidding on the Calhoun letter reached $1,700 before a bidder realized it had been stolen and notified authorities.

So what happens if you buy an item and only later discover it's stolen? Well, once it's recovered, the stolen item goes back to the original owner and you won't necessarily get your money back. How do you protect yourself? If you're on an auction site that offers buyer's protection, take advantage of it, at least for the big-ticket items. Also, use your common sense. Though I won't tell you that if something seems too good to be true it's because it is (duh!), I will encourage you to look long and hard before handing over your Andrew Jacksons to any potential Benedict Arnolds.

Q: In terms of privacy, if "what happens in Vegas stays in Vegas," why can hotel staff enter a room at any point if I've rented it for that period of time?

A: I won't ask what you were doing in that room, but I will tell you that hotel management has a right to enter your room to clean or perform maintenance whenever it likes. Additionally, if you are doing something illegal or disturbing other guests, the management has a right to come into your room and stop you. But the management is not supposed to let police into your room absent your permission or a search warrant. And by a hotel's own policy, it will likely not allow the desk to give out your room number to anyone but may offer to connect a caller to your room. You need not even be a celebrity trying to avoid paparazzi to be extended that convenience. (Though according to *People* magazine, when singer Wynonna Judd checks into a hotel room, she uses the pseudonym Anita Man . . . as in "I need a man." Clever. Kind of desperate, but clever.)

But if you have questions about your privacy, speak to the management at the hotel about its privacy policy and how it will work to ensure yours.

Q: **In the casinos you're not allowed to operate your cell at the tables—but the phones still work. Why don't the casinos just jam the signals?**

A: Because long before cell phones were invented, Congress passed a law—the Communications Act of 1934—making it illegal to operate transmitters designed to jam or block wireless communications. This is not the case in Mexico, where one priest who became so fed up when a groom's cell phone went off during his own ceremony that he later decided to use counterintelligence technology to jam phones in his church.

While there are now ads for these devices on the Internet,

don't think that it's legal to buy one in this country. The manufacture, importation, sale, or advertising of such devices is also
prohibited and the violator faces penalties up to $11,000 per
violation, forfeiture of the device, and imprisonment for up to a
year. That's a pretty stiff penalty for shutting down a ringtone.

Q: **Cn u txt-n-drive?**

A: Not in Washington, the first state to make a crime of DWT—
driving while texting. Seven other states have also banned it
(Alaska, Connecticut, Louisiana, Minnesota, New Jersey, California, and Arizona), and more than a dozen others are currently
considering legislation on the topic. One Arizona woman was
lucky the law had yet to take effect in her state when she hit a
parked car while she was trying to send a text. As it was, things
were pretty bad already, considering the parked car she hit was
a police cruiser with its lights flashing. Currently in California,
drivers caught texting (or speaking on a non-hands-free phone)
while driving face a fine of approximately $76 for the first of-
fense and $175 for each subsequent offense.

Even if the state in which you live has yet to ban texting
while driving, you can still face penalties for reckless and careless
driving when your conduct causes damage. So before you put
yourself and others at risk, ask yourself if sending that text message while you're operating your car is really so 9-1-1.

Chapter 6

Your Home

Your Castle, Your Casa, the Cage You Call Home

For many years real estate was the new porn in this country: the market was hot, huge, and any idiot with a few bucks in his wallet could get him some. So perhaps it shouldn't have been a surprise that people were so seduced by the notion of home ownership that many of our fellow Americans acted as irrationally as hormone-addled teens. After all, our homes are our refuge. They provide us with shelter, they offer us sanctuary, and perhaps most importantly, they give us a place to dump our junk. But whether you own or rent, live in an apartment, a mansion, or a shack in the woods, that place you call home comes fully loaded with rights and responsibilities. This chapter will explore both sides of that coin, and will discuss some of the best and worst ways to invest in your home any of the remaining shekels you haven't lost in it yet.

Q: I'm desperate for a new apartment and finally found a place I love but the landlord refused to give me a lease because of my bad credit. Isn't that discrimination?

A: By law, a landlord can't refuse to rent to you on the basis of your race, color, religion, national origin, sex, age, familial status, or mental or physical disability. He or she also can't say that an apartment isn't available when, in fact, it is. Landlords can, however, refuse to rent on the basis of valid business reasons like a poor credit rating. Under the Fair Credit Reporting Act, the landlord has to tell you that the rejection was based on the negative credit information and must disclose the nature of that information.

If you've been a victim of discrimination, you can file a complaint with the Department of Housing and Urban Development. But if you've been the victim of your own spending habits, hopefully that big flat-screen plasma you bought will at least throw you some shade. . . .

Q: Okay, so I got a roommate and moved into a new place. There's only one problem: she's *insane*. Worse, she's not paying her half of the rent. How can I evict her?

A: Amazing how quickly friends who become roommates can turn into dreaded enemies, isn't it? Unfortunately renting an apartment with pals isn't just a rite of passage, it's a cold hard contract. That means you and your roommates are jointly (together) and severally (individually) liable to the landlord to pay rent, which means you are each legally obligated to pay rent, but if one of you doesn't, the other has to make up the difference. So, here's a scenario: Single White Female moves out. The problem is, under the lease, if she stops paying, you're on the hook for the whole amount. While she is legally obligated to pay, it still falls to you to make up the shortfall now.

What happens if *you* want to move out midlease? Well, that's fine, too, but legally you're still obligated to pay the rent every month for the term of the lease, regardless of how soon you realize that the chucklehead you chose is unbearable. Regardless of how much notice you give your landlord of your intent to depart, you're obligated for the duration unless it's otherwise specified in the lease.

So before you put your name on a lease with your friends, figure out in advance what's your share of the rent; how you pay (either by electing a leader to write one check or by each paying the landlord individually); whether there's a house fund for food and necessities or if you each carry your own toilet paper; and how to resolve disputes before they ruin friendships. A landlord can evict a bad tenant—cotenants can't.

Q: My upstairs neighbor decided he wanted to go for a swim—in his bathroom. When his bathwater flooded through my ceiling, it wrecked my bed, desk, and computer. After I clean up the floor where my head exploded, who do I go after to pay for my stuff?

A: At a time like this it's probably hard to focus on the positive, but at least you can still sleep on your couch, right? Residents of one New Jersey apartment complex weren't so lucky. Fifty tenants of the building were left homeless when it was hit by its seventh fire in thirty years.

One of the most common misperceptions of apartment dwellers is that the landlord's insurance will cover them in the event of a fire or other damage the tenant did not cause. The landlord's insurance will pay for the damage to the building, but not to the tenant's personal belongings.

A recent survey found that despite the fact that renter's insurance is one of the least expensive policies, nearly two-thirds of all renters—50 million of 80 million renters nationwide—don't have renter's insurance. Renter's insurance is a package policy, which is a combination of personal property insurance to cover your belongings and personal liability insurance in case a guest of yours is, for example, bitten by your dog or trips over your lamp. There is also something known as a replacement cost policy that covers not what you paid for your property but what it will cost you to replace it.

Obviously the New Jersey tenants were lucky in that no lives were lost. But without renter's insurance, it is they (and you)—not the landlord—who will be paying out of pocket for the damage. In this case, though, if you can show that someone else's negligence caused your damage, you can file an action against him. That will require laying out the money for the court costs (which you may or may not get back) and proving that the damage was in fact caused by his negligence and not by faulty pipes or other issues that are not his fault. But if you want to sue—and you won't mind seeing him in the elevator every day thereafter—go for it.

Q: Say someone's fooling around in my apartment (never mind what he's doing) and gets injured . . . can I get sued for someone else's klutziness?

A: To paraphrase a former U.S. president, it depends what your definition of "fooling around" is. If there's a hazard on your property (a broken step, an icy sidewalk, a live wire) and you're aware of it, you *are* responsible to the people who get injured. In a case in Pennsylvania, a tax assessor visiting a home to judge its value slipped and fell on the unshoveled sidewalk in front of the house. In addition to raising the property owner's taxes, the T-man then sued the homeowners for $20,000, claiming they knew about the ice but failed to shovel.

In another case in Pennsylvania where the homeowners really must have questioned their karma, a nineteen-year-old man climbed over their four-foot fence, dove into their empty, winterized pool, and broke his neck. He then sued them, claiming negligence. The young man argued the pool owners should have foreseen the possibility of trespassers, and therefore should have made more strenuous efforts to keep him out. In this instance, the pool owners were not found to be liable because the court ruled they could not have foreseen that an adult would climb a fence and trespass in an effort to swim in the pool in the off-season.

However, if you own a swimming pool, you owe a duty to those who come onto your property to swim there. And if, heaven forbid, someone gets hurt, you are judged on the degree to which you took care to prevent such accidents. Simply putting up a sign that says "Swim at Your Own Risk" won't necessarily absolve you. It is still your responsibility to take other precautions—like putting up a fence or employing other safety procedures to prevent, say, children who can't read the sign from trying to swim. So put up a fence, lock the gate, and watch everyone on your property like a hawk to prevent both lawsuits and, more importantly, injuries.

Okay, now here's something else to consider if you're a pool owner: what if your neighbor asks you to host a middle school graduation party for her daughter so the kids can go swimming? While the prospect of hosting thirty fourteen-year-olds is never a pleasant thought, when you add the liability of a pool party to the mix you've got more to worry about than raging hormones seeping into the water.

Before letting anyone swim, check your homeowner's policy to make sure that in the event of an accident you are covered. Then consider the best way to avoid liability—by preventing injuries in the first place. Hiring a lifeguard for the party can help prevent lawsuits and, more importantly, injuries for the preteens who have no trouble finding trouble when the opportunity presents itself.

Q: **Well, what if someone dislocates his shoulder when playing an intense game of bowling on my Wii? Am I responsible for that, too?**

A: Assuming the injury didn't result from your precariously placed monitor crashing on his head, you're most likely off the hook. When trampolines were "hot" (don't press me on the exact dates for that phenomenon . . .), people frequently got injured when they didn't adhere to proper trampolining technique (and don't press me on what the hell that is, either). But in cases that were brought about trampoline injuries, judges ruled as to whether precautions had been taken to prevent them.

Leaving a trampoline in your yard when you know neighborhood kids will jump on it may not be considered reasonably cautious. But precautions like keeping a safety net around the

trampoline in a fenced-in yard and warning those who jump—
and their parents—of the risk of injury not only prevent successful lawsuits but actually prevent injury.

As for your injury-prone gamer friend, maybe you can encourage him to wear a helmet when he plays at your house. No,
that won't prevent shoulder injury, but it might make him so
self-conscious that the only thing he'll be likely to injure is his
pride.

Q: My lease is up and I'm moving out, but my landlord is being
dodgy about returning my security deposit. What gives?

A: You know what's more infuriating than trying to get your security deposit back from a landlord? Nothing. Fortunately for
you, there are laws in all states to protect tenants from unfair
practices by landlords.

State laws differ, but in most places landlords may not require more than two months' rent for security during the first
year of any lease. Thereafter, additional security may not be
more than one month's rent. Generally when a lease is up landlords must give a list of damages to the tenant within a certain numbe: of days after the end of the lease (typically thirty
days) if the landlord wishes to retain any part of the security
deposit. With the list of damages, the landlord must simultaneously return the difference between the actual damage to
the property and the security deposit. If he fails to do this,
the landlord forfeits the right to go after the tenant for additional damages and must pay double the security deposit to
the tenant. For more information, go to www.rentlaw.com/se-
curitydeposit.htm. Armed with knowledge of your rights, the

fight to get your money back shouldn't need to be such a pain in the a—partment.

Amy

A wise friend once told me that you can do everything you want in life, just not all at the same time. It's a philosophy that I have taken to heart, knowing well that there will be a time in my life to travel, do art, volunteer for good causes, and learn to speak a foreign language—now is just not that time. Another item in my personal "To Do . . . *Later*" list is good housekeeping. And when I say that good housekeeping is something I'll do "later," what I really mean is "don't hold your breath."

Early in our marriage when my husband, Len, was working as a prosecutor and I was at a big law firm in Philadelphia, we were both required to put in insane hours on the job. So when a friend gave us a last-minute invitation to her family's beach house one Fourth of July weekend, we jumped at the chance for a little rest and relaxation. Though we'd planned to spend the weekend at home, doing laundry and getting to all the chores we'd been neglecting around the house, the chance to escape to the beach was simply too tempting. We scrambled to find clean clothes amidst the chaos, then began the search for the suntan lotion. We dislodged most of the bottles, salves, and other ointments in the medicine cabinets, resolving to clean up what we'd upended once we got back. Bags packed, we jumped into the car and headed for the shore.

We did not, in fact, give the state of the house a second thought. Not when we got to the shore to stake our claim on the bedroom that was our weekend vacation spot. Not when we watched the sun turn to clouds and then to a thunderstorm at dusk that night. And not even when my cell phone rang. Until I saw that it was my mother, telling me that the thunderstorm had set off the burglar alarm at our house. Since the alarm company could not reach us, it called the police and the next name on our emergency contact list—my parents.

The police and my mother arrived at the same time, and both were stupefied at what they saw. One of the police officers turned to my mother, shook his head, and said, "The home appears to have been ransacked." My mother shook her head in disbelief and horror because she knew better. And because she knew her daughter. She also knew that this was not only a terrible reflection on me, it was, by extension, a terrible reflection on her, too.

After convincing the police that the house had not been burgled, Mom called me with a brief description of the events that led her to see the state of my house. She then made an offer that was—in a very sweet way—a reflection of her disgust: "How about I send my cleaning lady to your house? I think she has a free day." Mortified, I screamed that under no circumstances was she to allow *anyone* into our house, and that I was insulted at the insinuation that I was incapable of keeping my own home.

As the years have gone by and I now have a growing daughter of my own, I still adhere to the philosophy that in life you can do everything you want, just not all at the same time. I have also since adopted a second, perhaps more important mantra: if someone offers to send a cleaning lady, take her up on that offer.

Q: You know that tag on mattresses—the one that says "Do Not Remove Under Penalty of Law"? First of all, why is it there? And second, seriously, are the mattress police going to arrest me if I rip off the tag?

A: The answer to the question about why the tag is there is actually more icky than funny: in most states there is no law requiring that mattresses be made of all new materials. That means as long as the mattress materials are properly sterilized and approved by the health and safety department of your state, you, like Goldilocks, could actually be sleeping on someone else's old bed.

The good news is—under penalty of law—the seller must have a tag on all mattresses advising you if the material is all new or secondhand, or it faces a penalty for every single mattress without such a tag. So before buying a mattress, don't assume it's new merely because it's wrapped in plastic: read that tag! Once you've bought your bedding, though, you are free to remove the tag without fear of the mattress police.

Q: Screw city life, I want a beach house! Are there any differences between investing in a time-share condo and purchasing a property that's a "vacation interval"?

A: Ah, yes, you've come to the conclusion that some 3 million other people have: life's better on vacation. That's why investment in time-share properties has become so popular. As you mentioned, there are two types of time-share purchases. The first is known as a "time-share estate," where you actually own a deed to the property and get the benefits of ownership and equity. The other is called a "vacation interval" or a "right-to-use time-share." This option is less expensive because though you have a right to use it, you don't actually own it.

Generally time-shares are sold in one-week increments for a one-time cost plus annual maintenance fees—which may increase and often don't cover the costs of major repairs. Before you put any money down, learn if you are getting a time-share estate or a vacation interval. You should also find out what broker and closing-related costs you'll have to pay. Additionally you should learn whether there's a cap on maintenance fees, and find out about your rights to resell if you decide this side of paradise isn't the place for you after all.

Q: I just saw an ad on Craigslist for the most amazing house in Florida. The owners of this "3 bed 2 bath pool home on wide canal!" are facing foreclosure and I really think this could be the wide canal of my dreams! Are there any weird legal things I need to worry about when buying a foreclosed property?

A: You've heard the phrase caveat emptor (let the buyer beware), I'm sure. Well, I'm also sure a woman in Philadelphia wishes she'd been a little more aware when she bid on a property at a foreclosure sale, too. When she heard the property was coming up for sale, she drove past it, saw a beautiful home, and placed her bid. Turned out she was the sole and therefore successful bidder at the sheriff's sale. What she didn't realize was that the property she saw was actually *in front* of the property she bought, which was a useless water cistern that cost her thousands.

If you're considering buying a foreclosed property, first, you need to make sure that everyone with an interest in the property has actually been notified of the sale—all of the mortgage holders, the taxing agency, etc.—because if they haven't been notified, you take the property subject to those liens. Second, in many municipalities if a property is sold for tax delinquencies, the owner has a right to redeem for up to a year—that means if he pays, he can get his property back. So you'd get back the money you paid for the property, but you wouldn't get back money for improvements you've made. Finally, understand that once a house is up for a sheriff's sale you can't see inside the house to examine what you're really getting before you buy it. So it's always good to keep in mind that just because something's cheap, that doesn't make it a good deal.

Q: I saw the movie *Poltergeist*. If I want to buy a home, does the seller have to tell me if the place is located on an old Indian burial ground?

A: That would be nice information to have, yes, but whether the seller is legally obligated to disclose it depends on the state in which the house is located. Reminds me of one couple's story: they moved into an apartment building and soon discovered their new downstairs neighbor was a journalist; when they Googled her work, they discovered her last article detailed the horrific murder that had taken place in the very apartment they now called home.

When selling a home, state law governs what a seller is obligated to disclose. In general, sellers must disclose lead-based paint hazards and also known physical defects like a basement that floods and other physical problems that affect a property's value.

In some states, like California, sellers also need to reveal known nuisances like a dog that barks all night in the neighborhood or deaths that occurred on the property, and they must disclose the availability of the sex offender registry. But most states don't require such detailed disclosures. Most states do have a Megan's Law requiring disclosure on a Web site and by phone of registered sex offenders, but almost none mandate that a person selling a home in the neighborhood of a registered sex offender disclose this fact to potential buyers.

Ultimately the onus is on the buyer to ask the seller questions not only about the home's physical defects, but if there are any neighborhood nuisances, scary neighbors, or, say, horrific murders which took place around the property that could potentially affect your enjoyment of it. The seller for his part must answer your questions honestly, because, at least in some states, it would be fraud for him to misrepresent facts in an effort to get you to plunk down your money.

Q: **What's the story with these online real estate broker services? The ads say they'll save you tons of money when selling your house, but is it really just a scam?**

A: If you're thinking of selling your home, you can't turn on the TV without seeing commercials featuring people who listed with a do-it-yourself agent, saved money, and sold their homes in two minutes flat.

How do these cut-rate brokers operate? Well, real estate brokers and agents earn commissions on the services they provide. (The services and commission rates are spelled out in the listing agreement that you sign.) Traditional, full-service real estate brokers provide a broad range of services, such as making recommendations on the purchase price, publicizing the sale, arranging showings, and negotiating with buyers.

Nontraditional brokers offer many of the same services but on an à la carte basis, charging a fee for each service they provide. Still others, like Buy Owner, offer services to help owners who want to do a sale by owner transaction but use Web sites or other consultants for marketing help only. There can be a great savings to you if you choose to go with one of these services, but before signing up, do your homework. Ask how many homes the company has really sold in the past year. Ask what its total commission will be and if you could be liable for the fee to pay a cooperating broker. Finally, make sure you know what this person or service will really do for you to earn its commission and if it can provide references from previous clients. If it doesn't pass the smell test, chances are it's because the service stinks.

If you're considering selling your property yourself, remember that you're required to disclose defects that may affect the property. In most states, it's illegal to conceal major defects in the property like foundation settlement or basement floods. Many states also require a written disclosure statement, and, if your house was built after 1978, you must disclose all known lead-based paint hazards, which you can research on the EPA's Web site.

When it comes time to close, you will need the forms required for the transfer. Generally, the seller needs to provide the buyer with a deed, a standard affidavit of seller, a bill of sale, a certificate of real estate value, and a well certificate if applicable. Most of the forms are available for sale on the Internet, but make certain to get forms appropriate for your state.

You may also want to consider hiring a lawyer to prepare the forms just to make sure everything is 100 percent legal, and chances are that will still be less costly than giving a percentage of the purchase price to the realtor. . . . Probably wouldn't have guessed the lawyer would be a bargain, huh?

Q: During one of my moves, I found a moving company that seemed great . . . at first. They quickly and efficiently loaded all my stuff onto their van, but then told me they wouldn't unload it until I paid their tip in advance. Holding furniture hostage doesn't strike me as especially legal, but what could I do?

A: That's rough, though the story could have been worse, as one woman who found her movers over the Internet learned. She got an estimate, arranged for pickup, had her belongings loaded onto the truck . . . then never saw them again.

If you're moving from one state to another, the law requires the moving company to give you a copy of the consumer booklet "Your Rights and Responsibilities When You Move," which tells you about the movers' liability and dispute resolution. If you're given a nonbinding estimate, the mover can only require you to pay the amount of the estimate plus 10 percent at the time of delivery and you will have at least another thirty days to pay any remaining charges.

Don't sign off on the inventory until you've checked all your goods for damage—and report any damage immediately. If you notice damage later, you have nine months after delivery to report it, and by law the mover must acknowledge receipt of your claim within 30 days and either deny or settle the claim within 120 days. And remember, a tip is an "optional payment given in addition to the required payment." It is *not* something you are legally bound to give.

Robin

I moved into my first studio apartment in New York's West Village when I was twenty-three, and lived there very happily for many years. Even when I got a job that required me to move to Chicago, I held on to that little rental because I loved it. Loved it enough to brazenly flout the "No Subletting, This Means You" rule that I'd signed in the lease. I was sure my disregard for the law would not be a problem because over the years I'd formed a very nice relationship with my super, Hector. Hector and I had what you'd call an understanding. I understood that if I needed a favor, Hector needed money. And that worked well for both of us because I didn't see it as bribery, I viewed it as the Congrevian "way of the world." So when I told Hector I was going to be away for a little while, then handed him an envelope and said my friend Natalie would be over "a lot" to water the plants—wink, wink—we both smiled and nodded in understanding.

Unfortunately Doujon, the Maltese super who took over for Hector while I was away, understood less.

When I moved back in a year later, I saw this new super eyeing me suspiciously as I schlepped all remnants of my storage-stacked life back into my apartment. About a week after that, Doujon nabbed me as I stole up the stairwell. He said, "I don't know who you are, but I know you're living in Natalie's apartment, and dat, dat's illegal!" I smiled at Doujon and went on to explain who I was, and that what he must have incorrectly assumed to be Natalie's apartment was actually my own. My name was on the lease. My last name was even on the buzzer in the doorway, had been for the last seven years. I also explained that I'd told Hector Natalie would be staying there frequently since I'd been doing a lot of "traveling." I might have even winked at that point. But Doujon shook his head. He told me he knew what was going on. He wasn't stupid. More importantly he was honest. He said he could have me evicted for what I'd done: I was trouble, and he wanted no part of it. Apparently there was a new super in town, and much to my dismay, this one actually believed in the rule of law.

I was terrified. Not only was the idea of being kicked out of my apartment after I'd just moved everything back in horrifying, but as I said, I really, really loved that tiny, dark, back-facing place. Truthfully I wasn't sure what Doujon would do. Would he stick to his morals, do the right thing, and throw me out of my beloved Greenwich Village haunt? Or would he relent and let me stay, turning a blind eye to my illicit behavior? As the days passed and I devised methods for bolting myself in, barricading the door, and befriending the mouse in my kitchen, also now illegally subletting the place, I realized Doujon wasn't going to turn me in. He wanted to teach me through compassion, and it worked. I became the model tenant. I held packages for neighbors. I planted petunias in the dirt patch by the front door. I even cleaned out the gross lint bins in the communal dryers. As the months passed Doujon and I became friends, both of us complaining about the other disrespectful and dishonest crazies in the building.

Eventually, though, the time came for me to move on. I alerted Doujon that I would in fact be giving up the apartment for good, and he was kind enough to offer what I consider the highest form of Super Praise: "Why is it," he asked, "that only the good residents move out?" I was touched and I decided that the day the movers came I wanted to thank him for the good turn he did by letting me stay. I put together a little envelope with as much as I could give, in the same way I'd done for Hector. Doujon seemed a little unsure if this was appropriate—it seemed a little unseemly—but I pushed the envelope into his hands. Sure, it was a payoff of sorts, but that is the way of the world, isn't it?

The last thing the movers had to remove from the apartment was the air conditioner Hector had helped me install when I first moved in almost a decade earlier. But while I'd been away, my subletter had moved the unit to a different window. Unfortunately, whoever reinstalled it for her had neglected to attach it with the proper screws. So when the moving man opened the window, the air conditioner went sailing out of its fourth-floor perch. Thankfully it did not crash down onto the head of some unsuspecting pass-erby. Instead it went down an enclosed shaftway.

But before that air conditioner shattered into several large and dented pieces on the ground below, it took out every A/C unit beneath it, and the one it hit with the greatest impact was immediately below, the thousand-dollar unit belonging to my upstanding super, who thus brought home to me another lesson on the Way of the World: no good deed goes unpunished.

Q: Rolled up to my new condo in my company car—a sweet little Mini Cooper with a giant can of Red Bull bursting from the trunk—only to have the president of the homeowners' association tell me I couldn't park it in my driveway. What kind of red bull is that?

A: Though Mr. Rogers was always a friendly neighborhood presence, rules and regulations established by homeowners' associations—250,000 strong in the United States—can often make you feel less than welcome (especially if they're mocking your car).

The covenants, conditions, and restrictions (CC&Rs) dictated by a homeowners' association are rules you are subject to, rules on everything from the color you can paint your house to whether or not you can park your car on your own driveway or have to garage it. You may be surprised to learn that homeowners' associations often have powers so broad they can actually foreclose on your house for failure to pay your association dues.

Best advice—ask *before* you buy whether or not you'll be subject to a homeowners' association, and ask to see the CC&Rs

before you put down your money for the house or use that car to drive away.

Q: **My house is what you might call a "fixer-upper," though less generous souls might call it a "shithole." What should I know or do before hiring a contractor to fix it up?**

A: Anyone who has ever dealt with a contractor probably understands the frustration of a Pennsylvania woman who sued her contractor because during her home renovation, he left her personal property out in the backyard during a rainstorm, where it was ruined. He rented a backhoe that he didn't know how to use and broke her septic tank. He tore siding off her home. And finally, because he had not obtained the proper permit before he began "work," his operation was shut down in the middle of the project.

Here are things that you should do in advance of hiring a contractor to minimize the headaches home repair inevitably seems to incur:

1. Get more than one bid on a project, and then get references—which you actually call.
2. Make sure that the contractor is licensed and insured (ask to see the insurance policy to make sure it actually covers you).
3. Get a written contract spelling out the work to be performed and when it's expected to be completed.
4. Make payments based on milestone task completions rather than up front, and don't make the final payment until you are fully satisfied.
5. Do not pay cash.

6. Make sure you get receipts for the money you put out, both in advance of the work to be done and once it's completed and paid for.

Before you're in the position of losing your personal property and/or your sanity, know your contractor and know your rights. It also wouldn't hurt to make sure your contractor knows how to use a backhoe—or whatever other equipment he's using to make "improvements" on your home.

Q: Say a natural disaster blows my house down. Where do I start in terms of rebuilding?

A: Thousands of citizens have been forced to rebuild their homes and lives in recent years after devastating storms hit their areas. Making matters worse, scammers tend to prey on people at this incredibly vulnerable time. That's why the Federal Trade Commission has come out with recommendations about what to do and what not to do when repairing your home after a disaster. Here are a few of the suggestions it offers:

- First, verify that there's no cost for an estimate before you let someone into your home.
- Resist dealing with a contractor who demands 100 percent payment up front—one-third up front is standard.
- Be wary of temporary repairs and make certain you'll be able to pay for permanent fixes when they arise.
- Use workers who have a track record with people you know.
- If you suspect a scam, call your state's attorney general's office to complain.

Q: Mold! *Mold!* There's mold everywhere! What do I do?

A: Well, if you're like one judge in California who had mold in her courtroom, you'll sue. The judge took the county to court, claiming that toxic mold in her courthouse had caused her hair loss, dizziness, respiratory distress, and other ailments. (You can fill in the appropriate joke about how it's even possible to root out toxic mold in a courtroom full of lawyers.)

Exposure to mold has been linked to allergic reactions, infections, asthma, and other health effects, and homeowners have begun to fight back against what they claim is a defect in the design of the home or the use of substandard materials that lead to mold growth. More and more courts are finding in favor of homeowners, both against the builders and against the insurance companies that refuse to pay for mold damage, to the tune of millions of dollars.

But you need to look closely at your policy: insurance companies are insulating themselves from liability by excluding mold coverage in new policies and renewals of old policies that at one time did cover mold damage. . . . And you thought lawyers were toxic!

Q: My philosophy is usually live and let live, but my new neighbors are *the loudest, most obnoxious boneheads I've ever met.* Though I'm tempted to burn their house down, is there anything I can legally do to make them shut up?

A: Actually there's a new CD available on the Internet that might interest you. Entitled "Revenge," it is meant to settle scores with noisy neighbors and it comes with twenty tracks, including inhuman screams, unhappy dogs, and a rousing, full-throated cock-a-doodle-do. The CD also comes with earplugs.

If blasting "Revenge" isn't your cup of tea, know that virtually every municipality prohibits unreasonable noise levels. These regulations are designed to stop noise nuisances like dogs that bark all night long, contractors who start work at 5:00 A.M., and partiers who celebrate until all hours of the morning (including those who blast CDs as revenge for those transgressions).

Go online and check sources like www.nonoise.org, which lists noise ordinances for many cities. If a neighbor violates these ordinances you may call the police or animal control. But a smarter way of handling the situation with someone you'll still have to live next door to is first to ask them nicely to turn down their noise or to keep the pets in after 10:00 P.M. If that doesn't work, you can always put in your earplugs, blast your CD, and exact your own revenge.

Q: Jackass neighbor just had his lawn care people cut down branches on *my* tree. Then the jerk tells me I need to pay him for the expense! I said if he thought I'd reimburse him for chopping my tree, he should stop smoking the grass. Shouldn't *he* pay *me* for damaging my tree?

A: For suburbanites like me, it's not uncommon for branches of our trees to encroach on neighbors' properties. Though most folks aren't usually bothered by extra foliage, for any number of reasons, some are: the tree could be infested with bugs that get into a house, its roots could be burrowing under a patio, the neighbor could have an irrational fear of bark, etc.

Assuming your neighbor is not the cherry tree–chopping, George Washington type, he might hire a tree service to cut those branches back, and the law is very clear on who needs to pay here: overhanging branches constitute a trespass onto a neighbor's property as if the neighbor had climbed the fence himself. Therefore, the landlord whose property is encroached by overhanging tree branches has several options. First, he can trim the branches back to the extent that they intrude on his property. He can also collect the fee from the tree's owner if he spent money to have the work done. Or he can require the tree's owner to have those branches removed.

The law is similar if your tree is uprooted and falls onto his property during a storm: it's still considered "trespass" and you are still responsible for its removal and/or the cost incurred to remove it. Like George, though, I cannot tell a lie: it's not always the best policy to resort to the legal system to resolve differences. Work this one out rather than sue. After all, you never know when you might need to borrow a cup of sugar from that very neighbor to bake your cherry pie.

Q: Loud, nature-hating jackass neighbor just put up a fence, but I'm pretty sure he installed it on *my* lawn. What are my rights?

A: It was the poet Robert Frost who observed that good fences make good neighbors. But a misplaced fence can lead to bad blood and add a much darker meaning to the term neighborhood watch. If you're thinking of putting up a fence, first check to make sure where you plan to install it is actually on your property line. You can find the property line with certainty by hiring a surveyor to tell you the exact boundary. If you choose not to spend the money, ask your neighbors to agree to the boundary before putting up the fence. They will later have a hard time contesting a fence that they agreed should go there. (That said, once a new neighbor moves in, he may not be bound by the former owner's largesse.)

In this case, where the fence has already been erected, you can go to court to force your neighbor to take it down. You are also entitled to seek remuneration for the damages he did to your lawn when building it. Again, though, the bottom line is that it's always better to avoid a legal case if possible, so be a good neighbor and talk to him before you're forced to mend fences in a court of law.

Q: When I calculated the mortgage payment before buying my new home, I neglected to consider that I might have other expenses (like groceries). What happens if I apply for a loan, get it, and then can't pay it off?

A: Why, then, you'd be just like the millions other Americans who fell into the mortgage trap! Everyone who's ever been foreclosed on got a loan in the first place, so if you suspect you can't afford the property, don't assume the bank knows better. *Just because it gives you the loan, that doesn't mean you actually can make the payments.* Sadly, the recent credit crunch has been wrecking havoc with the housing market precisely because many, many, many home buyers were given loans in excess of what they could repay.

Let's look at the type of financing that's available when you decide to buy a home because there are several different types of mortgages. A *fixed-rate loan* generally has repayment terms of fifteen or thirty years. Both the interest rate and the monthly payments stay the same during the life of the loan. An *adjustable or variable-rate loan* usually offers an initially low rate, which fluctuates over the life of the loan, based on market conditions. That rate may or may not be capped, so ask what the highest rate you could potentially pay is during the term. When you're getting a loan you should also ask what the fees are to get the loan, what the other required escrows like taxes and insurance you'll also have to pay will be, and the estimated monthly payment.

Now, let's say repayment becomes difficult for whatever reason (loss of job, health issues, shoe fetish, etc.). Because the bank put out its money for you to buy the house, the bank holds a security interest in the house and can foreclose on it.

Foreclosures are governed by state law, and in most states there are notice requirements that oblige the bank to let you know when you are falling behind and the number to call to rectify the situation. If you get in arrears, call the bank to set up a payment schedule in order to prevent the foreclosure. (Keep in mind, the bank is not a realtor—it doesn't want your house—it wants your money.) And under no circumstances should you ignore its letters or messages. There are consumer advocates available to help you, so find your community legal services in the blue pages of the phone book to find them.

Be aware, though, not everyone who purports to help those in need really is there to help. Many who offer so-called help often want homeowners to sign documents that look like refinancing loans but actually transfer the ownership to the "lender." If you are asked to sign a warranty deed, a quitclaim deed, a contract or agreement for deed, or an assignment of a deed or leasehold, you should consult an attorney—signing those documents could cause you to be stripped of your equity *and* your home.

If you can't afford a lawyer, contact your local legal aid society to help you determine if you are getting actual refinancing help or are being victimized. You should never bury your head in the sand and ignore foreclosure notices; neither should you sign documents that you don't understand.

Q: **Is it true that even after you've lost your home due to foreclosure, the IRS can come after you to tax you on "gains" made through your debt?**

A: It is—how's that for maddening? You no longer have a pot to piss in, yet you still have to pay taxes on that old pot. How can that happen? Well, because if your house is foreclosed and the debt wiped out through the foreclosure exceeds the value of the property, the difference is considered taxable income.

If this happens to you—if you lost your home due to foreclosure and you also face a tax penalty because the value of the house you lost was less than the amount you owed on it—know that the IRS has unveiled a special rule to help you out. This new rule allows an insolvent (a.k.a. cash-strapped and now homeless) borrower to offset that income to the extent that your liabilities exceed your assets.

Go to www.irs.gov and you'll find a form you can use to request a payment agreement with the IRS. In some cases you may qualify to settle your tax debt for less than the full amount owed. It may not be as good as hitting the lottery, but it is at least a bit of good news when you could really use it.

Chapter 7

Your Pets

The Personal Petting Zoo

Scientists theorize that people began domesticating wild animals approximately ten thousand years ago, but explanations differ as to why they did so. Some suggest it had to do with the population explosion and the scarcity of food; others believe primitive humans just got a kick out of seeing dogs dressed in cavemen loincloths. We claim no authority on that subject, but we do know something about the people who choose to bring animals into their homes: they are a breed unto themselves. And we also know that when discussing issues concerning our animals, pet people are prone to getting emotional and then going ape-shit. What follows is our foray into the animal kingdom.

I loathe people who keep dogs. They are cowards who haven't got the guts to bite people themselves.

—August Strindberg, *A Madman's Diary*

Q: I heard Leona Helmsley left $12 million to her dog when she croaked. I can see Snoopy needing some cash to entertain his bitches, but $12 million?! Can you really leave money to your pooch?

A: You might not be surprised to hear a judge later ruled that Leona was "mentally unfit" when she made her will, and cut the dog's inheritance from $12 million to a measly $2 million. But though you can't leave money *directly* to your pet (because pets lack the capacity to acquire and hold property, and because they can't write "for deposit only" on the back of those checks), many states *do* recognize trusts made for pets like Leona Helmsley's lucky puppy. If you do want to pull a Helmsley and leave money to your four-legged best friend, you can earmark your cash for a person or an organization, like the SPCA, that will in turn use the money to care for the animal.

But my personal feeling is that the best way to handle leaving an inheritance to your pet is to treat it as you would any dependent unable to speak for himself: make an arrangement with a loving caregiver to take care of your pet, and leave a stipend for its health and welfare. And be smart; treat the caregiver well lest he be tempted to keep the cash intended for kibbles.

Q: My friend bought a dog from a pet shop. Then three weeks later, the dog bought the farm. Does my friend have any rights?

A: I'm really sorry for your friend; I know how rough it can be to lose a pet. And I'll bet she's worried that if she goes back and complains she'll be blamed for Spot's demise. The owner of a new puppy in Florida became so enraged when the dog died, he went back and stabbed the pet shop owner who'd sold him the defective pup. Obviously this isn't the recommended method for grieving a loss, but as a dog owner myself, I know how attached people can get to their animals.

Unfortunately puppies sold by pet shops are often sick—and frequently seem to die as soon as they've settled into the buyer's home. But that's why many states have disclosure laws requiring pet shops to tell you about a dog's health history before you bring it home.

Puppy "lemon" laws have been enacted in several states, including Arizona, Arkansas, Florida, Pennsylvania, North Carolina, and Virginia, requiring kennels and pet shops to guarantee that the dog is healthy on the date of the sale. If the dog is sick, the owner has the option of getting a refund of the purchase price, exchanging the dog for another that's healthy, or keeping the dog and receiving vet costs up to the purchase price if the animal can be cured. It takes a sick puppy to sell you a sick puppy, but at least the law is on your side.

Q: **What about insurance for pets—is it worth the purchase price?**

A: Look, health care—be it for your kid or your canary—is expensive. So to protect against unforeseen vet bills, purchasing pet insurance is often a good option. Be aware, though, that pet insurance does not cover vet visits for routine health care, and it doesn't cover elective procedures like neutering. It generally covers unforeseen illnesses or injuries, but often limits coverage to a certain dollar amount per condition or sets a ceiling for annual or lifetime payouts.

Before purchasing pet insurance ask the following questions:

1. Are claims subject to an annual limit or based on the condition?
2. Is the pet covered for hereditary conditions?
3. Are you covered against liability if the pet injures someone else?
4. Does the policy cover advertising if the pet goes missing?
5. Is there a payout at the animal's death?

These are things you'll want to consider when making the decision to purchase insurance, which can add another monthly cost to the food, grooming, and, if you're a certain kind of pet owner, wardrobe costs for your furry friend.

Q: Who gets to keep the kitty when a marriage busts up?

A: In a divorce, all marital property, ranging from dollars to dust mops, gets divided. But what most people don't realize is that animals are also considered property under the law. That means that, unlike children (who maintain a relationship with their parents through custody and visitation), dogs and other pets are treated like the china: they go to either one spouse or the other and the court will not impose visitation.

In ugly divorces this can add yet another layer of nastiness to the proceedings. In the messy divorce involving the founders of American Equity Mortgage Company, the husband, Ray Vinson, actually took his ex-wife, Deanna, to court over allegedly kidnapping their family dog. The incredibly acrimonious case cost husband and wife over a million dollars *each* and ultimately settled with Ray taking possession of the dog, Bogey, and Deanna getting the company. Who rolled over and got the short end of the stick, well, that's a matter still up for debate.

> *If you pick up a starving dog and make him prosperous, he will not bite you. This is the principal difference between a dog and a man.*
>
> —Mark Twain

Q: My neighbor's dog barks from sundown to sunrise. Aside from moving away, or leaving flaming bags of poop on the owner's doorstep, do I have any options or rights here?

A: The good news for you is that most communities have local ordinances about this sort of thing, so you don't have to resort to vigilante justice. Noise from dogs and other animals frequently cause what's known as a nuisance. I don't mean the common-parlance meaning of "nuisance," which most people think of as "a humongous pain in the ass." I'm referring to the legal definition of nuisance:

> Nuisance: "The unreasonable or unlawful use of property that causes annoyance, inconvenience, or damage to the property of another; or prevents another from the quiet enjoyment of his property."

In general, laws maintain community standards to prevent nuisances through a combination of zoning laws that determine the kind and number of animals you can keep on a property, and various other animal control laws. That means if you report the problem to the authorities, they'll be able to take action on your behalf. Your neighbor can incur penalties ranging from a simple warning by authorities, to a citation and fine, all the way up to a misdemeanor for nuisance violations.

Of course, as Mom always taught us, it's easier to catch flies with honey than with vinegar. So before you call the cops on your neighbor's pet and risk permanently souring your relationship, talk to your neighbor and let him know what's going on. Tell him Snarls Barkley is keeping you from your much-needed beauty sleep and you'd appreciate it if he'd take care of the problem. You might even suggest that he look into purchasing a citronella bark collar—a cruelty-free and environmentally safe way to spritz that bark right out of his dog.

Q: I really, really, *really* want a dog, but *technically* my lease has a "no-pets" clause. I heard that if I can keep the animal in my apartment for three months without the landlord saying anything about it, the pet is grandfathered in. True?

A: You're actually trying to tell me that you believe there is a law that says you can do whatever you want to flaunt your lease and it's legal as long as you don't get caught? Come on, did you read that in the journal of *"I Can So!"*?

In New York there *is* a law that says that if you keep a pet that your owner knows about for more than three months in a manner that is "open and notorious"—in other words "for all to see"—then you can't be evicted even if you have a no-pets clause in your lease. But that was created to prevent a landlord who knew you had a pet from kicking you out for another reason later. For example, if the landlord realizes neighborhood rental prices have gone up, he can't force you out by pointing to the no-pets policy if he's known all along you had a dog or cat.

So let's be perfectly clear: this law is not the "let's sneak Toto around that meanie landlord" rule. It only applies if the landlord knew about the dog—and only if you're living in New York. Keep in mind, most housing laws are municipal or township ordinances, so if you ever move, you'll need to check the Web site of your township or county and look up the laws that pertain to landlord-tenant rules there.

But if you are in breach of the lease, the landlord has the right to kick both you and your little dog to the curb. If others in the building have dogs, he *might* allow them for an extra security deposit. If he refuses, though, at least you'll know where he stands before you go violating the lease and risk facing the consequences.

Q: **My boyfriend's Great Dane, Mr. Big, likes to romp around his neighbors' lawn and leave behind "gifts" of his presence. The pissed-off neighbors believe it's a crime for the dog even to be on their lawn (let alone poop on it). They say he's guilty of trespass; I say they're tight asses. Who's right?**

A: You may be right that they're tight asses, but legally it's the neighbors who have the edge. Under the law you can be held legally liable for trespass if you enter the land of another or "fail to remove something you are under a duty to remove" (i.e., doodie). Additionally, most townships have codes that require leashes on pets—both cats and dogs—so call your township to find out what the statute requires. But if you allow your pets to roam freely and it craps in someone else's yard, you can be held legally liable.

In Wisconsin, seventy-eight-year-old Myrtle Maly thought she'd found the perfect way to keep her neighbor's cats from bounding onto her property—she poisoned them with d-CON rodent killer. This was not Grandma's wisest move. She was later arrested for animal cruelty and faced four counts of animal mistreatment after she admitted to the police that she purposely left out cat food she'd laced with poison. The *felony* charges for mistreatment of animals causing death were ultimately dismissed on the prosecutor's motion, but Granny Maly pled no contest to the two misdemeanor charges for giving poison to an animal. So even if you're feeling abused by a neighbor's pet, before you take the law into your own hands, remember that though being a vigilante might make you feel like an alpha dog, the animal you'll more closely resemble is a jackass in zebra stripes.

Q: **What's a person responsible for if his pet bites someone? (And does it matter if the bite-ee *so* deserved it?)**

A: One of my favorite cases of "animal bites man, man bites back" is that of Randy the cat. Randy was known to have a biting problem, which he demonstrated by biting his owner's brother. The bite caused an infection that led to complications. And this being America, *that* led to a lawsuit. The jury awarded the bitten brother $122,000, which his sister, Randy's owner, had to pay. How much does that bite, eh?

Now, you can't keep abnormally dangerous animals in either an apartment or a private home, and in some municipalities, you can't even keep a breed of animal with a propensity for violence (like a pit bull). But even if a particular dog is not of a breed that is known to be dangerous, the owner still has a duty to protect the public from getting hurt by the pet. Most states have what's called strict liability—if your dog or cat bites someone you are legally responsible.

A truly helpful resource for both pet owners and bite victims is the Web site www.dogbitelaw.com, which is maintained and written by attorney Kenneth Phillips. It explains that a dog bite victim may be entitled to money for all of the following things: "medical treatment such as first aid, emergency room, hospital, and ambulance; future medical treatment for scar reduction; psychological counseling to overcome the emotional trauma of the attack, fear of dogs, fear of being outdoors, and dealing with disfigurement; loss of earnings from work or the victim's business; torn clothing and broken glasses; medications; pain and suffering; and future disability." It adds, "Some dog bite victims are attacked with their dogs or other pets, which are injured or killed. Owners of injured animals may be entitled to compensation."

In the few states in which the pet owner isn't automatically liable for a bite, the pet owner may still have to pay up if the pet ever demonstrated any propensity for biting; if it was let off the leash; or if it was mistreated or poorly fed, in which case the owner is considered responsible.

It will be interesting to see how the courts rule on a case in Connecticut involving a pet chimpanzee that went on the attack. In February 2009, Travis, a two-hundred-pound chimp who was somewhat of a celebrity in his hometown, stole the keys to his house, unlocked the front door, and went on a rampage, critically injuring Charla Nash, a longtime friend of the chimp's owner. Though Travis's owner, Sandra Herold, acted to stop the ape when he attacked—repeatedly stabbing the animal—she could possibly face criminal charges, although it's unlikely since

Connecticut law does not prevent the keeping of primates as pets. But Herold now faces a $50 million civil suit claiming negligence and recklessness. Other important facts in this story are that two other people have come forward to say that Travis had, in the past, bitten their fingers, and that it was well known that the chimp had busted free before. In true sitcom form, Travis had even used his time away from home to direct traffic at an intersection. This is actually a crucial issue regarding liability: if the owner was aware that the ape could break free (and note that he used the key to unlock the door), then she arguably needed to take extra precaution to keep him caged despite the fact that this particular chimp had not demonstrated violent tendencies in the past.

Robin

My favorite "pet owner gone wild" story happened a few years ago in New York. The owner, Antoine Yates, was, by most accounts, a rather decent fellow, but his downstairs neighbor called the police on him because she said she'd grown tired of the tiger urine leaking through her ceiling. It was eventually discovered that Yates was keeping both a five-hundred-pound Bengali tiger and a three-foot alligator in his apartment. When the police came to check things out, they cut a hole in Yates's door, and as New York Police Commissioner Ray Kelly stated, the officers "saw the tiger lying by the window, contentedly licking its paws."

Yates said he'd raised the tiger, Ming, from the time she was just a cub and a tiger specialist confirmed that the animal was "well fed and in great shape." Still, perhaps not surprisingly, Harlem's very own Siegfried was arrested and pled guilty to reckless endangerment, which carried a sentence of up to six months in jail. Yates said that he pled to the charge in order to spare his mother from facing a charge of endangering the welfare of a child; it was claimed that she babysat a child in the apartment with the tiger. Ultimately Yates avoided jail time by staying out of trouble between the plea and his sentencing, and was given five years probation.

But my favorite part of the story is not that Yates was keeping these insanely dangerous animals in his apartment complex or that he thought they made great house pets (or even that his mother was babysitting in an apartment with a tiger). Rather, I'm just impressed that Yates's downstairs neighbor was able to identify the funky yellow seepage from the ceiling as tiger urine in the first place.

Q: **Why is it that some dogs are allowed to shop in supermarkets and others are kicked to the curb?**

A: As you know, Seeing Eye and other service dogs have long been exempted from regulations that bar dogs from certain places like restaurants and offices. But these days a lot of people appear to be pushing the legal limits of the definition of "service" dogs. Restaurants, apartment houses, and other businesses may now be legally required to allow not only dogs who help those with physical disabilities, but also dogs who provide "emotional" support.

True, every dog lover can claim that his or her pet brings emotional support, but while the definition of "support" animal is still hazy, legally a doctor must certify that a patient is keeping the pet for health reasons. Once you get your doctor's note, the

New York courts have ruled that emotional support is a valid reason to keep a pet even if the building has a no-pet policy.

Q: Why aren't hunters arrested for "cruelty to animals"? Killing for sport seems pretty, pretty, pretty cruel to me. . . .

A: Well, my dear liberal sister, though you may find it heartless, like it or not, game hunting is legal in every state. Still, each state has its own specific laws to regulate it: laws that concern the hunting seasons, permits, and weapon usage. For instance, in the state of Maine, you must be at least ten years old before you can shoot dinner. And every state does ban animal cruelty, which is defined as "the crime of inflicting physical pain, suffering or death on an animal, usually a tame one, beyond necessity for normal discipline. It can include neglect that is so monstrous (withholding food and water) that the animal has suffered, died or been put in imminent danger of death." Currently forty-four states consider certain forms of animal abuse a felony. (Ask former Atlanta Falcon and felonious dog-fighter, Michael Vick, about that one.) Some states go even further, with enhanced penalties for someone who harms an animal that's a companion (pet).

In one awful case, during a raging domestic brawl a father pulled his kid's goldfish out of its bowl then stomped on it in front of the child. That's right, nothing says "I'm your father and I deserve respect" like stepping on your kid's goldfish. Fortunately Bad Dad was later arrested for a host of domestic charges, *including cruelty to animals*. The defendant tried to argue that he shouldn't get the enhanced penalty for abusing an animal companion since a goldfish isn't a pet. But the judge ruled that you can't limit "animal companions" to dogs and cats; rather, domesticated animals (and apparently putting a fish in a glass bowl counts as "domestication") like gerbils, hamsters, hermit crabs, and other creatures can be considered animal companions.

Q: With all the crazy flight regulations today, can my dog still fly the "friendly" skies with me?

A: Some airlines do allow a pet owner to bring a pet into the passenger compartment rather than in the cargo bay. By FAA regulation, airlines are allowed to set their own rules on whether to allow pets into the passenger compartment. If they do, the pet must fit in a pet carrier that is small enough to be stowed under the seat in front of you, must be stowed before the airline doors are closed, and must remain in its carrier during taxiing, takeoff, and landing. *But even airlines that don't allow pets are still required to allow service animals.* So call ahead to the airline to find out its policy on allowing nonservice animals.

> The Department of Transportation has stated that support animals must be allowed on planes—even animals who aid people with emotional problems like depression or anxiety.

Q: Thinking about how many times the airlines have lost my luggage, what do I do if I get off the plane in Paris, and find they sent my caged turtle to Turkey?

A: Until recently, there was no way for the consumer to learn the statistics of such occurrences. But the Federal Aviation Administration recently passed regulations requiring air carriers to include incidents involving pets on the Department of Transportation's consumer report on airline safety. You can now see an airline's safety records for pets at http://airconsumer.ost.dot .gov—click on "Air Travel Consumer Report," and you'll find monthly updates on the number of incidents and the airlines involved.

According to the Air Transport Association, approximately five thousand animals are lost, injured, or killed on airplanes every year. And unfortunately, if you dig a little deeper into the facts, you'll see that according to the SPCA, "While the vast majority [of pets] arrive safely at their destination, serious and consistent problems have been documented on virtually every major airline." So just keep in mind, taking a pet—like bringing a child on a plane—is not an easy task. And even if you're allowed to do so, you may want to consider whether Rover really needs that vacation after all.

Q: I want to make sure Fluffy's getting only the best bits in his kibble, but I can't make head or tail of those pet food labels. What do the terms they use mean?

A: If you're not entirely sure what makes a "fancy feast," you're not alone. The U.S. pet food industry is big business—dog and cat food sales in the United States accounted for more than $14.3 billion in 2005, according to the Pet Food Institute (that's the public education arm of the U.S. pet food industry). That's why the FDA stepped in and started regulating pet food labeling.

For instance, now there's a "95 percent rule" for pet food products regarding their content of meat, poultry, or fish. That means a product advertising itself as "beef for dogs" must be composed of 95 percent beef. If the named ingredient is more than 25 percent but less than 95 percent of the product, the name must include a descriptive term, like "chicken *dinner* for dogs," or other descriptors like "platter," "entrée," or "formula." If the product says it's made "with" an ingredient, that ingredient must be at least 3 percent of the product. So if the can says "tuna cat food," the product contains 95 percent tuna—but "cat food *with* tuna" probably only contains 3 percent tuna. In other words, the bottom line is that understanding these labels may mean the difference between giving your beloved pet a lot of meat, or just a "spot."

Q: My friend's seventeen-year-old cat just passed away, and she wants to bury her under the tree where she always got stuck— seems like a fitting everlasting resting place. That's kosher, right?

A: I hate to add to her grief, but the answer is no. In most municipalities it's illegal to bury your pet in your backyard because it tends to attract wild animals. You thought the whole beloved pet death thing was mentally scarring enough on the kiddies? Try having them watch a fox dig up the body and carry it away. The money you save on the pet cemetery should go directly into an interest-bearing account for their future therapy.

Though it's unlikely your friend would get busted for a backyard burial, a lot of cities will pick up and dispose of a pet's remains for a relatively small fee. Best to call the city or county health department or community animal shelter to find out local policy if you don't want the vet to discard the body or to go the pricey pet cemetery route. But who knows? Maybe with some luck your friend will be able to find a discount pet cemetery, something like "Shady Pines: Because your best friend always knew you were a cheap bastard."

Amy

I believe that every dog has a lesson to teach us. For some dogs, their purpose is to teach people the true definition of loyalty. Or joy in the simple pleasures. Or unconditional love. As far as I could tell, our terrier Lucy's purpose was to teach our kids that we need to love and care for even the imperfect and ill-tempered among us. Also, beware of growling dogs because they ain't kidding.

Lucy matured the opposite of most. Rather than being a sweet playful puppy who eventually grew curmudgeonly as she aged, Lucy started off as a biter, then grew to a nipper, then to a mere (but frequent) barker, and finally into a tired but lovable old lady of a dog. At age eight, she became diabetic. When the vet told me why she'd been drinking excessively and peeing all over (another less than rewarding characteristic), I asked, "Gee, what does one do for a diabetic dog?" She replied, "You give her two shots of insulin a day." "You do?" I asked, somewhat incredulously. "No," she said, "*you* do." And much to my surprise, I did. Gave that dog two shots per day. It became our thing. She loved those shots because I rewarded her with a hot dog after she got it. All she had to do was hear me open the cabinet where I kept the needles and she would come running in, tail wagging excitedly. The dog received better medical care than some children in third-world nations. For another five and a half years, my day was naturally bracketed by the insulin shots I would give to Lucy; hers by the hot dogs.

By age thirteen, Lucy had become deaf and couldn't see well. She would take to walking into a corner and looking at it intently without moving for five minutes or so in an almost catatonic state.

It became clear to all of us that Lucy's days were nearing an end. And then finally the day came that I got home and found Lucy lying in the living room breathing shallowly. She looked up at me and took in one long breath, which she did not exhale. I knew little about dogs or death but what I could figure was not good. While I always knew that Lucy loved me, at that moment I understood in my heart that she had waited to see me come through the door before taking that last breath.

At that moment I did what came naturally: I scooped Lucy up in my arms, took her into the car, and frantically started driving to the vet's office in hopes of saving my dog. Anyone who has seen me driving my dented white minivan—the one with two hubcaps and a rear bumper held on with duct tape (no joke)—will tell you that I may not be the world's best driver on a perfect day. But there I was, a limp dog in one arm, steering with the other while simultaneously dialing the vet, the road obscured by the tears streaming down my cheeks as I prayed that no one was on the sidewalk. When I got the vet's receptionist on the phone I asked her a question she was probably not used to hearing: "Um. I am on my way to your office with my dead dog. Should I come?" "Yes," she replied without hesitation. "Well . . . why?" I asked, now starting to think through the logic. "What do you do for a dead dog?" "We need to make sure that she's really dead," she responded. "She's not breathing and she's not blinking. I'm pretty sure she's dead," I replied. "Okay," she said, "so we'll see you soon."

When I got to the vet, they confirmed what I already knew: my Lucy was no more. Then they discussed my options: I could pay a certain price for a private cremation, which came with a hand-carved box for the mantel (that would no doubt induce nightmares in my children), or I could pay a reduced amount for a public cremation. But funereal details were not something I was capable of deciding at that moment, so I told the vet I needed to talk it over with my husband and I'd get back to him.

I picked up some pizza before I went home to tell the kids what happened because I find most things are a bit easier to handle when melted cheese is involved. After feeding the kids and explaining what happened, we all cried and then, drying his tears, my eight-year-old asked, "Why did Lucy want to die?" "I don't think she wanted to die," I said, "but I do think she didn't want to be in pain anymore." He nodded. "Maybe she said, 'I don't want to feel bad anymore.'" My eleven-year-old added, "Or maybe she said, 'I don't want to take shots anymore.'" But my four-year-old shook his head. "Nope," he said. "I think she said, 'Good-bye. I will miss you all.'" And that ended our discussion because we all knew he was right—that was exactly what Lucy would have said.

Chapter 8

Your Ride

Getting from Here to There

How you get from here to there says a lot about you. Whether you're a hybrid-driving eco-nut, an SUV-loving planet hater, a subway-riding crowd surfer (who's too poor to own private transport), or a wheelie-popping badass biker (who's statistically likely to get into an accident soon), your ride is in many ways your destiny. So here is where we will consider issues that often crop up on your journey from point A to point B.

Q: My car! My beautiful caaaaarrrrr! Smashed! Crashed! Trashed! What am I supposed to do now?

A: Oy, auto accidents are definitely an annoying part of life, but believe me, the way you deal with your insurance company can either make it more or less awful for you. First and foremost understand that it's the job of insurance companies—even your own—to settle all claims as cheaply and quickly as possible. You are dealing with them when you're at your most emotional, so remember to stick to the facts when discussing the accident: when, where, and the other vehicles involved. If you're talking about injuries, realize that not all injuries are apparent immediately; so rather than saying you weren't hurt, state only that you're not currently in pain or report the treatment you have received up to the date of the conversation.

If you're asked to sign documents, understand what you're signing—you may be giving the insurance company the right to see your medical or employment records. And finally *remember that settlement is a negotiation: the first offer made by the insurance company may not be its best or final offer.* You thought it was tough negotiating for the car when you got it—you may be surprised to learn it could be even harder negotiating for the value of your old one.

Now, if you're worried that alerting your insurance company will make your rates skyrocket, you might also be wondering if you have to report the accident. In most cases, your insurance policy probably does require that you report the accident, or you may risk losing coverage. Even if the other driver tells you he won't report the accident to the police or his insurance company, think twice because it doesn't mean he really won't. After all, you don't know this guy from a hole in the wall (or the hole you just made in his fender . . .).

If the other party does wind up reporting the collision to his insurance company, they will then turn around and call your insurance company. And if he sues, you may be responsible for the legal fees, which your insurance company would have normally handled had you called. Therefore, if you know you're accident-prone and you don't want your insurance to be affected, my suggestion is to set your deductible so high that even if you report an accident, your insurance company won't step in—and the cost won't hit your premium—unless the damage level is high enough.

But what if the accident was the other guy's fault and he asks you to keep it quiet—maybe he even tells you it's still possible that your premium might go up despite your blamelessness? Is he right?

Well, it is possible—though unlikely—that come renewal time your insurance rates may go up if you've been in an accident that was not your fault. And should your insurance company hear about it from the other party's insurance company, it may be more difficult to prove later that the accident really wasn't your fault. The best bet is to file a police report about the accident, then call your insurance company and let them work it out. They work for you, after all. Let them earn their keep.

Q: **I lent my friend my car and he returned it washed *and dented*. His insurance pays for it, right?**

A: Nope, sorry to inform you that *your insurance pays for someone else's accident when your car is involved*. A third party is covered as a "permissive user" if you, the owner and "named insured," have allowed the person to operate your vehicle. You let your kid use the car, your insurance pays. The permission can be implied—

like tossing your keys to a designated driver—but the implication of permission only goes so far.

In the actual case of a fourteen-year-old who took her mom's keys and gave them to her driver-boyfriend, no permissive use was found. Similarly, the actual case of the repo man who took a car, crashed it, and then tried to claim coverage under the policy of the guy whose car he'd just repossessed lost the "permissive use" designation. The lesson of lending a car is like the old seat belt commercial: be cautious, the premium you save may be your own.

Q: **What about a case like in the movie *Ferris Bueller's Day Off*? The kids handed the keys to a valet parker and the valet damaged the car. Who pays when it's the valet's fault?**

A: Sounds like the real case of a man in England who gave the keys of his Lotus Exige to a restaurant's valet parker, who immediately smashed it into two parked cars. Now that's what you call an expensive dinner. . . . You pay car insurance not only for the purpose of having the insurance company cover damage to your vehicle, but also for the privilege of having their lawyers fight for you in a case like this. For a major accident involving a valet, you are best served to turn the claim over to your insurance company and let them handle it.

But for the more common scratches and dents that appear when the car is returned, you should fill out a claim form. While most valet companies do have policies limiting their liability for the contents of your car while parked, they usually can't limit liability while they are actually driving it. Make certain that you call attention to the damage *before you leave the garage*, though, or they will successfully argue that the damage didn't occur on their watch.

Q: The scariest part of any vacation for me is when I'm standing at the car rental counter and the employee in the ill-fitting vest leans over and says, "You want our insurance, *riiiiight?*" Then, when I turn it down, the guy goes, "Are you *suuuuure* that's a good idea?" . . . I don't know! Is it a good idea? Do I really need it, or am I already covered by my credit card?

A: Many people believe their own insurance covers an accident in a rental car, and this is probably true but only if you carry comprehensive *and* collision coverage. (Remember to check your policy before renting a car.) Some credit cards also cover accidents in rental cars, but generally only if you've charged the full amount of the rental car on that card. But not all credit cards do cover rental car damage, and some will only cover cars rented from particular companies, so again, check into these details before you rent.

For a fee, rental car companies offer something called a collision damage waiver (CDW). This is not technically insurance, but rather a guarantee that the rental agency will pay for all damage to the rental vehicle, including payment for the time they can't rent it while it's being fixed, which you'd otherwise be charged for. The CDW usually does not cover personal injury or damage to your personal property. That means if you decline the CDW, you're responsible for all damage, so best to understand what you already have in coverage before turning it down, to ensure you're insured.

Q: Drunk driving is bad, I know, and I won't joke about it. But I will ask how much I can drink before I'm legally considered blotto.

A: In every state you are currently considered too drunk to drive if your blood alcohol level reaches .08. (It's .02 if you're a minor and aren't supposed to be drinking anyway.) As I'm sure you're aware, alcohol is metabolized differently based on gender, weight, and whether or not you've eaten. The University of Oklahoma Police Department has a very helpful blood alcohol content (BAC) calculator available on its Web site, www.ou.edu/oupd/bac.htm, which will help you estimate "just how little alcohol it takes to put you on the 'wrong side of the law.'"

Some people who get pulled over and fear they are over the limit believe they can avoid a DUI (driving under the influence) or DWI (driving while intoxicated) conviction by refusing to take a breathalyzer test. In the case of one woman who was stopped by police, she was so adamant that she didn't want to take the test she resisted arrest and then bit the arresting officer. Did I mention she was the wife of a judge? Yeah, sometimes this stuff really writes itself. . . .

But while state laws differ, every state has an "implied consent" law, which says that any person who operates a motor vehicle on a public road is deemed to have given his consent to the taking of his breath for the purposes of determining the content of alcohol in his blood. If you refuse to take a breathalyzer test, you face automatic suspension of your driver's license under the implied consent law. Obviously, the best way to avoid a penalty if you've been drinking (even if you're sleeping with the judge) is to call a cab instead of risking the lives of everyone on the road.

Weird but true facts on drunk driving that will impress your friends at the bar

- You do not have to be driving and you don't have to be drunk to be arrested for drunk driving.

The musician George Michael was arrested in England after being found slumped in the driver's seat of his car, presumably under the influence of drugs. According to his own statement to the press, "I was in possession of Class C drugs, which is an offense, and I have no complaints about the police who were professional throughout."

But drug possession isn't the only charge he could have faced if he'd been caught in the United States. Here in the colonies, Michael could have faced the charge of driving while intoxicated even though he wasn't driving! That's because the way statutes are written, you only need to be in control of the vehicle to be arrested. So if you have the keys in the ignition but the car is in park, you can still be arrested even if you aren't moving when the cops show up.

It might also come as a surprise to learn that you don't actually need a blood alcohol level above the legal limit to be prosecuted. An officer must only prove that you are impaired by drugs or alcohol to arrest you. If you cannot pass a field sobriety test, you can be arrested even without proof your blood alcohol level was above the legal limit.

- You don't have to be driving a car or truck to be arrested for drunk driving. You can be arrested for drunk driving a lawnmower.

Police in St. Cloud, Minnesota, arrested a reckless mower after seeing him careening atop his mobile lawn clipper. They then seized the man's mower because of his previous drunk-driving convictions. The offense colloquially known as "drunk driving" is the crime of operating a vehicle with a blood alcohol level of more than .08. What people don't realize is that in most states, "vehicle" is defined very broadly and includes any device that is moved by power other than human power. That includes lawnmowers, tractors, golf carts, motorcycles, and motorized bar stools (no kidding). In one case, a guy was arrested for vehicular homicide after he hit and killed a pedestrian while intoxicated. He was driving a *bicycle* at the time. The charges were eventually dropped but the bottom line is that while drinking, you and your record—and innocent bystanders—are better off when you keep your bottom planted on a (stationary) barstool.

- You can be cited for alcohol-related charges even if you're just sitting in the passenger seat of a car.

Open container laws prohibit the possession of any open alcoholic beverage container and the consumption of any alcoholic beverage in the passenger area of any motor vehicle. If you have an open beer bottle, wine bottle, or any other alcohol container that has previously been opened—even if you are not drinking it in the car, you can be cited if it's in the passenger area (that is, not in a locked glove compartment or the trunk. Some states even make it a crime to transport any "unsealed" alcoholic beverage container in a locked glove box.). And both the driver and the passenger can be cited. So if you have alcohol, keep it in the trunk until you get to your destination.

- If you're "impaired" you can be busted on a drunk-driving charge, even if the only thing you've been drinking is cough syrup.

A Milwaukee woman discovered this when she was booked on charges of driving under the influence. When she hit a curb, she raised the suspicion of a police officer who witnessed it and he arrested her for DUI. But she hadn't been drinking: she'd simply taken over-the-counter cold medicine.

You don't have to be drunk on alcohol to be arrested, just

impaired. That impairment can come from alcohol, illegal drugs, or legally prescribed medications—even over-the-counter medicines. Better to read about potential impairment on the bottle before you take the medication than to see it on the police blotter after the fact.

Q: This guy tailgates me in traffic, then cuts me off, flipping me the bird, and *then* drives twenty miles per hour in front of me. I got so mad I nearly rammed his car. What would have happened to me if I did?

A: A sixty-six-year-old woman in Colorado, apparently angered that she had to "share the road with bicyclists," was arrested after she began honking her horn and swerving threateningly at the bikers. But as you've realized, incidents of road rage are not limited to grandmas with attitudes. AAA estimates that between 1990 and 1996, more than ten thousand people died in aggressive driving incidents, and another two hundred died in cases of actual road rage, when physical violence results from a disagreement between two drivers.

Cases involving road rage—including physical confrontations, attempts to bodily injure someone with your car, and other incidents that could lead to bodily harm—are criminal matters and will be prosecuted. In addition, your insurance is not obligated to cover damage that you do in a road rage incident. So if you think you're mad now, imagine how mad you'll be when the other driver's aggressive lawyer hits you where it really hurts: the pocketbook.

Q: Okay, now seriously: how do I get out of a traffic ticket?

A: That one's easy: prove you did nothing to disobey the law. Trying to get out of a ticket is so common, it's practically America's favorite pastime. Even the attorney general of New Jersey, Zulima Farber, was caught playing the game. Farber intervened in a traffic stop involving her boyfriend, Hamlet Goore. (That's right, their names are Zulima and Hamlet. They probably met at a support group for the Mercilessly Teased as Children.) Though Farber later claimed she didn't use undue influence to prevent her Hamlet from being written up and having his car impounded (for improper registration and driving on a suspended license), after an investigation Ms. Farber still wound up resigning her post because of the brouhaha.

So what should (and shouldn't) you do during a traffic stop? Well, if you get pulled over, *always* remain polite when speaking to the guy with the handcuffs on his belt—even if you believe the stop was wrong. If you intend to fight the ticket, plead not guilty within the time specified on the ticket. In most jurisdictions you have the right to request a copy of all documentation related to the stop to see if there are obvious holes in the evidence.

On the day of the hearing, arrive early and try to talk to the officer ahead of time to try to negotiate to see if he is willing to lower the charge for a lesser fee or no points. And keep in mind—this is a traffic ticket, not a career ender, unless you do something really dumb and make it one.

Q: My smoker friend threw her cigarette out a car window and got a ticket for littering. I found the whole thing pretty funny, but does she really have to pay the ticket?

A: It's like that old joke, "If I don't pay a jaywalking ticket, what will they do? Put a boot on my ass?" Here's what you should tell your friend: (1) Stop smoking! In case you haven't gotten the memo, it's a nasty habit and bad for your health. (2) Stop littering, you pig! Thankfully your friend's act of civil disgustingness didn't lead to much, but in 2004, when a man in China carelessly dropped his smoldering cigarette, the butt ignited and caused a fire that killed fifty-three people.

Littering is a crime that gets no respect, and people do it all the time. Every state has laws that forbid throwing cigarette butts and other trash from car windows, and you should realize that you are actually breaking the law when you do it. I think people don't take it seriously because as violations go, it tends to be listed as a summary offense: one that can cause a fine but rarely leads to jail time. But in the most serious incidents, like the case in China or in western wildfires, where a spark can lead to a massive conflagration, there are very serious consequences.

Remember, it takes the average cigarette butt twenty-five years to decompose because of the plastic in the filter and it costs states like Texas about $24 million every year to pick up litter from the roadside. So if you must smoke, at the very least try not to be a total butthead about it: use an ashtray to properly dispose of your coffin nail.

Q: **I bought a new car and it's a piece of shit—it never worked right despite several attempts to fix it. Do I have any legal recourse?**

A: As the old saying goes, if life hands you lemons make lemonade. But as the law goes, if a car dealership hands you a lemon, make a lawsuit. Under the law, consumers are protected against buying or leasing a new vehicle that is considered a lemon, and every state has its own lemon laws.

In most states, a "lemon" is defined as a vehicle that suffers a defect that substantially impairs the car's value or safety, that cannot be repaired after three attempts by a manufacturer-authorized dealership, or that is out of commission for a certain number of days during the first twelve months. The defect must generally be caused in the manufacture, and not as a result of an accident or poor maintenance. And note that the lemon laws generally only cover new cars.

Once a car is declared a lemon, neither the manufacturer nor the dealer can resell it without notifying you of its status as "nonconforming," so read the fine print carefully. You can also do a search of Web sites devoted to providing advice on legal recourse and listing makes and models of common lemons. Know your rights or you'll probably need a drink far stiffer than the lemonade you've been squeezed.

Q: Every insurance commercial I ever hear offers to save me 15 percent on my car insurance. On the seventh switch do I get it for free?

A: That's a really good question because most people don't realize what they are giving up when they swap insurance policies. Before you go switching your car insurance, you need to understand what those ads are actually promising, and what you'll be losing in exchange for that 15 percent.

There are many different forms of car insurance, and each may be purchased separately or wrapped together as a bundle of protection. So it's "easy" to save money—but you'll be spending less by getting less insurance coverage. State laws differ, but forty-seven states require that, to drive a car on a public road, you must, at the very least, carry liability coverage at a set minimum dollar payout. Liability insurance covers injuries that you cause to someone else. Remember, though, that in the event you are in a serious accident and you cause major bodily injury to others, you wouldn't be sued for the limit of your coverage, you'd be sued for all the damage you cause—and it would be terrible to lose your house because you have to pay the debt that your policy doesn't cover.

So not carrying enough liability insurance is one potential problem; another problem with purchasing only minimum liability coverage is that it won't cover other possible damage or harm. Personal Injury Protection (PIP) coverage is what insures for the medical costs (and in some cases the lost wages) of the driver and passengers in the policy holder's car. Then there is collision coverage for damage to your car, and comprehensive coverage that reimburses you for loss due to theft or damage caused by something other than an accident. That's coverage Ted Passon of Philadelphia probably deeply regrets not having. Passon's passion was baseball, and no one was happier than he when his beloved Phillies won the World Series in 2008. But Passon's delight quickly turned to horror when he returned to the parking lot after the final game and found his car had been flipped over by fanatical Phillies fans.

Since he didn't carry comprehensive coverage, Passon had no insurance to cover the total loss of his vehicle. But fortunately the man was creative and started a blog called Phillyfixmycar. blogspot.com, where he beseeched Phillies fans to donate $10 each so he could buy a new car. Luckily for him, Philadelphia

Phillies "Phans" came through, and he managed to raise more than $4,500, which covered the cost of a "new" used car for him—and enough to buy a car for another woman whose car had also been totaled in the festivities.

You, however, should not count on the big hearts of others to pay for damage to your car. So even though you might save money up front by buying only the minimum coverage, ask what the insurance you're paying for really covers (your medical costs? lost wages? harm to passengers? damage to the car or personal property in an accident? damage to a car through vandalism?), and then figure out if paying less now is a risk worth taking in the long run.

Q: Can you explain to me how the job of repo man is legal? Aren't these people basically just stealing cars?

A: A sheriff's deputy in New Orleans was probably asking the same thing when his car was repossessed. And how's this for adding insult to injury? After his car was taken, it was inventoried and found to contain marijuana, leading to the deputy's arrest, which then caused him to lose his job as a law enforcement officer. Yet it is strange that what a repo man does—hot-wiring cars and driving them away, often under the cloak of darkness—is perfectly legal.

Unless you pay cash when you purchase a car, you get a loan on which you make monthly payments. To secure that loan, the bank or dealership takes a security interest in your car, giving it the right to take the car back if you stop making payments. But there are laws governing repossession, the most important of which is that the repo man can't "breach the peace." That means he can't use bodily force or threats if confronted, and he can't risk a confrontation with you that would result in a breach of the peace. Moreover, a repo man can't break into a locked garage. He can, however, lawfully take your car in the middle of the night if it's on the street or in your driveway . . . even if the owner of the car is an officer in charge of preventing grand theft auto.

Q: **When I said good-bye to my old gas guzzler, I decided my new ride should be green. Can I get any Good Samaritan benefit for reducing my carbon tireprint?**

A: It's very possible that you can! If you are the original owner of a qualifying hybrid vehicle—one that combines an electric motor with a gas-powered engine—you may be eligible to claim a one-time tax deduction on your federal income tax return. But there are some big caveats on that: most important, *you have to be the first owner of a new car*, not a used car. This is because the government is trying to get the hybrid on the street, so once it's out already, the next owner doesn't get the credit. The credit also phases out in the second calendar quarter after that in which the first sixty thousand cars of that model have been sold. In other words, if you want to avoid missing the tax credit, check the IRS Web site to see which new hybrids are still eligible.

Now, if you want to avoid the high price of gasoline and go even greener, don't forget pedal power. That's right, I'm talking about the bicycle—it's not just for athletes touring de France anymore! If you are a cyclist, remember that in most states a bicycle is considered a vehicle, so the same laws that apply to other drivers also apply to you. This means that bicyclists must obey all traffic lights and signs; signal for turns, whether driving on a roadway, bike lane, or bike path; and yield the right-of-way when it is required. Bicyclists must drive with traffic, as driving against traffic is a leading cause of bike accidents.

Also, in many municipalities, helmets are required of bicyclists just as they are required of motorcyclists. Most violations of bicycle law are treated like traffic infractions: you're given a ticket and issued a fine—relatively speaking, not a big deal. Not following bicycle law, however, can lead to much greater harm. It's like I tell my kids when we see someone riding a bicycle without a helmet, "There's someone who doesn't value his head very much!"

Q: **I'd barely gotten over the fact that they didn't serve free pretzels on my flight when I was told the airline lost my luggage and canceled my connecting flight. Don't they owe me anything for the inconvenience and expense they cost me?**

A: Nothing says aggravation quite like the snafu on the flight that's supposed to get you to your relaxation destination. Unfortunately, contrary to popular opinion, airlines are not required to compensate passengers whose flights are delayed or canceled, unless you are bumped from a flight that is overbooked. (If it's a result of weather or mechanical failure you're out of luck.) In the case of overbooking, airlines are required to provide compensation in addition to a new flight, but it's up to you to negotiate with the airlines for extra flights, meals, and accommodations. (There are specific guidelines for reimbursing involuntarily bumped passengers based on the delay the traveler will face.)

But what if you do make the flight but *your bag* doesn't? While most airlines will reimburse you for misplaced or delayed

baggage, the amount they pay is again subject to negotiation.
Report a missing bag before leaving the airport so you can negotiate the compensation. Though with all the negotiating you
may need to do, it might be cheaper and easier to buy a used car
and drive. . . .

Q: **I'm about to leave for Paris—*ooh la la, j'adore Paris!*—but say
I drink too much champagne when I'm there and get *le sick*. If
I buy travel medical insurance, am I covered if I need to go to
the hospital?**

A: One of my favorite travel insurance cases was brought to us by a
twenty-five-year-old Canadian man who, while sober, was responsible enough to purchase travel medical insurance for his upcom-
ing Mexican vacation. Once he got to Mexico, however, he got
drunk off his ass and fell from his hotel's seven-story balcony. He
recovered but learned the very hard way that his travel medical insurance didn't cover costs of injuries associated with drinking. His
mother wound up having to raise funds for his medical expenses
despite the fact that he'd purchased travel medical insurance.

If you think you're being responsible by purchasing medical
insurance for a vacation since you'll be out of network on your
existing health care, do yourself a favor and ask the following
questions before buying: First, what's the co-pay and what's the
deductible? It might turn out to be more than what your current
coverage is for an out-of-network provider. Second, how long
is the benefit period? Some policies end coverage, even for a
lingering injury, and many won't cover preexisting conditions or
injuries caused by drinking or other activities you may consider
an integral part of your vacation.

Q: As if flying isn't frightening enough, now I have to worry about the airline itself going under before the plane takes off. Is there anything I can do to protect myself, financially speaking?

A: Oh, for the good old days when the only thing we feared when flying was a jumbo-size seatmate carrying a bag of salami sandwiches! With the rising cost of fuel, the ailing airline industry continues to suffer, and the pain trickles right down to consumers. Aloha Airlines, for instance, had to file for bankruptcy protection after it had emerged from bankruptcy merely fourteen months prior. The airline eventually stopped flying entirely in March 2008. Travelers who'd paid in cash or check in advance for Aloha flights after the airline ceased operation had to file a claim in bankruptcy court to get their money back. Aloha indeed.

Some good(ish) news first: if you already have tickets on a bankrupt airline you should not be affected in the short term. Though you probably shouldn't expect to be served orange juice that comes from real oranges, there are not expected to be great changes in routes or schedules in the near future. As for tickets in the longer term, there is greater risk of flight cancellations or route or time changes as the date of the flight is further in the future. And while the airlines want to maintain their loyal customers, you may want to think about using your frequent flyer miles sooner rather than later.

To protect yourself, always buy your ticket on a credit card and consider travel insurance—and make sure that the insurance covers you in the event that the airline isn't there anymore.

Q: You know how they tell you to turn off all cell phones and other electronic devices during flights? Aside from annoying your neighbor, what's the big deal and what's the worst that can happen to me if I disobey Stewart the Steward?

A: A woman on a domestic flight out of New York, whose cell phone was tucked into her carry-on bag, was surprised when it rang during takeoff. But she was more surprised when she received a letter from the FAA telling her that she was under investigation for using an electronic device on an aircraft and could face a fine of up to $2,500. That's because, according to the Electronic Code of Federal Regulations (e-CFR), the use of wireless devices is prohibited in flight because of potential interference to the aircraft's navigation and communications systems.

Now, though anecdotal evidence suggests that portable electronic devices (PEDs) such as cell phones, pagers, and two-way radios transmit signals that can interfere with the navigation system of a plane, hard evidence proving this theory has been difficult to come by. In fact, in April 2008, Air France became the first airline to run a trial allowing passengers to use their mobile devices in flight. The French airline reported no problems on the flight and said passengers liked the service save for some dropped calls (and probably a few shouts of "I surrender!" heard in the background). As technology continues to improve it seems likely that other airlines in Europe and Asia will soon follow suit and lift the cell phone ban on their planes as well.

But for now, FAA and FCC guidelines remain in effect here and restrict the use of PEDs on commercial airlines. There is a list of approved electronic devices that may be used once the aircraft reaches an altitude of ten thousand feet, but they must be turned off again during descent. Currently cell phones must remain off throughout the entire flight. And off means off, not just "not talking on." An individual can face a penalty of up to $2,500 for violating the regulations. So when the stewardess tells you to turn it off, power down and leave the electronic signaling to the pilot.

Chapter 9

Your Health

Body Issues

Good health tends to be one of those funny things you don't think about until it's taken away. But be it the first sign of sniffles, an upset stomach, or even a persistent case of hiccups, once daily life is affected by bodily malfunctions, it's hard to concentrate on anything else. Since we know navigating our health care system can be one giant pain in the ass, in this chapter we'll tackle questions about health care–related issues to help you steer clear of things that can figuratively (or literally) cost you an arm and a leg.

Life expectancy would grow by leaps and bounds if green vegetables smelled as good as bacon.

—Doug Larson

Q: I can't really afford health care now, and since I'm young(ish) and healthy, it's hard to justify paying several hundred bucks a month for bubkes. I don't want to be totally stupid, though, so I'm thinking of proposing to a friend that I'll pay her fifty dollars a month, and on the off chance I get sick, I'll just claim to be her at the hospital. Is that cool?

A: If by "cool" you mean "criminal," then yes, it's super cool. What you've just described is also known as "medical identity theft." At first blush that term sounds like a joke, doesn't it? *"Um, no, thanks, you can keep your high blood pressure. I'm going to stick with my arthritis."* But according to a study by the Federal Trade Commission in 2007, approximately 250,000 people were victims of medical identity theft in 2005, which is clearly no laughing matter.

The rising cost of health care is driving more and more people to utilize another person's medical identity and benefits card to obtain services like doctor visits, lab tests, and prescription drugs. (And this is done both with *and* without the consent of the payee.) A medical identity thief may rack up unpaid co-pays in your name or change your medical history—even providing a different blood type. Complicating the matter, medical identity theft is not as easy to detect as financial identity theft. To protect yourself, never carry around a social security card, don't leave your prescription card in an unattended purse or wallet, and ask your insurer for a list of benefits that have been paid in your name.

In this case, I'd also remind you that even when young(ish) and healthy, accidents do happen, and if you start racking up serious bills on your friend's account, she might just "accidentally" kill you.

Q: So what are you supposed to do if you get really sick and you're uninsured?

A: The number of uninsured people in this country is staggering. According to the last census in 2006, 47 million Americans were living without health insurance, which makes basic and preventative health care prohibitively expensive for many people. But the bottom line is that if you think your health is in serious danger because you have severe pain, a bad injury, a sudden illness, or one that is quickly getting much worse, you can get emergency care anywhere in the United States by going to a hospital emergency room. Will you have to pay for it? Yes. But since your health is quite literally the one thing that you can't live without, seek professional medical treatment if you need it.

Another thing that 2006 census revealed was that over 43 million others had received some sort of Medicare benefits. Keep in mind that anyone aged sixty-five or older and anyone on permanent disability is entitled to receive Medicare benefits. In the United States if you have Medicare you have certain guaranteed rights, whether you are in the original Medicare plan or a Medicare managed-care plan. You have a right to know what will and won't be covered, in language you can understand. You also have the right to get emergency care when and where you need it, without prior approval. And don't be afraid to fight for your rights as if your life depended on it, because realistically, one day it could.

Q: If you're a freelance or temporary employee and you get hurt on the job, who's responsible for paying your medical bills?

A: This may not be the answer you're hoping for, but you, the free-lancer/temp, will be the one footing the bills. Almost all workers' compensation insurance plans are limited to employees only. That's why if you're an "independent contractor," you should make sure that you carry enough insurance to cover you in the event of a work-related injury.

Q: But if I am an employee and I've signed up for the company health plan, then all of my medical costs will be picked up by my employer, right?

A: Not necessarily. Your company's health plan is intended to pay for your covered medical costs (some costs are not generally covered, like cosmetic surgery). But that company plan may not have to pay for costs of health crises that are covered when other insurance policies come into play. What does that mean? Well, if you get sick and need an operation, your employee health insurance policy would generally cover the cost of that procedure. But let's say the reason you need the operation is because of injuries you sustained in a car accident. Now there are several insurance policies that are in the mix: your car insurance, the other driver's car insurance, and the umbrella health insurance benefits from your company-sponsored health benefits. While people might assume your health insurance covers you since your health was affected, in fact the car insurance company is responsible for your medical treatment. Only after the car insurance has paid its limit would your health insurance kick in and hopefully pay the rest. The reason for that is to prevent you from being doubly or triply paid for the same injury. But sometimes a company-sponsored health plan will pay medical benefits first while the other insurance policies fight over who's responsible. This means that once it's decided which car insurance has to pay, you need to repay your company's health plan for the money it laid out.

Wal-Mart faced this very issue in May 2000, when one of its employees, Debbie Shank, was severely brain damaged after being hit by a truck. Wal-Mart initially paid her medical benefits (which totaled approximately $470,000). But after Shank won a lawsuit against the trucking company that caused her injuries, Wal-Mart sued the wheelchair and nursing home-bound Shank to get back the money it paid out. John Simley, a spokesman for the retail giant, called Shank's case "unbelievably sad," but defended the company's actions to recoup its money by stating that the health plan was bound by specific rules established to protect its assets for other members.

Q: **One of my friends suffers from bipolar disorder and he's nervous that if he submits medical claims through his company insurance plan, it could have an impact on his future with the employer. Is there any way he can protect his medical privacy?**

A: Your friend's concern is completely understandable. A lot of people fear that if they have company-sponsored medical benefits, their employer may learn about their treatment for conditions ranging from AIDS to pregnancy. Fortunately, thanks to the Health Insurance Portability and Accountability Act (HIPAA), a company health plan's disclosure of an individual's protected health information is greatly limited.

Under HIPAA, your company can't fire you because it improperly got word of your condition. So while employees with serious medical issues have a lot to worry about, fear of employer reprisals shouldn't be one of them.

Q: On some health plans, you get money back from your provider if you can prove you've exercised at a gym a certain number of times a month. Shouldn't the government also try to encourage something like this with a tax rebate for our nation of fatties?

A: Actually, the IRS has ruled that if a doctor recommends the purchase of home exercise equipment as part of the treatment for a particular condition such as obesity or hypertension, the equipment is deductible as a medical expense under Section 213 of the Revenue code. Moreover, you can use a flexible spending account to pay for the equipment so that it is a pretax expense.

But note that medical expenses are deductible only by the amount that they exceed 7.5 percent of your adjusted gross income. Additionally, the gym equipment may only be deducted if the physician recommended it for the treatment of a specific condition—not merely to benefit your general health or the appearance of your abs.

The IRS is also aware that some taxpayers try to take advantage of the medical deductions a bit too strenuously. One man actually tried to deduct the bills from his veterinarian as *his* medical expense. Though some men can be dogs, I think eyebrows were raised when they found deductions for prescriptions made out to Fido.

You may only deduct medicine if it is by prescription or if it's insulin. Over-the-counter medications are never deductible, even if they are reimbursable under your flexible spending account and/or recommended by a doctor. There are some medically related items sold over the counter—like blood sugar test kits, crutches, etc.—that may be deductible as well if they are related to medical care (so check on the IRS's Web site to be sure).

And in case you hadn't guessed, cosmetic surgery, if only intended to improve appearance, is not deductible. If needed to correct a deformity related to an injury, disease, or congenital abnormality, though, you may deduct it. But FYI, a crooked nose is not considered a congenital abnormality. . . .

Q: **Poor Heath Ledger! He took a combination of six prescription drugs and sleeping pills that together formed a lethal cocktail. How can I be sure the meds I'm taking won't combine to kill me?**

A: Heath Ledger's death in 2008 was tragic for a lot of reasons, not the least of which was its preventability. But especially when people are elderly and taking a lot of medication, the possibility of taking the wrong drugs in combination increases, and serious illness and death can result.

In a case somewhat similar to Ledger's, a Florida woman who suffered severe back pain was prescribed at least six different painkillers over several months and died as a result of the combination. But in her case the court ruled that her husband could bring a lawsuit against the pharmacy for negligence even though it had properly filled the prescriptions written by the doctor.

Until recently, it was considered the physician's duty to warn a patient of the side effects of the drugs he or she prescribed, and pharmacies were only held liable if they filled a prescription incorrectly. (And that's no small number: according to the *Journal of the American Medical Association*, more than 550,000 injuries and over 100,000 deaths each year are a result of errors in filling prescriptions. Of the 3 billion prescriptions filled yearly, an estimated 51.5 million mistakes are made.) But courts have begun to hold that pharmacists do have a duty to warn if there is a clear error on the face of the prescription or if there is a contraindication—where there is a dangerous interaction between two drugs—prescribed to the same patient.

Because pharmacists have more knowledge about drug side effects and dangers than the average patient, courts are more likely to hold them responsible. But the ultimate responsibility to make sure you are taking the right drugs at the right dose is still yours, because you'll be the one to suffer the consequences.

On the flip side of the coin, because of a marked increase in prescription fraud in recent years, regulators began a crack down on the broad group of crimes known as "pharmaceutical diversion." Pharmaceutical diversion is the illegal acquisition of prescription drugs for personal use or for sale to others. "Doctor shopping" falls into this category. Though the name "doctor shopping" probably calls to mind someone conscientiously looking around for the best physician, the government defines it as the practice of going to several doctors, emergency rooms, and pharmacies to get multiple prescriptions for an actual or feigned ailment.

Rush Limbaugh is a famous case in point: In 2006, he was arrested for abuse of prescription drugs and, as part of his plea, paid a $30,000 fine. He was able to avoid pleading guilty to a doctor shopping charge because he successfully completed a treatment program. Still, the Centers for Disease Control and

Prevention reported a 34 percent increase in written prescriptions in the last fifteen years, which indicates, among other things, a rise in doctor shopping across the board (as well as across party lines).

Q: **Seems like everybody has a tattoo these days. Me? I'm too scared to get a tat, not only because I fear cliché, but also because injecting permanent ink beneath my skin with sketchy needles seems dangerously stupid. Who makes sure tattoo parlors stay clean?**

A: According to the FDA, about 45 million Americans have gotten themselves inked (and according to a Harris poll, about 17 percent of them regret that decision). No doubt about it, tattooing is a big business and many people who contemplate getting the adornment should ask questions before it's too late. Not only questions like "That pretty Chinese character I'm about to have emblazoned on my skin doesn't really mean 'idiot,' does it?" but questions like "What are the legal regulations governing the safety of tattoos?"

Although tattoos are subject to the FDA's federal regulations as cosmetics, state and local agencies are in charge of regulating the practice of tattooing by salon technicians. That means the oversight of tattoo parlors varies widely from state to state. Some states merely prevent the tattooing of minors without parental consent, while others closely monitor the hygiene standards of salons.

Because tattoos can lead to bloodborne diseases (like hepatitis and HIV), skin disorders and infections, allergic reactions, and MRI and anesthetic complications, you should really think this one out before singeing that adorable little dolphin on your ankle. And if you decide the risks are worth it, make sure you ask the tattoo artist the following questions:

> How are the needles used?
> How are they sanitized?
> How are they disposed of?
> What does the salon do to ensure the equipment is sanitary?
> What dyes are used and what are the possible allergic reactions?

Lastly, do yourself a favor and ask how you're really going to feel about explaining to your grandchildren how the saggy skull on your biceps made you a real rebel back in the day....

Never go to a doctor whose office plants have died.

—Erma Bombeck

Q: **Aside from checking Awfulplasticsurgery.com, how do you know if the doctor you choose for your boob job is a reputable surgeon or a dangerous boob himself?**

A: Here's a sad story: In March 2005, Kelly Cregan flew to New York from Ireland to get a face-lift because she'd seen an article in her local newspaper about a particular surgeon there. Cregan wanted the face-lift to be a surprise, so before she left home she told her husband, Liam, that she'd be attending a business course in Dublin. It wasn't until Liam Cregan received a phone call from the Irish embassy telling him that his wife was on life support in a New York hospital that he even learned his wife had left the country. Unfortunately the article Kelly Cregan had read about the surgeon failed to mention that this doctor was the most sued plastic surgeon in New York, with a record thirty-three payouts for malpractice for botched procedures. Cregan died as a result of complications to her surgery, and the medical examiner in New York ruled that the faulty face-lift was a significant contributing factor to her death.

With the popularity of shows like *Extreme Makeover*, many who never contemplated plastic surgery are now considering it, and many wind up choosing the doctor with the lowest price or best payment options rather than the one with the best qualifications. If you're considering plastic surgery, be aware that though there is no national registry of malpractice complaints, every state has a medical board that requires all doctors to report lawsuits so it can keep records. In addition to the lawsuits, patients can also file complaints with the state's medical disciplinary board, which is a subsection of its medical board. These records are public and you can find the information online. Start at the home page of your state's medical disciplinary board (use a search engine and type in the name of your state and "medical disciplinary board"). On the state's medical board site, there is usually a link for consumers to follow that leads to the disciplinary section where a person can file a complaint or learn about a doctor's history.

You should remember, though, that there are also a lot of unethical lawyers out there willing to file frivolous suits against doctors. Despite the fact that all those lawyers on late night TV commercials make you think you can sue anyone for any reason, you actually do need to prove that someone was negligent and caused you harm. In the case of medical malpractice, you need to prove that the doctor or hospital failed to exercise the care and skill practiced by other professionals under similar circumstances. That's the difference between a bad outcome and malpractice. Don't take the simple fact that a suit was filed as concrete proof of malpractice. But if you find thirty-three payouts for malpractice from a particular doctor, you should probably get your head examined before you decide to go through with that surgery.

Q: **What's to prevent my doctor from blabbing about weird aspects of my body once I'm rich and famous ... or just when she's looking for a funny story to tell at the dinner table?**

A: Your relationship with your doctor is covered by doctor-patient privilege, which is comprehensive but not absolute. Doctor-patient privilege is meant to ensure that your medical conditions and health history cannot be divulged without your permission. Even a doctor's observations and opinions of you are covered by the privilege. But there are exceptions to this rule, as one Pennsylvania man learned after he was treated for an irregular heartbeat. While giving his medical history during an office visit, the man told his doctor that he regularly drank six to ten beers a day. Imagine his shock when Pennsylvania's Department of Transportation then sent him a letter telling him his license was being revoked because of a substance abuse problem.

You're probably aware that your medical information can be sent to your insurance carrier for billing purposes. If your medical condition is an issue in a lawsuit, your medical records might be released and entered into evidence. But a doctor is also released from the strictures of doctor-patient privilege if a patient tells a doctor of ongoing criminal activity in which he's engaged—drunk driving, for instance—or if a patient reports a condition that might "impair the ability to control and safely operate" a vehicle. Pennsylvania is one of six states that actually require a doctor to report on patients who might be unfit to drive.

But needless to say, if you think your doctor violated the privilege, there are any number of malpractice attorneys waiting for the privilege of fighting for you.

Robin

As a little girl who dreamed of one day getting to put her feet in a pair of stirrups, I can assure you my fantasy never involved me doing so while dressed in an unflattering paper gown as someone approached my private parts with a cold, lubricated speculum. In fact, to this day, I still find the prospect of a trip to the gynecologist less appealing than getting kicked in the head by My Pretty Pony.

But when I landed in the office of Dr. Real Name I Won't Tell You several years ago, I thought I'd finally found the perfect gyno for me. What made Dr. RNIWTY so great was that her practice was enormous and she clearly couldn't handle the number of patients she had to see on a daily basis. She therefore only spent about three seconds per patient doing a basic inspection, asked if you were sexually active, then sent you on your merry way. I'd routinely spend more time getting undressed and figuring out how to work the paper gown than Dr. RNIWTY spent in the room with me.

Year after year I'd have my annual three-second checkup, briefly contemplate the definition of "active," and then get the hell out of there. But one year I had to reschedule my annual exam because I was working out of town and was unable to get back to New York for the appointment. When I eventually returned to the city and went to Dr. RNIWTY's office, she glanced at my chart and saw too much time had lapsed since I'd last seen her. "Where have you been?" she asked, perhaps wondering if I'd been having an affair with another doctor. I explained that I'd been writing on a sitcom and had been living outside New York for a while. "Oh." She snapped on her latex gloves and then said, "I'm sure you've told me this before, but remind me how you got into comedy writing in the first place?" Equally sure that no, I'd never told her this information since after eight years as her patient we'd barely exchanged words beyond "spread 'em," I explained that I started out doing stand-up after college. This stopped Dr. RNIWTY in her tracks. She stared at me as I lay naked and spread-eagled on the table in front of her. "Really?" she asked incredulously. "But you don't strike me as the exhibitionist type." I lay there totally naked before her, my naughty bits thrust directly in the doctor's face. "Lady," I said, "what would it take to impress you?"

She gave no response.

Not a laugh, not a smile, not even a "pfft" of disgust.

And it was then that I knew I'd be looking for a new gynecologist. After all, the only thing that could make a gynecological exam even more painful for a comic is being forced to perform it in a cold room.

Q: I've started seeing a new doctor because my old one was a dud. New Doc wants to see an MRI I had done a few years ago for comparison purposes, but it's still in my file at old Dr. Dud's office. Can I get those records back, or are they the property of the doctor who made them?

A: Like going to a different hairstylist at the same salon, though it may be uncomfortable to ask your doctor for a copy of your records to show another practitioner, you have every right to see them. According to the American College of Physicians' *Ethics Manual*, 5th edition, you, the patient, are both ethically and legally entitled to the information in your medical records. "Legally, the actual chart is the property of the physician or institution, although the information in the chart is the property of the patient. Most states have laws that guarantee the patient personal access to the medical record, as does the federal HIPAA privacy rule." In other words, your doctor must either give you or a person you name the information you request.

As a case in point, the attorney general of Pennsylvania sued a diagnostic imaging center for the release of patients' medical records after the imaging center closed its storage facilities without giving patients the ability to collect their records. The patients eventually got their records back (which included X-rays, mammograms, and other tests) and were then able to do with them as they pleased. Whether they could actually read the doctor's handwriting once they got them back, now that's a different question.

Q: At what point is a health condition considered a disability?

A: Let's consider a condition like diabetes. According to the American Diabetes Association, almost 24 million Americans have the disease, which is about 7.8 percent of the population. It's clearly a big issue that affects a large portion of the population, but when considering if the condition meets the criteria of disability, another question needs to be asked: is this something for which an office will need to make reasonable accommodation?

A disease becomes a disability when it substantially limits

one or more of a person's major life activities, which are basic activities an average person can perform with little or no difficulty, such as eating or caring for oneself. Something is also considered a disability when it causes side effects or complications that substantially limit one or more life activities. Finally, something is considered a disability under the law if the condition does not significantly affect a person's activities, but the employer treats an individual as if it does. For example, the greatly improved treatment for HIV allows HIV sufferers to live for many years without developing full-blown AIDS. So even though the status of being HIV positive may not actually affect one or more major life activities, under the law it could still be viewed as a disability if the sufferer faces discrimination because his employer treats him differently from other workers because of it.

Inside some of us is a thin person struggling to get out, but it
can usually be sedated with a few pieces of chocolate cake.

—author unknown

Q: I'm having the girls over for a barbecue so I bought some "lean" beef to toss on the grill. Just in case those skinny bitches ask, is there a legal requirement for what "lean" must mean?

A: You know, you might want to rethink that menu since those skinny bitches are probably meat-shunning vegans . . . but that's a subject for another book. Now, when you read a food label and see the words "lean," "high in fiber," and "sugar free" you already know that in laymen's terms those words mean "tastes disgusting." But your weight-conscious friends will be happy to know the words actually do have a legally regulated meaning as well.

The FDA has defined and strictly regulates the use of eleven core terms on nutritional labels so that manufacturers can't deceive the public into believing the food they're selling is healthier than it is. Similar to George Carlin's list of "the seven words you can never say on television," these eleven words are strictly regulated by the FDA:

Lean
Extra lean
Light
Percent fat free
Low
Less
Reduced
Fewer
High
Good source
Fresh

The following definitions for these terms are taken from the FDA Web site, and can be found at www.fda.gov/fdac/special/foodlabel/lite.html.

Term	Definition
Lean	The food has less than 10 grams (g) of fat, less than 4 g of saturated fat, and less than 95 milligrams (mg) of cholesterol per serving and per 100 g.

Term	Definition
Extra Lean	The food has less than 5 g of fat, less than 2 g of saturated fat, and less than 95 mg of cholesterol per serving and per 100 g.
Light or "Lite"	Can mean one of two things: The first, that these nutritionally altered products contain one-third fewer calories or half the fat of the reference food. If the food derives 50 percent or more of its calories from fat, the reduction must be 50 percent of the fat. Second, that the sodium content of a low-calorie, low-fat food has been reduced by 50 percent. The term "light in sodium" is allowed if the food has at least 50 percent less sodium than a reference food. If the food still does not meet the definition for "low sodium," the label must include the disclaimer "not a low-sodium food."
Percent Fat Free	Products bearing "percent fat free" claims contain relatively small amounts of fat and must meet the definitions for low fat. The claim must also accurately reflect the amount of fat present in 100 g of the food. For example, if a food contains 2.5 g of fat per 50 g, the claim must be "95 percent fat free."

Term	Definition
Low	If a person can eat a large amount of the food without exceeding the "daily value" (www.fda.gov/fdac/special/foodlabel/dvs.html) for the nutrient, it's considered "low." "Low" claims can be made in reference to total fat, saturated fat, cholesterol, sodium, and calories. A claim of "very low" can be made only about sodium.
Less / Reduced / Fewer	A relative claim must include the percent difference and the identity of the regular product. However, "reduced," "less," and "light" claims can't be made on products whose nutrient level in the regular food already meets the requirement for a "low" claim. Reference foods for "light" and "reduced" claims must be similar to the product bearing the claim—for example, reduced-fat potato chips compared with regular potato chips. But the reference foods for "less" and, in the case of calories, "fewer" may use dissimilar products within a product category—for example, pretzels with 25 percent less fat than potato chips.
High / Good Source	To qualify for the "high" claim, the food must contain 20 percent or more of the daily value for that nutrient in a serving. Approved synonyms for high are "rich in" or "excellent source." "Good source" means a serving contains 10 to 19 percent of the daily value for the nutrient.

Term	Definition
Fresh	"Fresh" can be used only on a food that is raw, has never been frozen or heated, and contains no preservatives. (Irradiation at low levels is allowed.)

Occasionally you will hear about crackdowns on violators, like when the Federal Trade Commission looked into claims by KFC that its fried chicken is compatible with low-carbohydrate weight loss programs, then found those claims didn't fly. The Food and Drug Administration has also reviewed the labels of Russell Stover Low Carb mint patties, toffee squares, and pecan delights and found them to be misbranded. (Come on, you knew that one was too good to be true.) But can you guess what the legal definition of "low carb" is?

Now that you're thinking about it, you probably don't have a clue, do you? Well, don't feel bad because, my little thin mint, it turns out *there is no legal definition for "low carb."* The closest governmental agencies come to that is a standard for labeling: for a product to make the claim that it's low carb, it must have a lower carbohydrate content than comparable commercial products have. So if you say that your toffee squares are low carb, there is no magic number of carbs per piece—instead, your toffee squares simply have a lower carb content than other commercially available toffee squares. Stated more simply, even if it is "low carb," it still may not be such a sweet deal for your diet after all.

Q: **I hate reading about the fat content of my food. Are there any food products that are exempt from the tyranny of nutritional labels?**

A: You know those labels are there for your benefit—though this does call to mind the old laugh line, "I'm from the government. I'm here to help you." The answer to your question is that yes, there are certain categories in which federal nutritional labeling is not required by law in the United States (although some health-conscious municipalities like New York may require a restaurant to disclose the calorie count and other things you wish you didn't know). Exemptions include foods that are served for immediate consumption like at a hospital cafeteria, ready-to-eat foods prepared primarily on-site like at a deli, plain coffee and tea, and some spices. In England, one baker was forced by the government to rename her "novelty tarts." The confections had pictures of animals on them, but because she called one a Robin Tart, it did not pass muster because it contained no actual robin in the ingredients—ditto for her Pig Cake. Even her popular Paradise Slice Cake had to be renamed because—you guessed it—not from paradise. (Though in my book, any chocolate cake called paradise does constitute truth in advertising.)

In this country, with some of the strictest food labeling requirements in the world, that baker would not have been required to change the name. Foods prepared on the premises of a bakery are also exempt from federal government label requirements. If you have questions about what does need a nutritional label and what the label means, visit www.fda.gov.

Amy

While eating a dinner of barbecued chicken, my daughter, then age five and a half, looked up at me and said, "Mommy, isn't it funny that this dinner is called 'chicken' and that sounds just like the animal called 'chicken'?" My response should have been, "Hey! Who wants a Popsicle?" What I actually said was, "Yes, that *is* funny." But apparently I didn't say this quite convincingly enough because, cocking her little head to the side, she then followed up with, "But it's *not* the same, right, Mommy?" I took a deep breath and said, "Yes . . . it is."

My little girl was sure I'd misunderstood. "No, I mean like a farm chicken isn't *this* kind of chicken." I nodded. In disbelief she clarified, "This"—she pointed to her plate with her fork—"is a real chicken?" My head bobbed again. "And turkey?" she pressed, the scales falling from her eyes, "is real turkey?!" "Yes." Then, with true horror, she looked down at the family dog, Lucy, who was begging for scraps at her feet. "So that means *hot dogs* . . . ?" "No, no," I reassured her, "hot dogs are *not* from dogs. Probably." And thus ended my daughter's meat eating to this day.

Q: For a product to be referred to as "natural," does that mean it has to spring from the earth fully formed?

A: From natural health products to natural hair products, there is a booming business in selling and marketing goods that seem wholesome and eco-friendly. Indeed you can buy natural supplements to go with your natural beans to prevent the natural gas that will surely be produced.

But you may be surprised to learn that the term "natural" has not been defined by the Food and Drug Administration, and labeling a product "natural" is not regulated. In other words, that means anyone—from an organic hemp farmer to an industrial plastic maker—can use it. "Natural" is therefore just a marketing term designed to get you to think a product is made of wholesome ingredients, and that may or *may not* be true. Word to the wise: if you like the product, look at the ingredients, not the hype on the packaging.

Q: As a proud member of Gen X, a favorite movie moment comes from *Reality Bites*, when one hipster character stares at a bottle of water and says, "Evian is just Naïve spelled backward." Is there any standard for "pure spring" water, or is that just naïve thinking?

A: Indeed the FDA does govern what goes into a bottle of bottled water, and the EPA sets regulations for tap water. But over the years, the standards have sort of flowed together, and the level of allowable contaminants in both are very similar. As for what you're actually getting in a bottle of water, if the label says "spring water" it's water that comes from an underground formation and flows naturally to the surface. "Public water source," on the other hand, means it comes from the tap. Aquafina bottled water, which is made with tap water, now includes the words "Public Water Source" on its labels.

Is the bottle itself—and the environmental havoc it wrecks in our landfills—worth $1.25? Well, that's up to you. But don't be naïve in thinking you're always getting the purest water straight from the mountains just because the bottle bears a pretty picture of the Alps.

Q: On bottles of diet soda I'm always perplexed by the warning "Phenylketonurics: Contains phenylalanine." Seems a little specific, no? Are the beverage companies forced to write that (like cigarette warnings), or is it just because Mr. Coke and Mr. Pepsi have a special place in their hearts for the phenylketonurics?

A: Trust me, warning labels aren't applied because some executive started feeling warm and fuzzy. In the United States and Canada, products that contain aspartame (like Equal and NutraSweet)—made of the amino acid phenylalanine—must bear a warning label to alert those who are unable to metabolize it. The same is true for products that contain the eight most common allergens—*milk, eggs, finfish, shellfish, tree nuts, peanuts, wheat, and soybeans*. They must be labeled clearly, in plain English, so that allergens that go by less well-known names are identified (like whey or casein, both of which are milk products).

What you might find surprising is that although there are thousands of known food allergies, 90 percent are caused by the eight common allergens listed above. So just to be on the safe side, if you're having a dinner party, best to ask your guests in advance if they have any of these common allergies. Because if you serve curds and whey to a lactose-intolerant Miss Muffet, you might later hear cries of protest from her tuffet. . . .

Q: When I was on the subway, I saw an ad for a "diabetes wonder drug" (right between ads for a miracle weight loss drug and a miracle chemical peel). I know false advertising is illegal, but does anyone *really* get busted for it?

A: Traditionally, enforcement concerning drug advertisement has been relatively lax. However, in 2006 the Food and Drug Administration and the Federal Trade Commission sent over 180 warning letters and cracked down on eighty-four Web sites that advertise dietary supplements for diabetes. Regarding diabetes specifically, the agencies have also launched a drive to stop deceptive ads and sales of products that misrepresent themselves as cures or treatments. And in February 2009, the FDA and the attorney generals in twenty-seven states cracked down on Bayer HealthCare Pharmaceuticals for the ads it ran for the birth control pill Yaz. The FDA announced that the pharmaceutical company "overstated the drug's ability to improve women's moods and clear up acne, while playing down its potential health risks" and required the company to run ads to correct its deceptive claims.

As a consumer, you should always be on the lookout for red flags. With a disease like diabetes, for instance, major discoveries are front-page news, so be wary of any ad that talks about a scientific breakthrough you haven't heard of. Also, at the moment there is no cure for diabetes, so products that promise one are scams. Finally, don't take the phrase "money-back guarantee!" to mean something will definitely work or even that you'll definitely get your money back once you realize it doesn't. Unfortunately a lot of these little-known drugmakers are fly-by-night operations. So by the time you've figured out that the product is a piece of crap, many of these companies will have long since cashed your check, pulled up stakes, and walked away from whatever post office box you're petitioning to get your money back.

What's most important to keep in mind here is that even though lawyers at the FDA and FTC are investigating these frauds, it's your doctor who is up-to-date on your disease. You should always talk to him or her about any product that looks promising first before you waste your money and possibly endanger your health by using it.

Q: **Besides marijuana, are "herbal supplements" regulated at all?**

A: No, they're not. Completely unlike over-the-counter and prescription medications, the law allows the sale of herbal supplements without review for safety or effectiveness. (And I know you're joking, but just to be clear, marijuana, despite being leafy and green, is considered an illegal drug, not a mere herbal remedy.)

If you find yourself at the drugstore looking for something to relieve, say, your flu symptoms, you may not realize that there's a major difference both in substance and regulatory requirement between Zicam and Zithromax, or between Airborne and Afrin. Zicam and Airborne are two very popular cold remedies, but they're actually homeopathic and herbal remedies, and as a result they aren't regulated by the FDA. (If the FDA can affirmatively prove a "remedy" is harmful to consumers, however, it will step in, as in the case of the weight loss supplement ephedra.) Interestingly, the Federal Trade Commission—the governmental body that regulates consumer protection (as opposed to the FDA, which regulates foods, drugs, and cosmetics)—just settled a lawsuit against the makers of Airborne for the ad in which the makers claimed the supplement prevented colds. Because the manufacturers could provide no data to back up this claim, they can now make only a more general statement that it "helps" the immune system.

The big thing for consumers to know is that herbal remedies are often sold alongside medicines, so it's important to check the labels carefully and ask your doctor what you're really putting in your body in the name of better health.

Chapter 10

Your Death

Or, if You Prefer, We Can Call It "Your Relocation to a Farm Upstate"

If you thought dying would get you out of your legal responsibilities, think again, Casper. We regret to inform you there's still a great deal to think about even as you're making your final exit to the great beyond (or helping someone else make his). From elder care to wills, burial, and legacy planning, the law stays with you even after death's done you part. But we'll try to make this chapter as quick and painless as possible. . . .

> *I don't want to achieve immortality through my work;*
> *I want to achieve immortality through not dying.*
>
> —Woody Allen

Q: Here's an insensitive question: can you sign a loved one into a nursing home against his or her will?

A: I'm going to assume you're not referring to me there, junior. . . . But that is a tough question, primarily because nursing homes are rarely like the "Springfield Retirement Castle" on *The Simpsons*, which advertises itself as a place "Where the elderly can hide from the inevitable."

In real life, decisions about an aging loved one are no laughing matter, particularly when you're facing hard choices regarding a family member's care. To make decisions for another person, you'll need to get a *power of attorney*, which gives you the ability to act as that person's agent. And a valid power of attorney requires that the person understand what he or she is signing.

But what do you do if the person is already mentally incapacitated and therefore unable to grant you power of attorney? In this instance you must go to court and ask to be appointed a guardian. To find out the specific procedure for this in your county, call the clerk of the probate court and ask for the required forms.

It's obviously preferable (for all involved) if someone makes the decision about who they want to take care of them before they're in a position of need or are incapacitated and unable to make that call anymore. A *durable power of attorney* is the document you sign when you're in good health (or good enough to be making decisions yourself) which grants your agent authority to make decisions for you—like checking you into a nursing facility—should you become unable to make your own decisions.

State laws regarding guardians differ, but in general if you feel a person can no longer make good decisions, the correct step is to file a petition with the court to request the appointment of a guardian to handle the person's care, or a conservator to handle the person's property. (NB: Though you may believe your relative has never made "good decisions," we're talking about decisions like not taking medicine versus decisions about wardrobe or hairstyle.) The court will generally appoint an attorney to represent the proposed ward or to investigate the facts and advise the court. At that point the court can then choose to appoint a guardian to make all or limited decisions about the person's finances and/or health care. There are community legal services available to help you get the process started, so contact the court for a referral.

Q: **Does a power of attorney cover all decision-making aspects of a person's life?**

A: The two basic types of power of attorney are financial and health care and they are what you'd expect: the financial power grants someone financial decision making and bill paying power. The health care power names an individual to make medical treatment decisions and arrangements for the person's care at hospitals or nursing homes.

There are forms for sale that help you create the document, or you can, of course, see an actual attorney to help you craft one. Make sure to take into account your state law; and once you've created the document, sign it in front of witnesses and have it notarized. Some states require the form to be filed with the register of deeds, so know the requirements you need to fulfill so that the power of attorney you're granting gives true power to the person you'd like to have it.

Q: If someone gives you his or her power of attorney, do you essentially become like an adoptive parent, making you responsible for the person's financial obligations, too?

A: That's probably what a man named Eric Holloway should have asked when he signed his mother, Hattie, into Riley's Oak Hill Manor nursing home. Eric had no idea that when he signed his name on the intake form as the "responsible party" he became *financially* responsible to pay for his mother's cost of care. The nursing home wound up suing Holloway to collect the money his mother owed (and won).

While the Nursing Home Reform Act appears to forbid nursing homes from requiring third parties (like the son or daughter who checked the person in) to act as guarantors for a resident's bill, it does allow nursing homes to require the use of a resident's own funds for payment. But the contracts may be worded so unclearly that the resident's representative doesn't realize he is pledging his *own* money to guarantee payment. Even the nursing home employee signing your relative in may not understand what he's asking you to sign, so make certain that you get a statement in writing (and in plain English) that says that by signing the form you are *not* pledging your own money. Don't sign on the dotted line as "guarantor"; instead make sure you're the "agent for" that person and if you're in doubt consult an attorney with expertise in elder care.

Q: I know you can be arrested for neglecting your child, but can you face prosecution if you neglect your elderly relatives?

A: Well, in addition to the price you'll pay in hell, in most states, yes, there are laws making it a criminal violation for a caretaker to intentionally or recklessly cause injury by failing to provide care. While those laws are generally used to prevent neglect in nursing homes, individuals can be deemed legally responsible as caregivers if they provide care in exchange for the elderly person's pension or social security benefits. A man in Pennsylvania was arrested on charges of criminally neglecting his elderly mother, causing her to suffer serious bodily harm. Since he was living off her benefits, he was legally responsible for her welfare and it wouldn't have mattered if he'd tattooed "Mama's Boy" on his arm, the man needed to take better care of his mommy.

If you find yourself in the situation of caring for an elderly relative and using his or her social security checks to offset your expenses, you could be legally responsible as well. But every state has agencies that help the elderly get the care they need, so if you become unable to give proper care, look online or in the yellow pages to find them.

Q: I always hear stories about the elderly getting bilked out of their life savings when they're "estate planning." How can you make sure you don't wind up as one of those terrible tales on the TV news?

A: The sad truth is that scammers play on the fears of the elderly in trying to sell estate planning tools and living will kits. Oftentimes estate and financial planning solicitations start with a pitch for a free seminar that includes a presentation supposedly designed to help you avoid taxes or save money. At the end of the seminar, you're then "encouraged" to sign up for a follow-up appointment with a so-called trust or estate or senior expert.

The first thing to understand is that *these are pitches designed to sell you a product, not to provide you with impartial guidance.* Avoid high-pressure sales tactics that scare you and be wary of fill-in-the-blank–type documents, because "one size" doesn't begin to cover the myriad individual issues. Finally, don't go alone to these seminars and appointments. Ask a relative or friend to come so you can get an impartial opinion before signing up for a product that could cost you hundreds or thousands of dollars. If you suspect fraud, complain to your state attorney general's bureau of consumer protection, before you wind up appearing as the wronged party on your local news station's "Shame on You!" segment.

Q: I wrote an ill-conceived love letter as I was getting on a plane and promised my undying love—and all my worldly possessions—to the jackass who then cheated on me while I was away. Knowing him, he still has that napkin from the Admiral's Lounge. Is that a will?

A: The Pennsylvania Superior Court was asked to decide a case called "Estate of Norman F. Shelly." The family of the late Mr. Shelly submitted to the Orphans' Court a cardboard panel from a cigarette carton to probate it as his will. On the carton were the words "First, last and only will" and people's names, with arrows pointing to listed property, including: "Farm mach + tools" and "Money, Devide [*sic*] Michael Cooks sons." Was that writing on a cigarette carton a will?

The court said no. The court found that the arrows and the

language were so unclear that it could not even be determined if Shelly intended to divide the money between two people (Michael Cook's sons) or three (Michael Cook and his sons) or in what proportion. Among other grounds, the court noted that it was not a positive disposition of property, and therefore could not be considered a will by the court.

Your love note would also be unlikely to constitute a will because although most people wrongly believe that you have to get a will notarized (you don't in most states), you do generally need two adults who do not stand to inherit property (like your lawyer and her secretary) to sign the document after witnessing you sign it. There may also be a codicil that states that they witnessed you signing it while you were of sound mind and under no undue influence.

Q: Who gets your stuff if you kick the bucket before making out a will?

A: Ah, the question that launched a thousand dramedies! The answer is that the state decides who gets your belongings under what are called the "laws of intestacy." Those laws create a formula for figuring out who gets what if you haven't made your wishes known in a will. So even if your good-for-nothing son hasn't picked up the phone to call you in ages, if you don't have a will, you don't get the pleasure of cutting him out of it.

In an interesting case in my home state of Pennsylvania, a woman was accused of murdering her husband hours before he was set to travel to Morocco to visit his other wife. (He married wife #2 under Islamic law after he'd tied the knot to #1 under U.S. law.) As it turned out, the bigamist victim died without a will. So who takes that fortune? The accused murderer or wife #2?

Well, under U.S. law, wife #1 (a.k.a. the killer) is considered the only spouse since the second marriage isn't recognized in the United States. Usually any property that is jointly owned would therefore pass to the spouse. As for property owned individually, in the absence of a will it would go to the deceased's children or parents (except that an IRA or other fund with a designated beneficiary will transfer to the beneficiary regardless of the existence of a will). If, however, the man's parents were not alive and he had no children, in the absence of a will, his property would ordinarily pass to his widow.

But this case is somewhat different. Under the aptly named "slayer rule," a person who murders another cannot reap the benefits by collecting an inheritance. Like the old tale of the child who murders his parents then throws himself on the mercy of the court because he's an orphan, in this case the accused murderer/grieving widow will have legal battles on many fronts ahead of her.

Q: **Assuming your partner doesn't murder you, can you disinherit your spouse and kids?**

A: Actually you can't disinherit a spouse to whom you are legally married at the time of your death. A boiler room worker at a naval shipyard learned that the hard way. He had gotten married in the 1940s but soon drifted apart from his wife, though they never divorced. He moved and took up with a new lady in 1948 and they had six children. In the late 1980s—forty years later and almost fifty years from the last contact he'd had with his first gal—he was diagnosed with mesothelioma, a lung cancer caused by the asbestos to which he'd been exposed through his job.

The man filed suit and was set to receive a verdict of more than $1 million. It was an ending fit for O. Henry: a man who'd worked on the docks for forty years and struggled to support his family was about to become a millionaire on his deathbed. But to his horror, he was told by his lawyers that without a divorce, a part of that estate would go to the woman he left forty years earlier, a.k.a. his actual wife. The man quickly moved to begin divorce proceedings. Alas, it was too late. He died before the divorce was final.

I suppose that's the lesson of all this—you can't really shaft someone unless you divorce her first. As for kids, however, every state except Louisiana allows you to disinherit them as long as you do so expressly (lest the probate court just figure you simply forgot about 'em).

Q: **How do you protect yourself from vultures who might want to pull the plug on you so they can get their inheritance quicker?**

A: My first suggestion is to be nicer to them when you're in good health. But the best way to protect yourself is to get an advance directive, which is a legal document stating how you'd like to be treated in the event that you become too ill to decide your treatment later. It is governed by state law but there are generally two types: a *living will*, in which you state what kind of treatment you wish to receive under given circumstances, and a *health care proxy* (also known as the durable health care power of attorney I spoke of before), in which you authorize a person of your choice to make decisions for you in the event you become incapacitated.

Talk to a lawyer in your state or you can buy a kit that will guide you based on your state law. No one plans to become incapacitated, and no one should have health care decisions made against his or her will.

Q: What are your responsibilities if you're named the "executor" of someone's will?

A: Well, when baseball legend Ted Williams died, the executor of his estate became a party to the lawsuit between Williams's children over whether his body should be cremated or frozen. And while cryogenics is usually not on the list of executor responsibilities, what does it entail if you are named the executor of someone's will?

The executor's job is to protect the property of the person who died until all debts and taxes are paid and the remaining property and money goes to the people who are entitled to it. You don't have to be a lawyer or an accountant to do the job, you just have to act in good faith.

But before you agree to do it, you should know that the job carries a lot of responsibilities, among them locating the will, applying to appear before the probate court, managing the assets during the probate process (which can take up to a year), deciding whether or not to sell real estate, handling such details as canceling credit cards and leases, notifying the government and others, and setting up a bank account for the estate to pay continuing expenses. The executor is paid a fee either as stated in the will or determined by state law—but for heaven's sake, determine for yourself if all that work is worth it for the fee.

Q: Say you want to contest a will. How do you do that?

A: Okay, let's say, for example, that your new stepmom is named "Anna Nicole," and she was a day shift dancer at a strip club before your eighty-nine-year-old billionaire father married her. Let's also say Dad changed his will just before he died, leaving everything to her and excluding you and your brother from any of his billion-dollar fortune. What do you do?

You say, "Hello, lawsuit!"

If you object to a will and are an interested party with proper standing, you can bring a "will contest" in probate court. But you need specific legal arguments why the will should be contested—it's not enough that you're just unhappy with your take, or that someone like that ne'er-do-well brother of yours was given more than you.

Typical objections are that the will was drawn up improperly, that the person who died lacked the mental capacity to make the will, that there was force or undue influence involved, or that the will is a forgery.

The Anna Nicole Smith case, a legal battle that lasted for ten years, pit the *Playboy* centerfold against J. Howard Marshall's son E. Pierce Marshall. The case eventually made it all the way to the Supreme Court, where the justices unanimously decided in her favor ... but their decision did not pertain to whether she got to keep the billion. Rather, that judgment pertained to Smith's right to pursue her share in federal court. Ironically, as the battle over J. Howard Marshall's will raged on, both E.

Pierce Marshall and Anna Nicole Smith also died. The status of the litigation now rests with the heirs of the Marshall estate (Elaine Marshall) and the Smith estate (her daughter, Dannielynn, under the guardianship of her DNA-confirmed daddy, Larry Birkhead).

Q: Say I'm an inventor and I've patented my world-changing creation. Once I die, does the patent die with me?

A: As with personal property, patents and patent rights are assignable in writing. That means that an inventor can transfer them in a will if he does so explicitly. It's when the patent holder doesn't transfer those rights explicitly that he can run into trouble, as the family of Pat Oliveri—the original Philly Cheesesteak King—discovered. When Pat passed and left this mortal coil (and I'm not talking about the Eagles' stadium), both of his two grandsons wanted his patent and the keys to his cheesy kingdom. Unfortunately Pat didn't leave a detailed directive, something like, "You, Patty Jr., my favorite grandchild, will gain the right to call yourself the King of All Steaks Smothered in Cheese, and you, Leslie, get nothing, ya chucklehead." So absent an explicit declaration, rights are distributed according to the state's law on intestate succession and divided among the estate.

The best bet in any family dispute, of course, is to work it out without resorting to the court to see who has what rights. After all, blood, especially when filled with all that cheese, is thicker than water.

Q: **Does dying at least get you out of your credit card debt?**

A: You could look at it that way, I suppose. But I'll go out on a limb and say that when you're dead, you're not going to care much about harassing phone calls from bill collectors. You might, however, be worried that your debts will follow your loved ones from the grave—especially if you've received one of those misleading phone calls from credit card companies offering debt protection in the event of your death. They tell you that, for a fee, they'll make sure your credit card balance will be expunged and won't be passed on.

Companies offering debt protection in the event of death fail to mention this: you can't inherit debt. At least not directly. So your kids will not be sent to the workhouse to pay off your frivolous purchases . . . like winter coats. That said, the executor of your estate is required to post a death notice so creditors can make their claims. The estate you pass on to your beneficiaries will be reduced by the amount of your debts.

If your assets don't cover your liabilities, though, your beneficiaries are not obligated to pay off excess debt—regardless of what unscrupulous debt collectors may tell unsuspecting grieving widows. While you may be morally swayed by those collectors into clearing your loved one's name, you are not legally obligated to do so. Knowing your rights may be the best protection of all.

Q: **I hate to sound like a cheapskate, but dying costs a lot of money. Is there anything I can do to cut costs in advance?**

A: You know when Costco started selling caskets, death was officially big business. (I keep wondering, is buying a casket at Costco an impulse purchase people make at the register along with breath mints and *People* magazine?) Like the wholesale club, the Federal Trade Commission also got involved in the funeral business, in an attempt to aid consumers. The FTC brought a charge and later entered an order against the Virginia Board of Funeral Directors and Embalmers (no doubt a fun group of guys), because the group prohibited funeral directors from advertising discounts for "preneed" funeral products and services. That policy deprived consumers of truthful information about prices for funeral services and resulted in some consumers paying higher prices for funeral services than they otherwise would have.

As the consumer, you have a right to know prices of all the funeral services you buy in order to make an informed decision about what to purchase. If you think you've been treated in a deceptive manner, you can make a complaint with the FTC at www.ftc.gov, though you should do that before you're no longer just taking the casket for a test drive.

There's also something called burial insurance, which you can purchase to defray costs to family members when your time comes. For two to three dollars per week, many people are relieved to know that they may be covered for up to $5,000, allowing a loved one to pick out a lovely casket without the crushing debt. But keep in mind that though it's called burial insurance it's really a life insurance policy. A child or young adult in good health may get a better rate—with a higher benefit—by buying a regular life insurance policy instead, so do your homework. Also ask in advance if the burial insurance requires one to use a particular funeral home.

The Ohio Department of Insurance revoked the insurance license of the owner of a funeral home who was selling burial insurance because he'd misappropriated more than $180,000 worth of premiums. Thousands of policies for burial insurance are written every year. If you are thinking of getting one—or if it is your family's custom to buy one for the kids or grandkids—make sure you check with your state's department of insurance to see that the carrier is reputable and financially solvent. Needless to say, the last thing you want is trouble getting to your final resting place.

Q: **That reminds me, if I buy life insurance, how difficult is it to switch beneficiaries if I later decide I hate the person I named?**

A: It's very easy to switch beneficiaries, but the one thing you must do is do it! A husband and wife in Kansas applied for life insurance policies in the amount of $100,000. But they divorced and the husband subsequently remarried. When he died, he left everything in his will to his new wife. But who do you think was entitled to the proceeds of the life insurance policy? Here's a hint: the answer is probably making him spin in his grave.

To get life insurance, you make a contract with the insurance company—you pay money to them, and when you die, they pay money to the person you've designated in the contract as your beneficiary. If you want to change that contract to specify your money should go to someone else, you must make that change with the insurance company.

The reason for this is that though a divorce decree changes your relationship with your spouse, it doesn't change the contract with the insurance company. The statements in your will can't change the beneficiary either, because a will doesn't change the insurance company's obligation to pay money to the person listed in the policy. As I said, it's not hard to change the designated beneficiary, but you must do it in writing with the insurance company. I imagine there's little worse than knowing that your ex-spouse not only lived to see you dead, but now gets a windfall upon your demise.

Q: **I've read that health care for the last two years of life averaged almost $40,000 in New Jersey. Assuming your veins don't run green with moolah, what can you do to pay those costs as you're preparing to bow out?**

A: Well, I definitely can't recommend making your final exit in Jersey. But dying is a sad fact of life, and adding insult to injury, it's going to cost you an arm and a leg to do it! As you suggest, people with terminal illnesses are also often burdened with mounting medical expenses. One way to raise cash is with something called a "viatical settlement."

A viatical settlement is a transaction in which a terminally ill person who holds a life insurance policy sells it to a settlement company. The settlement company pays the patient a percentage of the policy's face value, takes over its payments, and becomes the beneficiary. Of course the people who had been named as beneficiaries will now no longer receive life insurance benefits—and you should notify them of this switch if they were counting on the money to pay funeral or other expenses. But if this seems like a good option to you, contact more than one settlement company before making a deal. It's clearly an emotional time and issue, but don't give in to high-pressure tactics. Check with your state's department of insurance to make sure it's an actual company before doing the deal, and finally, insist on a timely payment so you don't have to suffer any further.

Chapter 11

Rights You *Don't* Have

"*We* hold these truths to be self-evident, that all men are created equal, that they are endowed by their Creator with certain unalienable rights, that among these are life, liberty and the pursuit of happiness...."

Thomas Jefferson wrote those inspiring words for our Declaration of Independence, the cornerstone of the United States Constitution, the basis of our laws. Ask most Americans what those words mean and they will probably tell you that they are guaranteed certain rights, like the right to free speech, the right to practice a religion of their choosing, and ... some other stuff. In this chapter we hope to clear up some common misconceptions about our "unalienable rights" because what most people seem to forget is that the freedoms granted here are *only* protected against governmental interference. So if think you always have the right to say what you wish, the right to seek counsel, the right to privacy or to pursue happiness without inhibition, think again ...

1. You don't always have the right to speak to your lawyer.

Q: When I was accused of stealing a coworker's chair and demanded to speak to my lawyer (you), my boss laughed and said I couldn't. I countered by asking if he'd ever read a little thing called the U.S. Constitution. He replied by asking if I wanted to read a little thing called a pink slip. He can't deny me my right to representation, can he?

A: The problem is that the right to speak to a lawyer doesn't exist—at least not in this case. But believing you can see a lawyer is a notion that's so ingrained, people assume it's law. As it turns out, the right to consult with a lawyer only applies to official interrogations by the government, like when the police want to speak with you. It doesn't apply every time a private citizen wants to ask you questions.

Jack Ma, a physicist employed by TRW, Inc., a defense contractor in Los Angeles, California, learned this lesson at the expense of his job. Ma was asked to attend an internal security interview, which he refused to do without an attorney present. The company did not take kindly to Ma's demand, first suspending the physicist then firing him. But eventually Ma did find a way to get his lawyer involved: he turned around and sued TRW for wrongful termination. Ma's lawyer's claimed that refusing to allow him to have his attorney present at the interview violated established public policy. The court, however, flatly rejected the argument stating, "A public employer *may* terminate a public employee who refuses to answer questions directly, specifically, and narrowly related to the performance of the employee's duties." They ruled against Ma, which effectively kept the physicist canned.

Under the law, in criminal investigations and prosecutions by the police, the accused has the right to counsel—and as any TV watcher will tell you—if you cannot afford a lawyer, one will be provided for you. If your private employer wants to ask you questions, although you don't have an automatic right to have a lawyer present, you are more than entitled to keep your mouth shut. But you should also be aware that you will not be protected for refusing to speak.

2. *You don't always have the right to say what you wish.*

Q: I got so mad at a particular coworker that, after I threatened to pop him in the doodads and shave off his eyebrows, he went to the human resources department and tattled on me. But I told that big baby I didn't care because they can't do anything to me for saying my peace. After all, that's my First Amendment right, right?

A: Wrong. As you are aware in your calmer moments, threat of bodily harm is actually a crime, no matter how much this fella deserves to look like a wincing Mr. Potato Head. Moreover, as mentioned earlier, though the First Amendment grants you the right to freedom of expression, *it's only the government that must grant you this right.* It doesn't apply to private entities, which are within their legal rights to prevent you from freely expressing yourself on their time. It also means that they can fire you for the things you say to those around you—or the tone you take when you say them.

Here's something else you should know: you aren't allowed to say or print defamatory things about people either. *Defamation is the class of legal claims made of slander (based on the spoken word) and libel (based on printed material).* In a defamation claim, the moron-known-as-the-guy-you-defamed needs to prove that (1) you made a false statement of fact that was (2) published (that is, made public such that at least one other person hears it; you can pretty much write anything you want in your diary, as long as it's not the online variety, which *is* considered publication and is *very* public) and that (3) harms his reputation and ability to earn a living.

Jerry Seinfeld got himself into just that kind of hot water when he went on the Letterman show to promote his humdrum and overhyped *Bee Movie*. At the time, Seinfeld's wife was also promoting her new cookbook. Unfortunately Jessica Seinfeld's book happened to bare a striking resemblance to another recently published cookbook written by a less famous author named Missy Lapine. When Letterman asked Seinfeld to comment on accusations that his wife might be guilty of plagiarism, Seinfeld fired back, calling Lapine a "nutjob" and "a wacko." Not surprisingly, Lapine was *lapissed*, feeling Seinfeld had trashed her reputation on national TV. She decided to sue him for slander.

You may be wondering why I'm not concerned that I just defamed Seinfeld by calling his movie a piece of crap. The reason is because my statement is clearly just an expression of my opinion. In most jurisdictions, an opinion doesn't count as a false statement of fact because it's unlikely to impair a person's reputation. Though Seinfeld now claims that calling Lapine a "nut job" was meant as a humorous opinion, his accuser pointed to another statement Seinfeld made in the same interview: "Now you know, having a career in show business, one of the fun facts of celebrity life is wackos will wait in the woodwork to pop out at certain moments of your life to inject a little adrenaline into your life experience." That doesn't seem either like a joke or an opinion, and therefore lends credence to her claim of defamation.

But not every instance of name-calling is defamation. Take another *Seinfeld* cast member's bout with verbal diarrhea. After Michael Richards, who played Kramer, went on a tirade against hecklers at a comedy club, he morphed from beloved sitcom actor to reviled racist faster than you could say "YouTube." In addition to shouting the *n*-word at his hecklers, Richards very classily told them where he'd like to stick his fork.

The hecklers sought retribution: not just an apology, which Michael Richards uttered on every media outlet on the planet, but in the form of monetary compensation. (This made only one person even more of a villain than Richards: the hecklers' lawyer, Gloria Allred). Allred first floated the proposal that both sides should go before a retired judge to determine whether or not compensation was due; when that proposal was rejected she harrumphed loudly and went off to fight the next battle, sanctimoniously recognizing that not all moral outrage constitutes a valid legal claim.

3. You don't have the right to get out of jury duty.

Q: I'm way too busy to serve on jury duty now. Can I get out of it by saying I'm suspicious of everyone but the Amish?

A: You are entitled to postpone your service, but you can't refuse your civic duty indefinitely. And we all know people who say they're going to try to get out of jury duty by claiming they're either racist and/or insane. But if anyone suggests this strategy to you, you can tell him how well it worked for a man on Cape Cod. In a brazen attempt to get out of jury duty, the man wrote on his juror questionnaire that he didn't like African Americans, didn't like homosexuals, and was a habitual liar. Kind of the kitchen-sink approach to excuse making. But what he didn't realize is that when a jury is impaneled, it's sworn in. Therefore, when he told the judge he was a liar, the judge followed the logic: since the man was a professed liar, he must then being lying about being a bigot, which is why the judge then immediately had him arrested for perjury.

If you need to get out of jury duty, you do have some choices: politely explain your hardship, like child care or vacation plans, before your scheduled jury day; honestly tell the judge why you are unable to be a juror on the day of your duty; or suck it up and do your civic duty. But a word to the wise: it's far more preferable to be in the position of deciding someone else's fate than to perjure yourself, get arrested, and have someone who's truly civic-minded deciding yours.

4. You don't always have the right to name your child exactly what you'd like.

Q: If you were a mean son of a bitch and wanted to name your kid "4Real" (like two ding-dongs did in New Zealand), could you do that here in the United States?

A: Well, unlike in some countries where specific names are banned (in Germany, for example, a child cannot be named either Adolf Hitler or Osama Bin Laden), in America you can name your child *almost* anything you want. For instance, the proud parents of one baby boy chose to name their son "Lucifer." A fine name for a teenager I grant you, but what kind of knucklehead peers into a crib, counts ten tiny fingers, and then says, "Looks like a Lucifer to me!" And two *different* sets of "fun-loving" parents, one in Texas and one in Michigan, chose to name their sons "ESPN."

But according to Lowell Kepke, the deputy director of public affairs for the Social Security Administration, the U.S. government will only issue a social security card to a person whose name contains the letters of the alphabet, hyphens, and apostrophes (like the name "D'Angelo," for example). You *cannot* get a social security card with a number (like "85") or diacritical marks (i.e., accent marks) because of a 1987 federal ruling that banned them citing standards for government-wide computer security. In other words, you may name your child Renée (though her social security card will appear without the accent mark). But you can't name your kid 4Real, and you might want to reconsider the whole parenting thing in the first place if you think it's a good idea to do so.

Now if you happen to be little ESPN, and for some reason you decide you hate your name and want to change it, you can do that by petitioning a judge.

In many states, it's easier for women to change their names after marriage or divorce than to change their names for other reasons, like, say, believing your name change will help save the world. But with some persistence, two animal rights activists eventually did prevail in re-christening themselves for a cause: Chris Garnett, a PETA staffer, legally changed his name to KentuckyFriedCruelty.com, and Karin Robertson had hers changed to GoVeg.com. These two geniuses later petitioned to get their old names back, probably after realizing that while their new names inspired no one to become vegetarian, they did inspire practically everyone to think them idiots.

To complete a name change when your marital status changes, you need to get certified copies of the marriage license or divorce order to get a new driver's license and social security card. You'll then need to contact credit card companies and others with your new documents. If your name change is for any other reason, you'll have to petition a judge, and that sometimes involves putting announcements in the legal notice section of local newspapers to give fair notice to creditors. The process does take some effort and time, hopefully enough to give real thought to how it will look when you put YourNewName.com on a job application.

5. *You don't have the right to get a license plate telling cops to FCK OFF.*

Q: **Why don't you ever see vanity license plates with profanities?**

A: As it turns out, though specific rules and regulations are determined by the individual state's department of motor vehicles, for the most part you may not use a set of letters or numbers to spell things that are offensive to the people on the road with you. South Carolina, for example, refused to allow "quickie" on a plate. In addition, many states prohibit references to drugs, alcohol, or tobacco. That's what ultimately doomed the plate of a man in Seattle, Washington, whose license plate on his 2002 Audi read: C9H13N. While most people probably wouldn't have even realized that was a "special purchase" plate, any drug dealer worth his crystal would have realized that that spells the chemical compound for methamphetamine.

6. You don't have to be a Good Samaritan.

Q: I know we're all supposed to feel a certain responsibility to our fellow man, but when I lived in L.A., responsibility seemed to begin and end at the on-ramp of the 405. Is there any legal regulation about what we owe to our fellow citizens?

A: People in certain professions—firefighters, for example—have a professional responsibility to rescue people in danger. But in America, you have no duty to rescue someone in trouble, and that's still true even if you wouldn't be putting yourself in danger by helping. There are exceptions to this rule, such as when it's your job to rescue (like those trusty firefighters or members of a bomb squad). If you've created the danger, you also have the duty to rescue. And a parent has a duty to protect his child. But in other situations, you're not required to be a Good Samaritan.

Still, some people are Good Samaritans by nature, like a New Hampshire man who saw fire in a nearby building and entered it not once but twice to rescue elderly residents. Unfortunately, in the "no good deed goes unpunished" file, after the rescue, the man became disoriented and passed out. When he came to, he slugged the paramedics who were attempting to help him—and they had our hero arrested.

The bottom line is that you don't have to try to save your fellow man. But if you do, do no harm—you can't abandon him in a more dangerous position than when you found him. As for your other responsibilities, like the New Hampshire man, it's your heart and not the law that dictates what you must do in a dangerous situation.

7. *You don't always have a right to file a lawsuit.*

Q: **I am not happy about what's going on in this country and I'd like to sue the government. Should I go to D.C. to file my suit?**

A: Don't waste the bus fare. There's a legal principle called "sovereign immunity" that prevents an individual from suing the government without its consent as in, "Hello Government, this is Robin. May I sue you?" Government: "Hi, Robin. Um, no." A law called the Federal Torts Claim Act prevents a private citizen from suing the government at the planning level like when it makes a decision to act (i.e., passing a law to raise taxes). But it allows people to sue it at the operations level (i.e., once its plan is in action). So while you can't sue the government for raising your taxes, you can sue if a U.S. Postal Service mail truck carrying your 1040 form runs a red light and hits your car.

In addition to lawsuits against the government, there are other claims that you can't take directly to court. Although you may sue any individual representative of the government (the president included), you can't sue the government as a whole. You are also prevented from filing any type of discrimination or sexual harassment lawsuit in court without first filing papers with the EEOC and its counterpart state agency. The EEOC first gets to investigate the claim and attempt to resolve it through settlement. But it is only in the instance that the EEOC can't resolve the complaint through settlement, or it can't make a finding in either party's favor, that a plaintiff can then request leave to file a lawsuit in court.

Still, even without an actual suit, the damage is often done once the accusation is made. Just look at the case of former New Jersey governor Jim McGreevey. McGreevey was forced to resign amid allegations that he sexually harassed a male state employee. When the accuser, Golan Cipel, was later asked if he planned to sue for harassment, he said that since McGreevey had resigned, he didn't have to file a lawsuit. In truth, Cipel wouldn't have been able to file that suit unless he first went through the EEOC and the commission couldn't come to judgment.

Though learning you don't automatically have the right to file a lawsuit might be a surprise to you, most people would probably argue that there are still far too many lawsuits in this country anyway.

Chapter 12

Our Conclusion

The Actual Telephone Conversation . . .

ROBIN: Okay, Aim, I think we're close to done with the book here, but we've got to figure out a good way to wrap it all up.

AMY: What do you have in mind?

ROBIN: I'm not exactly sure, but it'd be great if we could tie all of these lessons together somehow, give people a few final words of wisdom.

AMY: Yeah, okay, that makes sense.

(Crashing noises. Children are heard screaming in the background.)

ROBIN: Um?

AMY: Hang on a second. . . . Did you just throw that? . . . At who? . . . Did it hit his head? . . . I gotta go, Rob.

Click.

Acknowledgments

Amy

This book would not have come to be without the love and support of my wonderful husband, Len Feldman, whose good cheer—despite taking a good deal of responsibility for kid pickup, pizza pickup, and general spirit lifting—helped make this possible. A man who can laugh as he watches you drive your car into the side of the garage and who dutifully adds "new tire" to the family budget as a line item is a good man indeed. Our three children, each an amazingly special individual, are the reason I get up in the morning. As for Robin, it is hard to believe that writing this book has brought us even closer, but this task has reconfirmed what I already knew: that she is an extraordinary writer, confidant, sister, and friend. And Melissa—the babysitter who is more like a big sister to my kids, who is multitalented in the ways of organization, cleanliness, and kindness—makes it possible for me to walk out of the house every day.

As with any other work that is worth doing, the success of this book is due in large measure to the people who have helped along the way. I am truly thankful to all my friends at the Judge Group, founded and led by my mentor, Marty Judge. Their often funny, quirky, torturous, real-life conundrums and work habits have provided a good deal of fodder for the book. And Marty's desire to control lawsuits, but never at the cost of eliminating fun in the workplace, should be an inspiration to all employers. I am also grateful to Jane Eisner, Paul Gluck, Joel Adler, David Yadgaroff, Steve Butler, Tracy Russell, Vince Hill, Steve Nikazy, Kevin Scholla, and all the people at KYW who gave me the opportunity to prove myself. The support I have received personally and professionally from Fox Philadelphia, including (but definitely not limited to) Kingsley Smith; MaryAnn Vaughn; Mike Cirigliano, MD; George; Torrie; Jodi; Berlinda; Becky; Sheinelle; John; Sue; and my friends in front of and behind the camera, has been invaluable. And no woman I know would be the person she is without the support of her girlfriends: Cheryl, Laura, Tracey, Dawn, Mindy, Allison, Michal, Liz, Marci, Nancy, Amber, and Julia.

Robin

A huge debt of gratitude is due to our incredible parents. Not only did they encourage us in the writing of this book, they've provided unconditional love and support throughout our lives. I've also been incredibly lucky to have the encouragement of Jay Dyckman, Renée Kaplan, Alison Pace, and Lynn Parramore: genius writers, hilarious wits, and great friends all. And when it comes to acknowledging sisters, I have to say, mine's the best. Not only is Amy the best lawyer I know, she's my favorite sister, too.

There are also several people we'd both like to thank for their inspiration, insight, hard work, and wisdom: our spectacular agent, Cynthia Cannell, and her super-smart assistant, Julia

Kelly; our amazing editor, Cherise Fisher, and her multitalented assistant, Jennifer Risser; Gary Mailman, Plume's crack lawyer; copy editor Sheila Moody, a master of usage; and our brilliant friend Tom Downey, whose sage advice helped us get this ball rolling.

Index

Abercrombie & Fitch, 5
Adjustable-rate (variable-rate) mortgages, 186
Administrative exemption, 39
Advance directives, 261
Advertising, 72, 115–17, 250–51
Airborne, 251–52
Airlines
  bankruptcy of, 223
  cell phones on, 224–25
  lost luggage, 221–22
  pets on, 200–201
Alcohol use, underage, 115–16, 122–23, 127
Alimony, 103, 112
Aloha Airlines, 223
American Express, 68
Americans with Disabilities Act, 29
Animal cruelty, 195, 199
Anticybersquatting Consumer Protection Act (ACPA), 154, 155
Apartment rentals, 163–65
Appearance, job hiring and, 4–5, 27
Artus, Angie, 43
Aspartame, 249
Association, freedom of, 34–35
Asthma medication, 118–19
ATM cards, 67–68
Auto accidents, 207–9

Background checks, 8–11
Bad checks, 59
Bankruptcy, 64, 83–84, 97, 223
Barter, 82–83
Beer advertising, 115–16
Better Business Bureau, 94, 159
Bicyclists, 220–21
Biting pets, 195–97
Blood alcohol level, 211–13
Blum, Leslie, 110
Bombeck, Erma, 116, 235
Bottled water, 248–49
Bouncing checks, 58–59
Breathalyzer test, 211
Broken engagements, 99–100
Burial insurance, 266–67
Butcher, George, 95
Buttons, Red, 124

Car insurance, 207–9, 217–18, 229–30
Car rentals, 210
Casino winnings, 74
Celebrity divorces, 109–10, 134
Cell phones
  on airlines, 224–25
  privacy and, 37–38, 160–61
Chalal, Gurbaksh, 120, 121
Charitable contributions, 74–77
Charney, Dov, 18–19

Cheney, Dick, 34
Child care, 46–47, 115
Child labor, 120–21
Child support, 62, 112, 132–34
Children, 114–36
   alcohol use, 115–16, 122–23
   child labor, 120–21
   child support, 62, 112, 132–34
   coaching sports, 117–18
   college expenses, 84–85, 130–31
   divorce, 131–35
   financial costs of, 115
   litigious parents, 117–18
   in loco parentis doctrine, 127–28
   medications in schools, 118–19
   parenting plan, 134–35
   property damage, 124–25
   television commercials, 116–17
   travel with, 119–20
   visitation rights, 135
Christmas parties, 20–21, 49
Cigarette smoking, 28, 215–16
Cipel, Golan, 280
Circuit City, 151–52
Civil Rights Act of 1964, Title VII of, 16
Coaching sports, 117–18
Codes of legal ethics, 108
Cohabitation, 106
Collection agency calls, 59–60
College expenses, 84–85, 130–31
Collision coverage, 216
Collision damage waiver (CDW), 210
Collyer brothers, 95
Common law marriage, 106
Communications Act of 1934, 160
Comp time, 40
Complaining at work, 48
Computer Fraud and Abuse Act, 52

Constitution of the United States, 33, 34, 79, 80, 270, 272
Consumer protection statutes, 142
Contractors, 180–81
Controlling the Assault of Non-Solicited Pornography and Marketing Act (CAN-SPAM), 153
Cosmetic surgery, 235–36
Costco, 4, 266
Covenants, conditions, and restrictions (CC&Rs), 179–80
Craigslist, 86, 93, 142
Crashing parties, 101–2
Credit cards
   disputed charges, 68–70
   dying and, 265
   joint, 111–12
   online shopping, 143–44
   teenagers and, 125–26
Credit freeze, 145–46
Credit rating, 65–67, 163
Credit reporting agencies, 145
Creditors, 59–64, 111
Cregan, Kelly, 235–36
Cregan, Liam, 235–36
Criminal records, 9–10
Cybersquatting, 154–55

Dangerous animals, 196–98
Data destruction, 52–53
Dating sites, 141–42
Death and dying, 253–69
   elder care, 256–57
   estate planning, 257–58
   funeral expenses, 266–67
   life insurance beneficiaries, 267–68
   nursing homes, 254, 256, 257
   power of attorney, 254–56
   viatical settlements, 268–69

wills, 258–64, 268
Debt collectors, 59–60
Declaration of Independence, 270
Defamation, 272–74
Diabetes, 118, 240, 250
Disabled people, 29
Disclosure issues, on homes, 173–75
Discriminatory hiring practices, 3–5
Disinheritance, 260–61
Dittmer, Karen, 123
Divorce, 105–13, 131–35, 191–92
Doctor-patient privilege, 237–38
Document collection, 94–95
Domain names, 154–56
Dress codes
    jobs and, 4, 30–31, 49–50
    teenagers and, 123–24
Drinking age, 127
Drop catchers, 156
Drug advertising, 250–51
Drug testing, 27–28
Drug use, zero-tolerance policies
    for, 118
Drunk driving, 210–14
Durable power of attorney, 254,
    261–62
DWT (driving while texting), 161

eBay, 73, 74, 85, 86, 158–59
Elder care, 256–57
Electronic Code of Federal Regula-
    tions (e-CFR), 224
Electronic Funds Transfer Act
    (EFTA), 68
Employment at will, 1, 6, 25, 55
Employment handbook, 25
Enron, 63
Ephedra, 251
Equal Employment Opportunity
    Commission (EEOC), 5, 29,
    279, 280

Equifax, 145
ESPC, 140
Estate planning, 257–58
Eviction, 164
Executive exemption, 38–39
Executors, 262–63, 265
Exempt employees, 38–40
Exit interviews, 52
Experian, 145
Expression, freedom of, 33, 272
Extended warranty, 70–71

Facebook, 5–7, 138
Fair Credit Billing Act, 69
Fair Credit Reporting Act (FCRA),
    66, 163
Fair Debt Collection Practices Act
    (FDCPA), 59, 60
Fair Labor Standards Act (FLSA),
    38
Fair Trading Act, 71
Family and Medical Leave Act
    (FMLA), 43
Farber, Zulima, 215
Federal Aviation Administration
    (FAA), 200, 224
Federal Bureau of Investigation
    (FBI), 150
Federal Torts Claim Act, 279
Federal Trade Commission (FTC),
    66, 76, 126, 143, 145, 153, 181,
    227, 245, 250, 251, 266
Federline, Kevin, 134
Fences, 184–85
Fifth Amendment to the Constitu-
    tion, 79, 80
Financial aid, 84, 112–13, 131
Financial identity theft, 85, 144–46
Firings, 51–53
First Amendment to the Constitu-
    tion, 33, 272

Fixed-rate mortgages, 185–86
Food allergies, 249
Food and Drug Administration
  (FDA), 154, 201, 234, 242, 245,
  248, 250, 251
Food labels, 241–46
Forcible touching, 24
Foreclosed properties, 172–73,
  186–87
401(k) plans, 96, 97
Free Application for Federal Student
  Aid (FAFSA), 84–85, 112
Freelance/temporary employees,
  health care and, 228–29
Funeral expenses, 266–67

Gambling losses, 76
Game hunting, 199
Garnishment of wages, 61–62
Gift certificates, expiration of, 72–73
Gift tax, 130
Good Samaritans, 278–79
Goore, Hamlet, 215
GPS systems, privacy and, 37
Grandparents, visitation rights of,
  135
Greene, Bob, 84
Guy, Richard, Jr., 127
Gynecological exams, 238–39

Hayes, Mike, 84
Health, 96–97, 226–52
  bottled water, 248–49
  company insurance plans, 229–30
  condition as disability, 240–41
  cosmetic surgery, 235–36
  doctor-patient privilege, 237–38
  food allergies, 249
  food labels, 241–46
  freelance/temporary employees,
    228–29

herbal remedies, 251–52
  medical deductions, 231–32
  medical identity theft, 227
  medical malpractice, 236–37
  medical records, 239–40
  natural products, 247–48
  prescription drugs, 232–34
  tattoos, 234–35
  uninsured people, 228
Health care proxies, 261–62
Health Insurance Portability and
  Accountability Act (HIPAA),
  230, 240
Heating oil, 64–65
Helmsley, Leona, 189
Herbal remedies, 251–52
Herold, Sandra, 196–97
Holidays, working on, 35–36
Holloway, Eric, 256
Home office deduction, 78
Homeowners associations, 179–80
Homeowner's insurance, 167
Homes, 162–87
  apartment rentals, 163–65
  contractors, 180–81
  disclosure issues, 173–75
  fences, 184–85
  foreclosed properties, 172–73,
    186–87
  heating oil, 64–65
  homeowners' associations, 179–80
  housekeeping, 169–70
  mattresses, 170–71
  mold damage, 182
  mortgages, 185–86
  moving companies, 176
  natural disasters, 181
  no-pets clauses, 193–94
  noise nuisances, 182–83
  online real estate broker services,
    174–75

refinancing loans, 186–87
security deposits, 168–69
subletting, 177–79
swimming pools, 166–67
time-share properties, 171–72
trampolines, 167–68
tree care, 183–84
Hood, Canieva, 79
Horkey, Amanda, 59
Hostile work environment sexual
harassment, 16–18, 20
Hotel privacy, 159–60
Housekeeping, 169–70

Identity theft
financial, 85, 144–46
medical, 227
In loco parentis doctrine, 127–28
Internal Revenue Service (IRS),
73–75, 78–80, 96, 112, 115,
130–32, 187, 231
Intestacy, 259

Jackson, Michael, 103
Jefferson, Thomas, 270
Jobs, 1–56
asking for raise, 48–49
background checks, 8–11
child care, 46–47
comp time, 40
complaining at work, 48
credit rating, 66
criminal records, 9–10
data destruction, 52–53
discriminatory hiring practices,
3–5
dress codes, 4, 30–31, 49–50
drug testing, 27–28
exempt employees, 38–40
exit interviews, 52
fear of firing, 51

firings, 51–53
freedoms of speech, expression,
and association, 33–35
medical leave, 42, 43
medical testing, 28–29
noncompete agreements, 11–12
office morale, 31–32
office parties, 20–21, 49–50
online postings, 5–7, 29–30
overtime pay, 38, 40
performance evaluations, 50–51
personal hygiene, 30–31
personality tests, 2–3
personnel files, 32
policy manuals, 25
political associations, 34
privacy rights, 36–37
progressive discipline, 51
safety conditions, 41
severance, 54
sexual harassment, 16–25
sick days, 42
two weeks' notice, 55
unemployment compensation,
55–56
weight gain, 26–27
working on holidays, 35–36
Jordan, Juanita, 104
Jordan, Michael, 104
Judd, Wynonna, 160
Jury duty, 274–75

Kentucky Fried Chicken (KFC), 245
Kepke, Lowell, 276
Knauss, Melania, 102
Krueger, Scott, 128

Lapine, Missy, 273
Larson, Doug, 226
Leahy, Patrick, 34
Ledger, Heath, 232

Leedham, Bradley, 36
Lemon laws, 216–17
Liability insurance, 218
Libel, 273
License plates, 277–78
Life insurance beneficiaries, 267–68
Limbaugh, Rush, 233
Litigious parents, 117–18
Littering, 215–16
Living wills, 261
Loans, 62–63
Lockard, Rena, 22–23
Lotteries, 61
Low Income Home Energy Assis-
    tance Program (LIHEAP), 65
Lying on resumes, 9

Ma, Jack, 271
Mackey, John, 140–41
Maly, Myrtle, 195
Marijuana, 251
Marriage (*see* Relationships)
Marshall, E. Pierce, 263–64
Marshall, J. Howard, 263
Massachusetts Institute of Technol-
    ogy (MIT), 127–28
Masturbation, 21
Mattresses, 170–71
McGreevey, Jim, 280
Medical deductions, 231–32
Medical identity theft, 227
Medical leave, 42, 43
Medical malpractice, 236–37
Medical records, 239–40
Medical testing, 28–29
Medicare, 228
Medications, in schools, 118–19
Megan's Law, 173
Michael, George, 212
Minimum wage, 38
Mold damage, 182

Money, 57–97
    ATM cards, 67–68
    bankruptcy, 64, 83–84, 97, 223
    barter, 82–83
    bouncing checks, 58–59
    casino winnings, 74
    charitable contributions, 74–77
    collection agency calls, 59–60
    college expenses, 84–85
    credit rating, 65–67
    creditors, 59–64, 111
    disputed credit card charges,
        68–70
    document collection, 94–95
    expiration of gift certificates,
        72–73
    extended warranty, 70–71
    financial aid, 84, 112–13, 131
    garnishment of wages, 61–62
    heating oil, 64–65
    loans, 62–63
    pensions, 97
    postdating checks, 58
    rebates, 71–72
    retirement, 95–97
    scams, 85–93
    social security numbers, 85
    taxes, 73–81, 95, 112, 115, 130–32,
        187, 220, 231
    vacation packages, 93–94
    work-from-home opportunities,
        82
Mortgages, 185–86
Moving companies, 176
Mujerm, Stephen, 99–100
MySpace, 6, 29

Names, 275–77
Nanny cams, 47
Nash, Charla, 196
Natural disasters, 181

Natural products, 247–48
No-fault divorces, 108, 109
Noise nuisances, 182–83, 192–93
Noncompete agreements, 11–12
Nude Olympics, Princeton University, 128–30
Nursing Home Reform Act, 256
Nursing homes, 254, 256, 257

Occupational Safety and Health Administration (OSHA), 41
Office morale, 31–32
Office parties, 20–21, 49–50
Oliveri, Pat, 264
Online issues, 137–59
Online pharmacy sites, 153–54
Online postings, 5–7, 29–30
Online real estate broker services, 174–75
Online shopping, 143–44, 158–59
Open container laws, 213
Outlaws Motorcycle Club, 34–35
Overtime pay, 38, 40

Parenting plan, 134–35
Passon, Ted, 218
Patents, 264
Paternity, 133–34
Pensions, 97
Performance evaluations, 50–51
Permissive visitation statutes, 135
Personal hygiene, 30–31
Personal Injury Protection (PIP) coverage, 218
Personality tests, 2–3
Personnel files, 32
Pets, 188–205
    on airlines, 200–201
    animal cruelty, 195, 199
    barking dogs, 192–93
    biting, 195–97

dangerous animals, 196–98
death of, 202–5
divorce and, 191–92
food, 201–2
insurance, 190–91
no-pets clauses, 193–94
sick puppies, 189–90
support animals, 198–200
wills and, 189
Pharmaceutical diversion, 233
Phelps, Michael, 139
Phenylalanine, 249
Phillips, Kevin, 196
Pizza Hut, 22
Plastic surgery, 235–36
Policy manuals, 25
Political associations, 34
Polumbo, Amy, 6–7
Pornography, in office, 19–20
Postdating checks, 58
Postnuptial agreements, 104
Power of attorney, 254–56
Prenuptial agreements, 102–4, 113
Prepaid phone cards, 125
Prepaid tuition, 130
Prescription drugs, 232–34
Privacy rights, 36–38, 47, 137–60
Probate, 262
Professional exemption, 39
Progressive discipline, 51
Property damage, 124–25
Provenzino family, 125
Puppy "lemon" laws, 190

Quid pro quo harassment, 16

Raises, asking for, 48–49
Ranch Dressing (Epstein), 13–15
Rebates, 71–72
References, 53–54
Refinancing loans, 186–87

Refund anticipation loans (RALs), 79

Relationships, 98–113
  alimony, 103, 112
  broken engagements, 99–100
  cohabitation, 106
  common law marriage, 106
  divorce, 105–13, 131–35, 191–92
  joint credit cards, 111–12
  postnuptial agreements, 104
  prenuptial agreements, 102–4, 113
  sexual relations, 100–101

Renter's insurance, 165
Replacement cost policy, 165
Representation, right to, 271–72
Restrictive visitation statutes, 135
Resumes, lying on, 9
Retirement, 95–97
Richards, Michael, 274
Rison, Andre, 132
Road rage, 214
Rowe, Debbie, 103
Ryan, Jack, 109–10
Ryan, Jeri, 109–10

Scams, 85–93, 131, 144
Securities and Exchange Commission (SEC), 141
Securities laws, 140–41
Security deposits, 168–69
Seinfeld, Jerry, 273
Seinfeld, Jessica, 273
Severance, 54
Sexual battery, 24
Sexual harassment, 16–25
Sexual relations, 100–101
Shank, Debbie, 230
Shelly, Norman F., 258–59
Shin, Elizabeth, 128
Sick days, 42
Simley, John, 230

Sixteenth Amendment to the Constitution, 80
Slander, 273
Slayer rule, 260
Smith, Anna Nicole, 263–64
Smoking, 28, 215–16
Snipes, Wesley, 79–80
Social host law, 123
Social Security Administration, 81
Social security numbers, 85, 276
Soloway, Robert Alan, 152–53
Sovereign immunity, 279
Spam, 152–53
Spears, Britney, 105, 134
Speech, freedom of, 34
Spock, Benjamin, 114
Stored-value credit cards, 126
Subletting, 177–79
Support animals, 198–200
Surveillance video, 150–51
Swimming pools, 166–67

T. J. Maxx, 143
Taboh, Victorine, 99–100
Tattoos, 234–35
Taxes, 73–81, 85, 112, 115, 130–32, 187, 220, 231
Texting while driving, 161
Third-party sexual harassment, 23
Third-party visitation statutes, 135
Tiffany, 158
Time-barred debts, 60
Time-share estates, 171
Time-share properties, 171–72
Tracking cookie, 147
Traffic tickets, 215
Trampolines, 167–68
Transportation, 206–25
  airlines, 200–201, 221–25
  auto accidents, 207–9
  bicyclists, 220–21

car rentals, 210
   drunk driving, 210–14
   hybrid cars, 220
   lemon laws, 216–17
   littering, 215–16
   repossession of cars, 219–20
   road rage, 214
   traffic tickets, 215
TransUnion, 145
Travel insurance, 222, 223
Travel with children, 119–20
Tree care, 183–84
Trump, Donald, 102, 104
"Truth about Frivolous Tax Arguments, The" (IRS), 80
Two weeks' notice, 55
Typosquatting, 155

Unemployment compensation, 55–56
Uniform Commercial Code, 58
Uninsured people, 228

Vacation intervals, 171
Vacation packages, 93–94

Veritas, 8, 9
Viatical settlements, 268–69
Vick, Michael, 199
Video Voyeurism Prevention Act, 139
Vinson, Deanna, 191–92
Vinson, Ray, 191–92

Wal-Mart, 33, 230
Warranties, 70–71
Wedding rings, 113
Weight gain, 26–27
Western Union, 86, 158
Whole Foods, 140–41
Wild Oats Markets, 140–41
Williams, Ted, 262
Wills, 189, 258–64, 268
Wiretapping, 47, 149–50
Work-from-home opportunities, 82
Wrongful death lawsuits, 127–28

Yates, Antoine, 197

Zicam, 251
Zoeller, Fuzzy, 146